GAIN®

The Dynamics of Successful Economic Outcome

A Primer on
PRODUCTIVITY CLASS® ECONOMICS*

The economics of gainful prosperity
for the
**Working Class, Middle Class, Small Business Class,
Administrative and Specialized Professionals**

Also for **corporations**, **investors**, and **governments**
for productivity and ethical framework reference.

A TRUE WORKING HANDBOOK

A Productivity Class® 'Reference Book'

GAIN explains clearly
the *underlying 'cause-and-effect' and 'application' principles*
that actually generate into existence the very subject of economics.

The 'how it works' and 'how to live an **ethically gainful** life'
left out of academic 'theory only' texts.

*Productivity Class® Economics...

...is a **gainful 'activity'**, not a *'study'* of something –
an activity in which *all of us* **'participate'** together and succeed *'productively'*.
Productivity class® economics is the economics of
participate, contribute, and **prosper.**

This is a 'print on demand' 'beta' version of this text.
~~The $14.65 price is estimated to be one half of the future 'alpha' version.~~

Print on Demand service furnished by IngramSpark

The purpose of presenting this 'beta' version for sale is to earn the
financing for the professional services required
to bring this text to a full 'alpha' version state –
ghost writer
editor
proofreader
layout specialist
– at which time, such version will become available
through a major commercial publisher through bookstores
at an expected list price of approximately $29.00 to $35.00.

Thank you for your purchase and contribution to this project.
Further donations can be gifted at productivityclass.*info*

GAIN® and **Productivity Class®**
are registered trademarks.

ISBN 978-1-7347088-0-6

BISAC: BUS044000 / BUS039000 / BUS069000 / BUS069030

THANK YOU!!!
BRAINYQUOTE.COM for being such a great resource for quotables.

CONTENTS

Get The Most Out of This Text
Go to
ProductivityClass.*info*
and
Print and Use the Accompanying
Chart of Economic Operating Dynamics

It Goes With The Book – and *It's FREE!*

This 11 x 17 inch poster-chart shows
the entire 'clockwork' of all economic activity –
its 'driving force', its 'human capacities employed', its 'operating dynamics':
Basic Purpose
the Five Primary Axioms
the Twelve Elementary Activities/Primary Operating Dynamics
and all of the Derivative Subordinating Operating Dynamics
of economics.

As you apply what you read to real life,
use the chart of operating dynamics
to help you see how
every *economic principle* and *dynamic activity* you learn *fits in*
and *effects* the whole 'clockwork of economic dynamics'
operating and functioning all around you.

It's FREE at ProductivityClass.*info* [*not* .com]

CHAPTER 0
PREPARATORY
Principles and Techniques

This text is not just 'an informative read'. It is a 'working handbook'.
These 'preparatory principles and techniques' are how
you make it work for you.

This Primer is also Your Handbook

"We are to admit no more causes of natural things than such as are both true and sufficient to explain their appearances." Sir Isaac Newton

*This is a true 'subject basics' handbook. You use it.
The principles contained herein are intended to be
observable self-evident truths – axioms and basic working principles.*

Therefore, the material herein requires no prior study to understand and put to immediate use. Further, everything herein is *openly observable* in everyday life.

The reader is expected to look for and observe
these working principles and activities in real life
and, within their own level of experience and understanding,
succeed economically by putting them into their own immediate practice.

In fact, all principles delineated in this text are so basic as to *require only reading and practice to learn and understand.* Successful application at ground level should take only basic literacy.

As this is a **working handbook**, the point is *application.*
Nothing in this text is intended to be understood as theory alone.

Economics is *not* a discipline to be practiced by only academic or analytic elites. The whole point of this text is to show that economics begins at the *cause-and-effect* and *application principles* successfully applied by the **productivity class** – and to add the learning and practice of those principles to the subject of economics at *every* activity point, including the *productive base.*

In further fact, every principle in this text is *required* for a more complete and successful understanding of economics, no matter how fundamental or sophisticated your level of living, working, or purpose of application.

Dictionaries and Definitions:
Important Notice

Educational Axiom:
You cannot understand the meaning, or subject matter, of a communication
if you do not *precisely know* the *meanings of the words* communicating it,
or how the words are *used for that specific communication!*

You, therefore, cannot *learn* and you cannot *do*
what the communication [text] provides
unless you know the intended meanings of the words.

Learn a lesson from **Benjamin Franklin**
(In a letter to his adapted 'niece', Mary 'Polly' Stevenson, on May 16,1760)

"...as many of the terms of science [*economics is a science*] are such as you cannot have met with in your common reading, and may, therefore, be unacquainted with, I think **it would be well for you to have a good dictionary at hand**, to consult immediately when you meet with a word you do not comprehend the ***precise*** meaning of. This may <u>at first</u> seem troublesome and interrupting; but it is a trouble that will daily diminish, as you will daily find less and less occasion for your dictionary, as you become more acquainted with the terms; and in the meantime you will read with more satisfaction, because [*you will read*] with **more understanding.**" [The Way to Wealth, Skyhorse Publishing. Kindle Edition. (underline, bracketed notes, and bold emphasis mine.)]

Also, some current definitions extant on the subject of economics are inadequate for **productivity class** purposes. Therefore, we provide such words with *productivity class definitions*, prefaced with "*For our purposes...*". Further, throughout this text, *when you see an asterisk in a dictionary source – e.g. (SOED*) – it means I have slightly modified that definition in brackets [...] <u>for better contextual clarity</u> without changing that dictionary's meaning.*

Productivity Class™ recommended dictionaries are:
- o the **Shorter Oxford English Dictionary** (SOED);
- o the **New Oxford American Dictionary** (NOAD); and
- o the **WordWeb Dictionary** [by Princeton University]

*[All three dictionaries are available at **WordPro.com**]*
*A '**Glossary of Vital Words**' is provided at **productivityclass.info**:*

Should, at any point, the material in this text confuse you, ***stop reading!*** – go back and *find the point you where you begin to feel confused*, and just before that there will be a word that begins that confusion. Look that word up in the glossary or dictionaries above. When you find the definition the author had in mind, your confusion will clear up. Always remember, there are no concepts in this text beyond the understanding of anyone of average intelligence.

Understanding Principles and Standards
and
How They Work

There are 'cause-and-effect' and 'application' principles that apply to every aspect of living life. And there are 'standards' by which to judge the *value* or *correct measure* of all things – also in every aspect of living life.
You must *know*, *apply*, and *live by* them if you wish to live life successfully.

This section is about what 'standards' and 'principles' are.

In Productivity Class® Economics, There Are Two Kinds of Principles:

- **'Causation' principles** [also called 'natural' or 'cause-and-effect' principles], and
- **'Application' principles** [also called **'operating' principles** (principles of *applying* or *operating with* the cause-and-effect aspects of a subject or in a field of endeavor)].

Cause-and-effect [causation] **principles** are *those natural cause-and-effect characteristics of how a thing functions or how its phenomena occurs.* These are the *natural laws* – the physics and physical *mechanisms* – of anything in nature or the physical universe.

Application [operating] **principles** are how we *use* a known **cause-and-effect principle** to *cause the effect intentionally* to accomplish a desired result. It is the **application principles** that begin the 'discipline', 'profession', or 'skills' of a field of knowledge – the field of knowledge consisting in its totality of *all* of the *truths, facts and factors*, and the **'causation'** *and* **'application' principles** employed to operate effectively with it.

Important Note: If proper *'cause-and-effect'* principles and corresponding *'application'* principles of a subject or field of activity are known and proven, and one applies that *'cause-and-effect'* [causation] function with the proper *'application'* [operating] principles, *one always gets the same, proper result or outcome.*

Correspondingly, if one does *not* get the proper result or outcome, and one gets a poor, or wrong, or no result, then one has *misapplied* that principle, or the principle is false or faulty* – the only exception being 'other factors' that may be influencing the activity. [*See **scientific method** below to correct false or faulty principles. *Keep in mind that if everyone else using such principles get consistently positive outcomes, and you do not, it is not the principles that are faulty.]*

Every Subject Has at Its Core, Its Base 'Fundamental' Principles

All sciences, all spheres of knowledge, all subjects of study have at their foundation *those truths, factors,* and **principles** *of causation and application that give rise to the subject's existence.* They are the founding core truths, factors, and principles that *the entire subject from there on up is built upon* – and upon which all further developed **principles** are *derived from,* and must *comply with* and *subordinate to,* or will cause that subject to run askew and bring failure.

The job of all developed advanced and sophisticated principles of any subject is to make the fundamental activities *function better,* to *serve the purpose of the subject's existence,* and to do so within *all variant circumstances.*

In fact, *everything in life or science* has its **causation** and **operating principles** and primary fundamental *truths* and *factors* that make up that aspect of life or that part of the physical world we live in. Certainly, everything *economic.*

> *'Causative' and 'application' principles are the basis for all successful 'actions'.*
> **It is *actions* that get the results, cause the effects, create the outcomes.**
> **Economics is a set of *actions* based upon a specific set of *causation* and *application* principles.**

True Standards – of anything – are defined in **productivity class** economics as...

- o 'accepted measures for accomplishment – *proven through successful experience'*;
- o any *'proven valid basis'* for the comparison of one thing to another thing;
- o the correct way of doing a thing, proven through successful experience.

The Scientific Method

The Scientific Method: (Dictionary.com*) noun: a method of research in which a problem is identified, relevant data are gathered, a hypothesis is formulated from these data, and the hypothesis is empirically tested [through direct observation and experiment].

When dealing with **principles, factors, standards**, etc., you have to know you've got them right. The method used to ensure the correctness of human knowledge and understanding is the **scientific method**. The **scientific method** is a method that *scientifically establishes the trueness or falseness or the accuracy or inaccuracy of a hypothesis* – 'a supposition or proposed explanation [of something] made on the basis of limited evidence' (SOED*).

The word 'scientific' makes it sound complicated, sophisticated, or advanced. It is not. It is very basic and fundamental to *how humans understand or determine the trueness of anything* – including laymen, and even children.

The *Basic* **Scientific Method** is:
- Make an **Observation** of some phenomenon, event, or activity.
- Ask a **Question** about it – how it occurs; why it occurs; how it works when it does occur; what factors are necessary for its occurrence; etc.
- Based on your *observations*, create a **Hypothesis** that should answer your question.
- **Experiment** to substantiate, prove, or disprove the hypothesis.
- **Analyze** the results.
- Draw a **Conclusion** based on the results of your experiments and analysis.

If you just look at it, *its innate human 'figuring something out' process can be easily seen*: *You see something; you get an idea or wonder something about it; you suppose what the answer probably is or propose a probable answer; you do something that will show whether or not your supposed or proposed answer is true; you analyze what you've done; and draw some conclusion about it – maybe you keep doing this over and over until you figure the thing out.*

And that is the *basic* **scientific method**. Only the **standards** we apply, and the complexity of the subject matter, is what makes it difficult or requiring. The process itself is just the basic *innate human 'figuring something out' process.*

What are missing in *basic* **scientific method**, however, are *Valid Evidence, Confirmation*, and *Documentation*. One can do the **scientific method** and *flub* it.

Therefore, we must add:
- '**Determine what is needed to be known**' as the true first step;
- Gather only *Valid Evidence* – '**something that shows something else to be true or valid**'. In order for something to *be* **evidence**, it must actually *show* that something is '*true*' or '*likely to be true*' – *that makes it 'evident' the thing is true*. Beware of all bias;
- **Confirmation** of results – through *'repetition' by others* or *'consistency' of real-life results and outcomes under varied conditions*, as the last step; including
- **Documentation** of all activities, factors, observations, conditions, etc. – that means *everything*.

Understanding this explanation of **principles** and **standards** and how they become established through **scientific method** will be necessary for you to use the materials in this handbook.

[A fully '**extended scientific method**' *at productivityclass.info.*]

General Introduction
to
Productivity Class Economics

"*Human well-being is not a random phenomenon*. It depends on many factors... [including] economics. ...clearly, there are scientific truths to be known about how we can flourish in this world." Author: Sam Harris: Neuroscientist, Non-Profit Executive

Productivity Class Economics:

Economic Theory Statement

It is upon *cause-and-effect physical dynamics* that all things in the physical universe exist and operate. It is upon *cause-and-effect biological dynamics* that all *living* things exist and operate. These are the functioning 'causative principles' of *physics* and *living things*, and they exist with or without human knowledge, belief, or understanding.

Application principles [aka operating principles] come into existence only when humans discover a set of these naturally occurring *cause-and-effect dynamic phenomena, activities,* or *processes* and utilize them to produce their own desired results or outcomes. These are the 'specific actions with required concepts and reasoning' to effectively '*operate*' or '*apply*' these cause-and-effect dynamics to produce a desired result – in physics, productivity, or in living life. We therefore call them 'operating' or 'application' principles – principles for 'applying' the 'cause-and-effect' dynamics.

'Causation' principles *are not mutable* – causation principles are naturally occurring and are *not* susceptible to change. 'Operating' or 'application' principles are susceptible to improvement, but may not be ignored or poorly or sloppily applied without lessened, negated, or adverse outcomes.

Further, all *founding* fundamental principles, both causative and operating, of *any* subject *generate by their activity all further causative and therefore also operating principles on that same subject* – the dynamic activities of *foundational* principles generate into existence all *further* dynamic principles.

Only when one knows and understands the true founding *purpose* and *causative* and *operating* principles of a subject can they then know how to understand and correctly apply the rest of that subject to the true, full, and proper purpose of its existence in living life or as a human endeavor.

i.e. Without the founding principles and purpose for the existence of a subject, one does not know the proper context in which to apply the further generated principles of that subject, nor the proper purpose toward which to apply them – ethically or consequentially.

Productivity Class® [productivity] economics
establishes the actual *'purpose for the existence'* and *'founding principles'*
of the subject of economics. The activities of which generate into existence, and
form the *basis* and *underlying purpose* of,
all further economic principles.

Productivity Class Economics:
an
Overview

Economics is *not* a human invention.
It is a set of *naturally occurring innate human dynamic activities*.

You really need to get that. We are *born* with the innate *drives* and *capacities* to do the *activities* that together add up to *economics*. Materially, *all humans* survive through this *same innate set* of dynamic fundamental activities.

The Material Aspect

Every human living dynamic has its *material* aspect. In everything we do, we use some material '**thing designed for that particular function or adapted for some purpose**' (SOED*) to better succeed at that 'function' or 'purpose' and, therefore, at that human dynamic:

The handling of the material aspects of
our human dynamics is economics.

Every material aspect of every dynamic in living a human life requires skillful handling of this *same simple set of human **productive** activities* or a person or group fails on that dynamic endeavor, or at least comes up short of where they should have succeeded more fully.

The activities of economics are inherent to *all* human cultural development. *All* economic fundamentals show up in one form or another in *every* human social or cultural system, from rain forest tribes to the most highly sophisticated civilizations, now and throughout all of human history.

And the 'bedrock basics', the fundamental purposes and principles that govern all economic activity, are, because they are innate to all of us, the same for every possible way humans can come together to form a culture, a society, or an economic system.

Understanding The Subject You Are Reading About

To begin with, in the word 'economics', the prefix 'eco' originates from the ancient Greek word 'oikos', meaning 'house' or 'household'. 'Nomics' comes from a combining of the ancient Greek words 'nomos' [meaning in this case *the functional and operating principles of a subject,* sometimes referred to as the 'laws' of a subject] and 'nemein' [distribute], which together as 'nomics' mean 'the laws of production and distribution'. So originally the literal meaning of the word 'economics' ['ta oikonomika' in ancient Greek] was...

'The operating laws [principles]
of production, distribution, and income in a household'.

And yet, no texts delineating such principles were ever written. Aristotle wrote only about the *ethics* of 'ta oikonomika', not its **causation** or **application principles**. Adam Smith, John Maynard Keynes, Karl Marx, etc., never delineated the **cause-and-effect** or **application principles** underlying the complex management strategies and controls they were famous for.

A situation we hope is resolved with this text. This is important stuff.

TWO SPECIAL NOTES:

At the time of this writing, what is considered the 'fundamentals of economics' is actually an attempt to *string together* some of the *recognized phenomena* of economics into a *foundational base* upon which to build further economic under-standing. It may not be a proper base to us **productivity class**, but it is to a good degree *'workable'* for *academic* economists.

What has been built upon that foundation is an often brilliant capacity to analyze the broad, complex web of myriad economic activities, the further myriad of resultant simultaneous outcomes that go with them, and the overall collective resultant effects, trends, etc. – allowing *analytical economists* to *predict* and *advise* on the **management** of economic institutions, various economic systems, and the many segments thereof.

To avoid confusion between the three economic approaches – *academic, analytical,* and **producer** – let's look at the academic's and analyst's *'academic theory'* approach first, then segue from there to the **productivity class** approach of **primary** and **derivative** *'operating dynamics'.*

FURTHER: No actual overall or single agreed upon primary basic theory of economics exists in academic or analytical economics, only the 'theoretical picture', given below. Note the attempt to string together recognized phenomena into a base upon which to format or present all further understanding:

Academic and Analytical Economic Theory Statement

Every populated geographical area has productive resources - natural, human, and capital - which are utilized to produce the products and services required to serve the needs and wants of its populace. *This establishes the 'need of resources' and 'production of products and services' as fundamental economic principles.*

However, since *resources* are always *finite*, and human material wants and desires are always *infinite*, resources are always considered '*scarce*' by comparison. *This establishes the concept of 'scarcity of resources' as a fundamental economic principle.*

And since *resources* are always considered *scarce*, humans have to make determinations – '*choices*' – of how to handle *three basic questions*:
- What products and services will be produced?
- How will those products and services be produced?
- Who will consume those products and services?

This establishes the concepts of 'human choices' and the 'three basic questions' as fundamental economic principles.

Further, as a result of the '*scarcity*' of resources, every time a *choice* is made to expend a *resource* on one thing, it is considered that some other alternative thing that could have been done with that *resource* has to be given up – to do or have the one thing *costs the opportunity* to do or have the other thing – a *trade-off* has to be made to forgo one thing in order to do or have the other. *This establishes the concept of 'opportunity cost', also known as 'trade-off', as a fundamental economic principle.*

Managing and dealing with scarce resources, the three basic questions and determining trade-offs in the economically productive activities of a real life populace creates the need for an economic system [which is usually '*centralized*' (aka '*command – government controlled*') or '*decentralized*' (aka '*market determined*') or a 'combination' of the two]. *This establishes the need for 'economic systems' as a fundamental economic principle.*

The 'management tools' of economics are its basic operating principles: supply, demand, and pricing; absolute and comparative advantage; cyclic flows of currency; scarcity of resources; the principles of competitive markets; the principles of profit maximization; etc.; also scientific method reasoning and the use of economic models to show and determine standard economic causes and effects.

The concern of economics, and therefore economic systems, is to ensure that every geographic population makes the best choices on how to most effectively utilize its limited productive resources to best serve the needs and wants of that populace.

The Productivity Class Position on Academic and Analytical 'Basics'

In and of itself, the above 'model' and 'outline' describes a *valid* and *true* statement of basic economic *construct* – there is nothing actually 'untrue' about it. This foundational 'construct', however, does *not* include any actual economic *'causation'* or *'operating' principles*. It is a *still life picture* of economics – and an *incomplete* one, at that.

By **productivity class** standards this academic and analytical foundation for economics is simply too devoid of the base *capacities*, *activities*, and *principles* of economic *function* to be of much use. And in being so it creates more of an *'academic's' conceptual, theoretical, 'study of'* point of view of economics, rather than the point of view of an *active participant*, a **producing / consuming** *'economic entity's'* point of view.

This 'study of' approach to economics is not without its virtues. It has been, and will continue to be, the source of discovery of many of the known *'derivative'* **operating dynamics** we'll explain later in chapter three, and it has developed most of the understanding of how to make them work correctly and **ethically**. In doing so, this 'study of' contribution to economics in general has also contributed greatly to the question most important to the **productivity class**:

> *What are the dynamic 'causative principles' that make up economic activity,*
> *and how are they to be 'applied' for economic success?*
> [What are its *'cause-and-effect'* and *'application'* principles?]

Therefore, in **productivity class** economics, with the focus primarily on **producing** and **gainful** advancement, we tend to dismiss 'scarcity', 'choices', and 'opportunity costs' as **unproductive** economic principles. **Producers** tend to view 'scarcity' and 'opportunity costs' in their traditional definitions and, therefore, as *variable economic* or **operational** *circumstances*, not actual **productive** or *economic principles*. For example, for the **productivity class**…

> A 'trade off' is having to choose between *equal <u>needs</u>*
> due to limited **resources**.
> Choices between *unequal* needs is not a 'trade off' or 'opportunity cost',
> it is *prioritizing* [choosing which comes *first* or is *most important*].
> 'Trade off' or 'opportunity cost' does not apply to <u>*wants*</u>.
> Choices between equal wants is choosing from *options*.
> Choices between unequal wants is, again, *prioritizing*.

In **productivity class** economics, we handle the '*the limitations of resources*' by the '*disciplines of efficiency*' and the '*principles of trade*': *efficient usage* and '**supply and demand**'.

Additionally, in *academic* or *analytical* economics, all things economic appear to begin with '*resources and the scarcity thereof*', when in actuality, *all things economic begin with 'produce'* – **productivity** [as we'll explain later].

And we tend to view '*choices*' as a '**marketing**' or '**consumer demand**' variable –

part of the understanding necessary for successful **marketing** and **producing**.

Further, **productivity class** economics rejects *'human choices'* as a *cause-and-effect* or *application principle* of *anything*. Once the concept of *'choices'* is considered a principle of any 'cause-and-effect' based discipline, that discipline tends to diminish the importance of 'causative' and 'application' principles and gets lost in the quagmire of human psychology. In truth...

> **It is upon the actual *cause-and-effect* dynamic principles of a discipline**
> **that we develop effective *application* principles –**
> **correct methods of *application* that produce desired outcomes**
> **in that area of activity.**
> **And it is the *actual cause-and-effect dynamics* of a subject that**
> **determine the outcomes of our 'choices' and 'behaviors' –**
> **of whether or not we effectively applied correct 'application' principles.**

Finally, *academics* and *analysts* observe ['study'] the actions of **producers** and **consumers** to determine economic *principles*, *trends*, and *conditions*. They are *observers* that *study* the economic activities of the *active participants*.

The **productivity class**, however, *are the active participants* the academics and analysts are *observing* and *studying*. And if the **productivity class** is to operate successfully, they must operate from *cause-and-effect* and *application* principles. The very purpose of human knowledge and thought is for *effective doing*. There is no room for non-productive, ineffective, or 'conceptual only' thinking in *productive* economics.

Answering The 'What Is Economics' Question:

This question is also answered later in covering the **five primary axioms**. But it is covered from a **productivity class** point of view. In *academic* and *analytical* economics, the answer to that question is very different – and currently, a poor help to anyone who doesn't *already know the subject*. Every academic and analytical description of 'what is economics' is vague and non-descriptive of what it actually is:

"Economics is the <u>study of</u> how individuals and societies use their scarce productive resources to obtain goods and services."
Harlan R. Day, Grade school primer: 'What Economics Is About" National Council on Economic Education distributor

"Economics can be more specifically defined as *the social science concerned with how limited resources are used to satisfy people's unlimited wants and needs*".
Mark A. Selzer and Ian R. Gibson, From 'An Economics Primer' MIB Publications

"A distinguished British economist named Lionel Robbins gave the classic definition of economics – *'Economics is the <u>study of</u> the use of scarce resources which have alternative uses.' In other words, economics studies the*

consequences of the <u>decisions</u> that are made about the use of land, labor capital and other resources that go into producing the volume of output which determines a country's standard of living..."
Thomas Sowell, 'Basic Economics' Basic Books Publishers

"...economics is, to its very heart, the <u>study of</u> people. It is an inquiry into how people succeed, into what makes us happy or content, into how humanity has managed over generations to become more happy and prosperous... Economics <u>examines</u> [studies] what drives human beings to do what they do, and looks at how they react when faced with difficulties or success." [brackets mine]
Edmund Conway, From '50 Economic Ideas you really need to know' Quercus Publishing

"Economics is a social science that is at once broad in its subject matter and unified in its approach to understanding the social world. An economic analysis begins from the premise that individuals have goals and that they pursue those goals as best they can. Economics <u>studies</u> the behavior of social systems – such as markets, corporations, legislatures, and families – as the outcome of interactions through institutions between goal directed individuals."
From 'Undergraduate Economics at Harvard - A Guide for Concentrators' economics.harvard.edu

Note the approach to economics by *academics*:

- Most of the *academic* and *analytical* definitions of economics define economics as '*a study of*' economic activities, and does *not* approach economics as *the economic activities themselves*.
- The *academic* and *analytical* approach primarily '*studies*' the *generated phenomena* of an economic system *that is already up and running* – but not the underlying principles that put it there.
- Therefore, academics and analysts '*study*' *derivative* phenomena and the activities of participants *but not cause of the existence of the phenomena, nor do they study the 'base' principles and applications required to participate successfully.*
- Academics approach economics from a '*study from the <u>outside</u>*' point of view, and does not take an '<u>insider</u>, active participant's* point of view' – all is 'still life' theory only.

Therefore, the above '*definitions*' of economics by academics, for an economic *producer/consumer, any real economic participant*, just won't work.

The Productivity Class® Definition of Economics:

Economics is the <u>active application</u> of a specific set of intrinsic human *capacities, activities*, and *principles* required for success in *securing the <u>material</u> requirements of a worthwhile quality of survival, successful material contribution to all the dynamics of human living,* and *consistent improvement of* *living conditions.*

This specific set of intrinsic human capacities, activities, and principles are expressed as: human *'material basic purpose'*, the *'five primary axioms'* of economics, and the *'twelve elemental activities'/'primary operating dynamics'* of economics, and all resultant *'derivative operating dynamics'*.

It is only with the above definition and application of the corresponding **productivity class** economic principles, can **producers**, lawmakers, and economists effectively direct their efforts toward the successful **administration** and **management** of economic conditions for any institution or populace.

What are *'material basic purpose'*, the *'five primary axioms'*, and the *'twelve elemental activities'* – aka *'primary operating dynamics'* – of economics and all resultant *'derivative operating dynamics'*?

Well, that's the whole point, isn't it.

CHAPTER 1
BEDROCK BASICS

THE BASIC PURPOSE
of Economics
This is Where it all Starts

and

THE FIVE PRIMARY AXIOMS
of Economics
This is Where it all Becomes a Productive Activity

ATTENTION:
If you have not read the preceding **"Preparatory Principles and Techniques"**,
if you normally skip such things, ***go back, and read it all now***.
*It contains the **preparatory information** necessary
to understand and apply the material in this text.*

THE BASIC PURPOSE
of
All Economic Activity and Endeavor

About The Basic Purpose of Economics:

Productivity Class Economic Theory Statement

Every dynamic of human life has its material aspect – i.e. all humans use material things to better succeed on every active pursuit required for living life. The BASIC PURPOSE of *all* material activity [the reason it genetically evolved into existence] is to *'secure the material requirements necessary* to...
- *achieve a worthwhile quality of survival,*
- *successfully pursue the dynamics of living,* and
- *improve living conditions with consistent regularity'.*

From rain forest tribes to the most sophisticated civilizations, we all share this same fundamental material drive – this same BASIC material PURPOSE to use material things to succeed in living life.

As humans have evolved to utilize the resources around us to produce all the *material things* we *need* and *want* in order to accomplish every fundamental requirement of living a human life, this BASIC PURPOSE, then, is *'the fundamental incentive or drive'* for *all* material decisions and actions.

Further, the need to meet the *material requirements necessary to survive, pursue the dynamics of living,* and *improve living conditions* generates the need to consume. The need to consume generates the need to produce – *which further generates all other elemental activities of economics.*

As the *evolutionary reason* for material 'BASIC PURPOSE drive' is *'material contribution to the success of human living and well-being',* 'BASIC PURPOSE' as stated above is also the basis for economic *ETHICS.*

About The Basic Purpose of Economics:
an
Overview

Productivity Class Causation and Application Principles

In **productivity class** economics, all **causation** and **operating principles** begin from **basic purpose** drive generating the need to **produce** and **consume**:

- It is the human **basic purpose** drive that generates the *activities* of economics. We describe that process using...
- **five primary axioms** to delineate the human capacities employed to create the actual *activities* of economics; which are...
- the **twelve elementary activities / primary operating dynamics;** which also further generate...
- the *derivative* or *subordinate* **operating dynamics** – utilized for their success.

[That may seem a little confusing right now because we haven't yet covered what those activities are. *This is where using the online diagram can help.* It shows the whole thing very clearly. In any case, if you get the idea that it all starts with **basic purpose** drives, bringing into play certain innate human capacities to do certain **elemental activities** that become and remain the **primary operating dynamics** of all economics, and that they further generate, by their activities, **derivative** or **subordinate operating dynamics**, well then, you've got it.]

Always Correctly Define The 'Purpose' of an Activity

The most important thing you need to understand about *any field of applied knowledge*, including economics, is its fundamental *purpose* – what is it *for*, why does it exist in the first place – in *nature* and in *human life*. Only when we know the purpose for which an activity or behavior evolved into existence can we know how to correctly *apply* that subject toward the achievement of its true reason for existence – in nature and in human life. *This principle is what guides the creation of all proper 'application' principles for all fields of knowledge.* [see ' **Principles and Standards**' in Introduction]

The Basic [*Founding*] 'Purpose' of Economics

In Chapter Two we explain the innate application of **twelve elemental human activities** that *every* human practices in order to achieve *all* material needs and wants. The active application of these **twelve elemental activities** all together *is* the activity of *economics* – *is* *economics* itself [see full diagram at **productivityclass.*info***].

And it is through economics, as these **twelve elemental activities**, that we fulfill the material requirements necessary for our *quality of survival,* our *successful pursuit of the dynamics of living,* and *achievement of improved living conditions.*

The *material needs* required for *basic purpose* success
is the purpose for all **productive** and **consumptive** activity –
the reason these activities, *economics itself,* evolved into existence.

FACT: The active employment of the **twelve elementary activities** toward the successful achievement of this **basic purpose** _is_ the economic activity – is 'economics'. Further...

All **dynamic forces** in economics are **basic purpose** 'at work' –
i.e. is **basic purpose** _compelling into utility_
all of the different _functions_ and _operating activities_ necessary to accomplish
a worthwhile quality of survival,
successful pursuit the dynamics of living, and
consistent improvement of living conditions.

FACT: Without understanding its **basic purpose**, you cannot recognize when economics is being inverted, corrupted, abusive, or just plain 'gone off its rails' – or for that matter, how to just _apply_ its _cause-and-effect principles_ to a fully appropriate and **ethical** outcome.

IMPORTANT ETHICAL NOTE:
All human social drives extend outward from ourselves
toward all other aspects of human and other forms of life.
These same _social drives_ also guide our _material **basic purpose** drives._
That's why **gain** at the expense of others, other living things,
or the environment is an _**inversion**_ –
it generates the _opposite_ of the proper **basic purpose** effect.

About Basic Purpose:

Characteristics and General Factors

Basic purpose is the foundation of _all_ economic activity. It is the drive that generates and compels into existence all other fundamental economic **operating dynamics**. Below are but a sample of the more important characteristics of the '**basic purpose**' of economics.

Basic Purpose Is The Basis of Economic Ethics

Every human being is _born_ with the innate gifts of **basic purpose** drive, the _five primary economic capacities and behaviors_ [expressed in the **five primary axioms**], and the ability to wield the **twelve elemental activities** required to successfully achieve all **basic purpose** _needs_ and _wants_ – albeit each of us to varying degrees of potential and talent. This is simply how nature evolved us to succeed in providing materially in living our lives.

Exercising these capacities freely and without obstruction
is _fundamental and necessary to successful human survival._

*Therefore, the basis of economic **ethics** is to ensure that*
***basic purpose** is not opposed, hindered, obstructed, or prevented*
for individuals, groups, populaces, and even environments
effected by any economic activity.

Organized economic frameworks, then, must include incentives, regulations, and laws that ensure this.

Although **basic purpose** principles form the *basis* of economic **ethics**, it is principles of **symbiotic exchange** that form the *functioning structure* upon which economic **ethics** is actually carried out – **organized trade** and **productive** *behaviors* and *structuring* that ensure '**mutual benefit'** to all parties, life forms, and environments effected by any economic activity. Together they complete the foundational working principles upon which economic **ethics** can be carried out and expanded upon.

Basic Purpose Graduates from *Needs* to *Wants* – from *Necessities* to *Desirables*

We start by fulfilling our *needs* for basic or essential *survival*, ensuring we have all the essential *necessities* to live. At the same time, we also ensure our ability to successfully *pursue the most basic dynamics of living*, usually also considered *necessities*. Finally, and again *concurrently*, we ensure that we have safe and secure *living conditions* to do it in. Once again, a *necessity*.

Once this *minimal* level of **basic purpose** is achieved, we *instinctively drive forward* and begin work to *improve* upon that. We pursue **gainful** *'advancement of standards'* on whatever our **basic purpose** conditions are – to fulfill our desires for *more, better*, and *pleasure* – to *wants*.

Once *essential survival* is achieved, it is our innate basic purpose drive to immediately begin *working to improve upon that*. We now strive to *gain*.

Completion of Purpose

All things economic begin with produce.
We produce to fulfill basic purpose *needs* and *wants*.

Therefore, if the **basic purpose** of material **productivity** is to better *survive, pursue the dynamics of living*, and *improve the conditions of living*, then the **productivity** is not actually complete until its *purpose* is fulfilled – until a **product** or **service** completes its reason for being **produced** in the first place – serving someone's **basic purpose** *needs* or *wants*.

THE FIVE PRIMARY AXIOMS
The Beginning of All Economic Activity

About The Five Primary Axioms of Economics:

Productivity Class® Economic Theory Statement

The Basic Purpose drive for *material needs* and *wants* compel into utility all of the different functions and operating activities necessary for accomplishing *a worthwhile quality of survival, successful pursuit the dynamics of living*, and *consistent improvement of living conditions*.

These functions, capacities, and activities, when in coordinated operation, coalesce into the entire applied field of knowledge and activity we call 'economics'. The *founding* application of these functions, capacities, and activities are postulated and stated in 'Five Primary Axioms'.

The Five Primary Axioms of economics are together a statement of the application of *five primary human capacities* humans apply in creating a *single clockwork* of 'Twelve Elemental Activities' necessary to successfully achieve all human material needs and wants – the operations of which generate *all* further 'Derivative Operating Dynamics'* and functional economic principles. [*Dynamics 'derived' from the activities of other dynamics.]

By their *founding* and *primary* nature, these 'Twelve Elemental Activities' function as the *'Primary Operating Dynamics'* of *all* economic activity no matter how expanded or sophisticated that economic activity may get.

The Five Primary Axioms of Economics are:

Primary Axiom One:

In order to secure the *material* requirements necessary to
achieve a worthwhile quality of survival,
successfully pursue the dynamics of living, and
consistently improve living conditions,

humans actively PRODUCE what we *need* and *want*,
actively CONSUMING *when* we PRODUCE,
and through expenditure or utility, *what* we PRODUCE.
[Capacity: *productivity* – including the ability to **invent**, **innovate**, *create*, etc.

what is needed or wanted to achieve **basic purpose** drives).]

Primary Axiom Two:

In order to actively PRODUCE what we need and want,
we humans EDUCATE ourselves
so to become *knowledgeable* and *skilled* in
the 'causation' and 'application' principles of PRODUCING
which requires as a precursor we
locate, obtain, and develop for use all possible RESOURCES.

Active, but limited, TRADE and concepts of ETHICS begin here.

[Capacity: to *educate*, *be* educated, and develop *skills*.]

[**Trade** at this point is primarily to obtain **resources** – **material** and **capital**.
Ethics here is to prevent human conflict and are simple, uncodified agreements
of fairness, honesty, and rightful interactions and behaviors in **trade**.]

Primary Axiom Three:

As humans we are endowed with all the physical and mental capacities
necessary to PRODUCE and provide beyond our own
individual and family *essential* BASIC PURPOSE needs.

Thus material GAIN and
asset accumulation begins.

With GAIN and asset accumulation comes indefinite expansion of
TRADE and concepts of ETHICS.

Active, but limited, EMPLOYMENT begins here.

[Capacity: the ability to *produce gainfully – i.e. beyond consumptive needs*]

[**Employment** at this point is considered **trade** for occasional assisted **labor**.]

Primary Axiom Four:

In order to be more *efficient, productive,* and most especially *consistent*
in producing for BASIC PURPOSE needs and wants,
we humans create *patterns* and *systems* of doing things.

Thus, concepts and methods of ORGANIZATION begin,

and therefore also, SPECIALIZATION, EMPLOYMENT, and CURRENCY.

Also, with the development of ORGANIZATION,
all TWELVE ELEMENTAL ACTIVITIES
develop into full, expanded, and ever more sophisticated use,
and become established as, and more properly referred to as,
the PRIMARY OPERATING DYNAMICS of economics.

[Capacity: the ability to *create patterns and systems* (of doing things).]

[**Employment** here is considered *routine* and *consistent* '**trade** for **service**',
no longer limited to 'occasional assisted **labor**' as above.]

Primary Axiom Five:

Humans are social, cooperative beings and therefore
survive and thrive only in SYMBIOTIC patterns and systems,
and suffer and decline in INVERTED [antagonistic] or *primarily* ALTRUISTIC
patterns and systems.

A *primarily* ALTRUISTIC economic system tends to over burden itself
over time and eventually must revert back to a SYMBIOTIC EXCHANGE
based system in combination with ALTRUISTIC *support* activities.

Properly worked in and applied ALTRUISTIC <u>support</u> activities
strengthen SYMBIOTIC EXCHANGE based systems,
making them more stable and resilient.

[Improperly applied or excessively **ALTRUISTIC** patterns and systems tend
over time to cause similar effects as **INVERTED** patterns and systems
through the reduction of responsibility levels of whole segments of the populace
and extracting excessive resources from the **SYMBIOTIC EXCHANGE** system.]

SYMBIOTIC principles properly alloyed with ALTRUISTIC support structure
– *designed to provide successful participation in SYMBIOTIC EXCHANGE* –
completes the *structural principles* required for economic ETHICS.

[Capacity: to exchange productive value in *mutual gain with others*.]

These 'five primary axioms' *flow one into the other*, are dependent upon
each other to function successfully, and as such their 'primary operating
dynamics' are all done as *one set of coordinated actions*.

The very doing of these twelve elemental activities/primary operating
dynamics *is* economics and is what the subject is actually about:

PRODUCE, CONSUME, EDUCATE, RESOURCES, TRADE, ETHICS,
GAIN, ORGANIZE, EMPLOY, CURRENCY, SPECIALIZE, SYMBIOSIS

Economic Theory Statement Expanded:

When humans set out to achieve **basic purpose** needs and wants, these are the *five primary capacities and behaviors* that *all* humans employ to do so. The active use of these capacities is to employ **twelve elemental activities** through which we accomplish *all* material **basic purpose** needs and wants.

Therefore, the **five primary axioms** of economics can be best understood as: a statement of the *five primary capacities and behaviors* that *all* humans employ to create a *single clockwork* of **twelve** *interrelated* **elemental activities** necessary to *successfully achieve all human material needs and wants*.

Due to the *founding* and *primary* nature of these '**twelve elemental activities**' to accomplish *all* **basic purpose** material needs and wants, they always remain the '***primary operating dynamics***' of *all* economic activity no matter how expanded or sophisticated economic systems or conditions get.

About The Five Primary Axioms:
an
Overview

The Foundation of *All* of Human Economic Activity

Basic purpose and the **five primary axioms** with the **twelve elemental activities** are *innate* to each and every one of us. They are our material *nature*. The **twelve elemental activities** are the *real world **operating dynamics*** we *all* apply to accomplish our **basic purpose** *needs* and *wants*:

- o *All humans* are born with the capacity and drive to **learn** [**educate** themselves and others] to *locate, obtain,* and *develop for use* all possible **resources** necessary to **produce** what they need to **consume** in fulfillment of **basic purpose** *needs* [and soon thereafter, *wants*];
- o *All humans* are born with the capacity and drive to ***produce** more than they need to **consume**,* **trade** their excess **productivity** for the **productivity** of others, develop **ethical trade** agreements that avoid human conflict, and thus create material **gain** that advances **basic purpose** *conditions*;
- o *All humans* are born with the capacity and drive to **organize** into *patterns* and *systems* all material activities: including utilizing a material or commodity as an intermediate **currency** to make **trade**

more efficient; **productively employing** others or *be* **employed**; and **specializing** in their **productivity**;

o   *All humans*, as social beings, create **symbiotic trade** relationships with others, and further create **altruistic** behaviors that support the well-being of others [but can learn to **invert** these behaviors].

Really get that!

That is *all* any of us ever do to accomplish our *material* needs and wants. All societies that have ever existed anywhere in any time in human history, from a single family surviving in the rain forest to moguls and corporations, have been using these same fundamental human drives, capacities, and activities to provide for material *needs* and *wants*.

*Therefore, the very doing of these **twelve elemental activities** <u>is</u> economics and is what the branch of knowledge is actually about.*

About The Five Primary Axioms:

Characteristics and General Factors

A *Single Set* of Coordinated Actions

The **five primary axioms** are *not*, taken individually. Each is *not* a complete economic principle in any way functioning on its own or randomly done. Like the gears of a clockwork, *it is the set together that is the complete single functioning construct.*

Any one 'element' or 'activity' can be worked with or acted upon alone, *but only in the context of ensuring that it functions with, and contributes to, the forward motion of all the others as a whole, and always toward the accomplishment of **basic purpose** needs and wants.*

Natural *Capacities* are not Necessarily Real World *Capabilities*

The **five primary axioms** with their **twelve elemental activities** are *born* to each and every one of us. They are our *nature*. And we are born to *use* them as defined in the **axioms** by *doing* the **elemental activities** – *born* to it. One only need to *look* to see every human being in every culture at every economic level from the rain forest aborigine to modern corporate leaders all abiding by the same innate **basic purpose** drives, applying the same fundamental capacities to do the same **elemental activities** in order to fulfill their material requirements for a *worthwhile quality of survival, successful pursuit of the dynamics of living,* and *improvement of living conditions.*

However, having the innate *capacity* to do something doesn't necessarily mean one is innately born to do it *well*. Real *capability* implies a level of *competence*, some level of **education**, **training**, and/or **learning** experience that develops some level of *expertise*.

Competence is the key factor in the success of anything.

The **five primary axioms** describe the mental and physical *capacities* all humans use to perform and practice the **twelve elemental activities** of economics. To apply these as real world *capabilities*, one needs some type of **education** and *real world successful practice*. [More on this in Chapter Two: **The Twelve Elemental Activities** in the section on **Education**.]

CHAPTER TWO

The
TWELVE ELEMENTAL ACTIVITIES
of Economics

also known as

The
PRIMARY OPERATING DYNAMICS
of Economics

INTRODUCTORY STATEMENT:

So... How fundamental is this, *really*?

As advanced as we are today, it's easy to forget that all we see around us in its earliest beginnings started from tribes of people living off whatever natural **resources** were available to them in their particular environments in the remote past – no different from aboriginal tribes living in the rainforests or other remote areas of the world today.

What has advanced humanity in all of our many various economic sagas throughout the world and time has been the drive for **gainful basic purpose** advancement through both **productive** and **organizational** *inventiveness* and *innovation*.

And just underneath that, from those early aboriginal tribes to the most sophisticated civilizations of today, you can observe the same fundamental *drives*, *capacities*, and *activities* underlying *all* material successes – from human community to human community, civilization to civilization, we all do the *same* fundamental things to succeed materially – that is, *economically...*

THE PRINCIPLES of
The TWELVE ELEMENTAL ACTIVITIES
of Economics

"Economics should be defined in terms of what it is about. It should be about how people produce things, how people exchange them, how people earn income, how they pay taxes, how the government provides infrastructure with tax revenue, and how it conducts monetary policy. The subject has to be defined in terms of the object of inquiry."
Author: Ha-Joon Chang, Author of pragmatic economics [very recommended reading]

About the Twelve Elemental Activities of Economics:

Productivity Class Economic Theory Statement
[Includes partial review of the **Basic Purpose** and the **Five Primary Axioms**.]

The 'Basic Purpose' of *all* economic activity is to *secure the material requirements* necessary to *achieve a worthwhile quality of survival, successfully pursue the dynamics of living,* and *consistently improve living conditions.*

The drive to achieve Basic Purpose brings to bear the five primary human capacities – stated in Five Primary Axioms – employed to create a *single clockwork* of Twelve Elemental Activities necessary to successfully achieve *all* human material needs and wants.

These 'Twelve Elemental Activities', *no matter how sophisticated and advanced the economic system*, are *always* the 'Primary Operating Dynamics' of *all* economic activity – the operations of which also generate *all* further 'Derivative Operating Dynamics' and economic working principles. These 'Twelve Elemental Activities' are:

PRODUCE, CONSUME, EDUCATE, RESOURCES, TRADE, ETHICS,
GAIN, ORGANIZE, EMPLOY, CURRENCY, SPECIALIZE, SYMBIOSIS

These Axioms and Twelve Elemental Activities *flow one into the other*, are dependent upon each other to function successfully, and when in action, are all done as *one set of complimentary and contributive coordinated actions* – operating as a 'clockwork-like' set.

The very doing of these Twelve Elemental Activities *is* economics and is what the subject of economics is actually about.

About the Twelve Elemental Activities of Economics:
an
Overview

These **twelve elemental activities** are the material **activities** that *all* humans do naturally to *survive, pursue the dynamics of living,* and *improve their living conditions. None of these **activities** are 'thought up' human concepts:*

Each of these twelve elemental activities,
as well as their interrelationship as a single coordinated activity,
are the *evolutionary attributes humans have developed*
in order to secure the *material requirements* of *living a human life.*

The Twelve Elemental Activities

PRODUCE, CONSUME, EDUCATE, RESOURCES, TRADE, ETHICS,
GAIN, ORGANIZE, EMPLOY, CURRENCY, SPECIALIZE, SYMBIOSIS

Another way of picturing the **twelve elemental activities** [so they are not understood as just some random list to memorize]:

Axiom 1	*Axiom 2*	*Axiom 3*	*Axiom 4*	*Axiom 5*
Produce	Educate	Gain	Organize	Symbiotic
Consume	Resources		↓	Exchange
	↓			↓
	Trade		Specialize	[alloyed with
	Ethics		Employment	Altruistic
			Currency	Support]

These **twelve elemental activities** are *not just a list* of individual activities packaged together because they all happen to be economic fundamentals. The **twelve elemental activities** are fundamental dynamics of a *single mechanism* – a clockwork of activities that interrelate, interact, and function together to form a single larger activity providing for material needs and wants: *economics.*

Further, each **elemental activity**, although never independent of the others, is still an **'educational'** and **'specialized'** subject unto itself, having *its own fundamentals* that must be **learned** in order to do *each* of them well enough to succeed at *all* of them as a whole. **Education** answers all of this.

The 'Core Four'

The first four of these **twelve elemental activities** are so inter-related that you cannot discuss one without discussing the other three – you cannot *do* one without *doing the other three* – **produce, consume, education**, and **resources**. *Each exists only because the others exist. Each is active only when the others are also active.* These can be considered the **'core four'** activities upon which all the other activities are based – most especially ***produce***.

One Complimentary and Contributive Coordinated Set of Actions

Again, to drive the point home, all **twelve elemental activities** when in action, are all done as *one complimentary and contributive coordinated set of actions*. Any **elemental activity** out of context and alignment with all of the others will get 'lost' [misdirected or **inverted**] and become noncontributing and, therefore, *counter-***productive**. When out of context with the others, the energy expended on any 'misdirected' activities is wasted and all of the other activities become less effective or possibly completely *in*effective. *Ineffective* translates to failure to achieve **basic purpose** needs and wants – for an individual, group, or even entire economies.

Each Elemental Activity Has Its Own Set of Principles

As stated earlier, *"the **five primary axioms** are not, taken individually. Each is not a complete economic principle in any way functioning on its own or randomly done. Like the gears of a clockwork, it is the set together that is the complete single functioning construct."*

The **axioms** are statements of how the **twelve elementary activities** are generated into existence. However, each **elemental activity** has its own set of *'causative'* and *'operating'* principles. You don't do the same things to **produce** as you do to **consume**. Each must be operating *under its own correct applications*, but fully *coordinated with each other* and in order to generate **gain**. As stated earlier, "Any one 'element' or 'activity' can be worked with or acted upon alone, *but only in the context of ensuring that it functions with, and contributes to, the forward motion of all the others as a whole, and always toward the accomplishment of **basic purpose** needs and wants."*

So, since each **elemental activity** has its own set of *cause-and-effect* and *application* principles, let's look at each one...

THE PRINCIPLES of PRODUCE

"I find that the harder I work, the more luck I seem to have."
Author: Thomas Jefferson 1743-1826

Primary Axiom One:

In order to secure the *material* requirements necessary to *survive*,
pursue the dynamics of living, and *improve living conditions*,
humans actively PRODUCE what we *need* and *want*,
actively CONSUMING *when* we PRODUCE,
and through expenditure or utility, *what* we PRODUCE.

About Producing:

Productivity Class Economic Theory Statement

Producing is the elementary activity of bringing a resource of *value* or *potential value* into actual human consumptive basic purpose service.

All things economic begin with nature's fundamental requirement that we must materially produce what we need and want in order to *survive, pursue the dynamics of living*, and *improve living conditions*.

In order for *anything* to be consumed for basic purpose, it must *first* be produced. However, production itself *cannot occur without* consumption, education, and resources: the *essential purpose* of 'educate' and 'resources' is to '*produce*' for 'consumption'. Economically, they *exist* to produce.

The activities of consume, educate, and resources, therefore, are not the *cause* of economic activity. Only *producing* for consumption, for self or others, begins actual *economic* activity.

All things economic begin with produce.

Further, the basic purpose need for *continuous* consumption generates the need for *continuous* production of 'needed but expended' products and services – generating into existence a *self-perpetuating cyclic system* of continuous production and consumption.

Therefore, all economic *systems* begin as
'any *continuous cycle* of production and consumption'.
[and always remains so no matter how sophisticated.]

About Producing:
an
Overview

Natural Born Producers

Economically, life can seem like one long demanding **productive** pursuit for **basic purpose** *needs* and *wants*. Prospering, even a small amount in life, requires tough, **productive** action. Nature provides us with every **resource** we could materially need or want to live any lifestyle we choose, and all the *capacities* for the *capabilities* necessary for success. But we must actively *produce* if we are to fulfill the material requirements for success along all the dynamics of human living.

As we strive for what we need and want in life, we get to *have* only equal to what we can **produce** – in our careers, our life dynamics, and our living conditions. Any *achievement* of any kind will be only in proportion to what we can **produce** – *in volume and in value.*

We either produce equal to our needs and wants, or suffer the lack of it.

No one should be daunted by that. We are *made* for this.
It is a *fundamental* that humans are *natural born* **producers**.
It is our innate nature to succeed in life through productivity.

About Producing:

Characteristics and General Factors

**The first three factors of *producing* are
the other three 'core' elemental activities:
consumption, *education*, and *resources*.**

Producing Requires Consumption

There is no **producing** without **consuming**. One of the first things we learn about **producing** is that, not only do we **consume** *what* we **produce**, but that **producing** itself **consumes resources**. This connotes the important relationship of *efficient consumption* to **gainful productivity**:

Production *expends* resources. *Inefficient* **consumption**
increases **costs** and therefore *reduces* the revenues left for **gain**.

Producing Requires Education

There is no **producing** without knowing *how* to **produce** – we must be

educated to it. From *self*-**education** of trial and error experience, to every generation of parents, mentors, or teachers who taught and apprenticed their next generation, *the skills of* **producing** *for* **basic purpose** *needs and wants must be learned by each and every generation.* We are *not* born *knowing.*

However the capacity to *learn, retain knowledge and capability,* to *think creatively,* **invent** and **innovate,** and through practice become *skilled* and *competent* in any and every possible handling of a **resource** is the *capacity* that allows humans to adapt to almost *any* environment and still achieve **basic purpose** success. And that we *are* born with.

Producing Requires Resources

There is no **producing** without **resources**. All **products** are made from something. Those somethings are **resources**. What we can **produce** is limited by the type and amount of **resources** we can access and how well we can manipulate those **resources** into needed and wanted **products** and **services**. To the degree we can *locate, obtain,* and *develop* **resources** *for use* – and *expand* our **resource** capacities – we improve our lot, and we **prosper.**

'Develop for use' means to take a **resource** of little or no **value** in its raw form, and, by whatever means, work it into something *useful* and *valuable* that serves human **basic purpose** drives. This is the aspect of **producing** that requires **inventiveness, innovation,** and **educated** *competence.*

The 'Complete Production Cycle' [of Economics]

The complete **production cycle** is:
1.   **Educate** [on **productivity**]
2.   **Resources** [locate, obtain, develop for use, and make use of]
3.   **Produce** [*needs* and *wants* as **products** and **services**]
4.   **Trade** [includes **Ethics** as 'Symbiotic (mutually beneficial) **Exchange**']
5.   **Consume** [realize **consumptive** benefit]

Note the *complete* **production** cycle is *the completion of* **axiom one** *and* **axiom two** *in service to* **basic purpose.**

From the viewpoint of a **business** endeavor, **producing** [a **product** or **service**] is considered the beginning of the **production** cycle, and **trade** is usually considered the end of the **production** cycle. However, *economically* the purpose of any **productivity** is to serve **basic purpose** benefit.

The **product** was made to do something. When it completes or is serving that purpose – when it has achieved *consumptive benefit* by **producing** *its intended purpose* – then and only then is the **production cycle** complete.

Producing 'Evolves' [*Continuously*]: *Discovery, Invention,* and *Innovation*

Producing, among other things, is a *technological* subject. Therefore, even simple usages of the most basic '*thinking fundamentals* of *exploratory* and *creative thought*' – **discovery, invention,** and **innovation** – continuously *evolves* what we **produce** and how we **produce** it:

A primitive forest dweller **discovers** a stone that breaks off with a sharp cutting edge [e.g. obsidian, flint, etc.]. He *develops* a **product** to cut meat and clean animal skins for leather. An **innovation** puts a wood handle on the stone to prevent the user from being cut by the stone. Yet another's *creative thinking* '*evolves*' placing the stone with a 'sharp cutting point on the end of a wood staff' – a spear – **inventing** a new hunting weapon.

A tribal gatherer **discovers** that certain plants have fibers that, when twisted together are very strong [e.g. hemp, flax, etc.]. Using her innate capacity for **invention**, she separates the fiber from the plant and *develops* it into rope or twine to tie things together. Another's **innovation** meshes the twine into a net to catch fish. Yet another's *creative thinking* '*evolves*' use of the twine into a 'new use' – the tension of a sapling along with the twine and some twigs can be used to catch small animals for food – **inventing** the new **productivity** of 'trapping'.

Another individual gets the idea to *reconfigure* both of these two trends of **discovery, invention,** and **innovation** into a bow and arrow – a new weapon – yet another new **invention**.

And so it goes with **productivity** *evolving* across every '*dynamic of living*' in order to make those dynamics more *successful* and more *enjoyable*. No matter how sophisticated we get in our **productivities**, we are still only performing this same fundamental function.

All through the entirety of human *material* endeavor *there has never been anything else going on*. Advancement is just a matter of sophistication.

The Other Eleven Elemental Activities and 'Produce'

With the exception of **consume**, *all other **primary operating dynamics** [twelve elemental activities] exist for the sole purpose to serve or expand upon **produce*** – as **produce** *directly* serves the **basic purpose** need to **consume**, and **basic purpose** is the very *driving force* of all material **productivity**.

If you re-read **basic purpose** and **axiom one** in Chapter One, you will see how **basic purpose** *requires* and *naturally leads to* **axiom one**. If you re-read the four proceeding **axioms**, you will clearly see that every **axiom** *serves* or *expands upon* **produce** [**productivity**].

It is the volume and value of our productivity that determines
the success of our material contribution to our entire living experience.
This is the significance and the importance of produce – productivity.

About Producing:

Principles and Concepts Important to Success

You don't get paid for the hour. You get paid for the value you bring to the hour.
Author: Jim Rohn, prolific author of books on living a better life.

All Value Has A Basis [a *quality* or *attribute* '*contributive to living life*']

In order to judge whether or not anything is of any true **value**, there must be a *basis* by which that **value** is determined.

Productivity class® basis for *economic* **value**:
The quality of outcomes on human basic purpose experience or conditions
derived from producing and utilizing a product or service in living life.

Without such *contribution* or *quality of outcome*, a **product** or **service** has no *actual* **value**.

However, economic **value** isn't always determined by '*reason*' or '*actual*' **value**. In fact **value** is *usually* determined by '*perceived*' contribution to **basic purpose** needs and wants – not *actual* contribution – including the influences of **marketing** forces. In fact, *inaccurate perceptions of value* often cause adverse effects upon our **basic purpose** pursuits.

"I conceive that the great part of the miseries of mankind are brought upon
them by false estimates they have made of the value of things."
Benjamin Franklin

In academic economics, **value** is usually measured as **price** or **market value** [**trade value**]. In everyday *real* life, each individual person has *their own basis* for determining what a 'quality of outcome' or 'well-being' actually *means* or *is* – most without thinking much about it. In **productivity class** economics, **value** is measured as '*economic value*' above, which may include **price** or **market value**, but primarily, contribution to **basic purpose** success.

The Different Types of Value in Economics:

Actual **Value**

Everything **produced** has an *actual* [aka *true*] **value** determined by...

a. Tangible contribution to the **volume** or **value** of a **producer's productivity**, or

b. Tangible contribution to a **consumer's** *actual* **basic purpose** *needs* and *wants*.

This is *not* **value** as measured by **price**. This is strictly **value** – *the worth, usefulness, or importance of a thing* – as contribution to **producing products** or **services** or to **basic purpose** outcomes.

Market, Price, or *Trade* Value

The second measure of **value** is *market* value, sometimes called *trade* value or *price* value. In order to understand **market value**, we must first understand what **demand** is. For now, we will define economic **demand** as *'people's desire* and *willingness to pay* to acquire particular **products** and **services***.

Consumers desire to acquire what they *perceive* as needed or wanted – aka **consumer demand**. And by the *strength* or *intensity* of that **demand** consumers have a higher or lower **price** limit they are willing to pay for that **product** or **service**. **Producers** on the other hand set **prices** according to what **consumers** are willing to pay, but *in* **competitive balance** with their **competitor's prices**. The **volume** of **supply** provided to the **consumer** by **competition** drives prices down as **producers compete** for the **consumer's** business. This balance between *'intensity of demand'* and *'competitive pricing of supply'* sets the **price** in the *market* – aka *market value*. [More in Chapter Three]

Value Measured as 'Quality'

Quality is measured by *'how well a thing is made'* – that is, how well a thing is constructed to perform its intended purpose; how well it holds up in expected or required use, or difficult circumstances of use; and how *lasting* a thing is in performing its intended purpose.

Additionally, a ***productive*** *tool*, an *appliance*, a *machine*, etc. – a **capital resource** – in **addition** to the above *must also allow for acceptable **gain** from **productive** usage*. The more lasting, the better the performance and usefulness [**quality**], and the more **productive gain** from usage, the more **value** to the **producer** or **consumer**.

Value Measured as 'Quantity' [or 'volume']

The *value* of **quantity** – volume of **production** – is measured in the difference between *production costs* and the *volume of products produced*. If *more volume* can be **produced** with '**capital resource** *a*' at an *equal* **cost** to '**capital resource** *b*', the greater potential for **profit** is with '**resource** *a*' – it produces '*more*' at the same **cost**. **Producers** work from **profit margins**, but **consumers** must also consider the **productivity** of their *household* **capital resources** [home appliances, car, power equipment, etc.]. [More on this in Chapter Three].

Also, in general, 'more' of something for the 'same **price**' is considered a better **value** [even if you don't want or need it. Hmm...].

'Creating' and 'Adding' Value

The whole point of 'creating **value**', or 'adding more **value**', is creating a more **profitable product** or **service** *through improved basic purpose outcomes for the consumer* from their having or use of that **product** or **service**:

Creating **value**
- This is '*making new things from raw materials or basic components*' [raw or basic **resources**]; it is manufacturing **products** and **services**, and also includes **discovery** [of new materials (**resources**)] and **inventing** new **products**, **services**, and **resources**. Where there was nothing of useful value, there now is.

Adding **value**
- This is '*adding to things usually already of value*': improving quality; *altering, modifying,* or *expanding* the capabilities, usefulness, or usability of an existing **product** or **service**; improving appearance to increase desirability; etc. – anything that **consumers** would **value** more and therefore pay a higher price for, or will now purchase when they otherwise would not. This is *re-invention, innovation**, and *discovery*. [*The first sail on an ancient boat was an **invention**...everything after that was **innovation** after **innovation**...until there were great schooners and sailing ships.]

Productive 'Volume' – 'Quantity'

The value of 'volume' also has its basis:
profit, gain, and contributive effect.

The *initial* **value** basis for **productive volume** is higher or more **profit** and **gain**. Assuming that you can **trade** whatever **volume** you can **produce**, more **volume** of **production** usually means a higher **volume** of **revenues** and, therefore, **gain**. [This principle extends to **working producers (employees)** who rightfully expect to be paid more if they **produce** more than other **employees.**]

However, in order to make that work, a **producer** must be able to **trade** what he or she **produces**, and must not **produce** more than they can **trade**. To do so creates waste. Therefore, *again we come to efficiency. Inefficiency and waste increases costs and unnecessarily* reduces **profitability** – reduces **gainfulness.**

More, **However, Is Not Always** *Better*

When pursuing **basic purpose** drives, **volume** can get a little tricky – because *more* is not always *better…*

'More' is '**volume**'. 'Better' is '*improved **basic purpose** outcomes.*'
So *more* is not always *better.*

Productively speaking, **invention** and **innovation** is the true key to 'growth'
– the true key to *better.*

Once a particular quality of life has been achieved, *more* and *bigger* no longer contribute to an improved life experience. *And **basic purpose** requires material contribution to improvements in the living experience.* At some point, *better* is no longer *more* or *bigger* material things, but contribution to *better living* from material things – *improved* **products** and **services.**

THE PRINCIPLES of CONSUME

"It is incumbent upon each of us to improve spending and savings practices to ensure our own individual financial security..."
Author: Ron Lewis, British Labour politician

Primary Axiom One:

In order to materially *survive, pursue the dynamics of living,*
and *improve living conditions,*
humans actively PRODUCE what we *need* and *want,*
actively CONSUMING *when* we PRODUCE,
and through expenditure or utility, *what* we PRODUCE.

About Consumption:

Productivity Class Economic Theory Statement

The need to meet the *'material basic purpose requirements necessary to survive, pursue the dynamics of living,* and *improve living conditions' generates* the need to consume. It is the need to consume that generates the need to produce.

All consumption *starts* when *resources are consumed* in order to produce the products and services that will be then consumed for basic purpose needs and wants.

Further, in order for something to be consumed, it must first be produced. Accordingly, consumption can never exceed production. However, production can exceed consumption and therefore produce gain.

Accordingly also, all who would consume must first produce. Therefore, it further follows that the capacity to produce, in volume and in value, determines capacity for economic consumption and basic purpose success.

The drive for 'basic purpose' consumptive *needs* and *wants* is the primary *driver* of *all* economic productive activities – including the drive to *gain.*

About Consumption:
an
Overview

It is through **consumption** that **basic purpose** is achieved. We **consume resources** to *survive, pursue the dynamics of living*, and *improve and maintain our living conditions*. **Consumption**, however, also *depletes* and *expends* **resources**. **Consumption** is an *expense* – whether expended on **productivity** or directly on **basic purpose** *needs* and *wants*.

Therefore, effective **consuming** requires application of the principles of *economy, efficiency*, and *utility*. We must maintain what we **consume** at levels *less than* what we **produce** in order to create **gain**. The first thing we learn about economics is that *expenses* [**consumption**] *must always be less than income* [**productivity**], no matter how we work that out. *Gain can only be created when* **consumption** *for* **basic purpose** *needs and wants is* <u>*less*</u> *than what we* **produce***.* **When our production is in** *excess* **of our consumption, we gain.**

> *Economically*, **when the** *value* **of one's productivity is higher than the** *value* **of resources consumed, one gains.**

> *Tangibly*, **when the value or volume of one's productivity** *advances basic purpose conditions*, **one** *gains.*

In **business**, this factor, or principle, must not only create **gain** for the **business** itself, but it must create enough **gain** so that the **owners, operators**, and **employees** can each create **gain** in their *household* economics.

Skilled **consumption** improves **basic purpose** conditions – *tangible* **gain** described above. Remember, **basic purpose** drives require a <u>*worthwhile*</u> quality of survival, <u>*successful*</u> pursuit of the dynamics of living, and the <u>*improvement*</u> of living conditions. To achieve that, we must be skilled at **producing** *and* **consuming**. Once we are successful **producers**, only as *skilled* **consumers** can we ***gainfully*** improve upon our **basic purpose** conditions.

Consuming Requires 'Prioritizing'

The root word of *prioritizing* is 'priority', of which the root word is 'prior', meaning in this case '***comes before others in order***'.

> **Prioritizing is determining which comes first in order of importance.**

Prioritizing our needs and wants in order to **consume** within our **productive** means is always a primary consideration when contemplating our **consumptions**. We do it every time we are in '**consumption** mode' –

whenever we are purchasing, **producing**, utilizing assets, or focusing our time – we determine our *options* and *prioritize*.

Effective Consumption Requires 'Budgeting'

Every economic entity requires a budget. A 'budget' is a simple **organizing** and **accounting** activity – a tool. It always sounds more complicated and burdensome than it really is. But if you understand its correct context, you are more likely to use it as a *tool for basic purpose objectives* and make it work for you. A budget is not burden or a monetary restraint. It is a *plan*, a *tactical tool*, to '*account*' for how **money** and **resources** are '*expended*' in order to reach **basic purpose** objectives or targets. If you get that, you hit your targets, you achieve your **basic purpose** objectives.

Budget: A summary of intended [or predicted] *expend*itures [necessary to achieve specific purposes] along with proposals for how to meet [or achieve] them [WordWeb*].

Skilled Consumption and Credit

Essentially, the meaning of **credit** is the recognition that a person can be '*trusted to live up to a certain standard'* in some area of life – that a person's word or reputation is worthy of being considered '*credible*' – in this case, '*trust to repay what is loaned*' or '*to fulfill an economic commitment*'. **Credit** is discussed here because all **capitalizing** is a form of **credit**. And **production** and **consumption** are **capitalized** via [but not limited to] *financial lending* – aka *commercial* and *consumer credit*.

[**Note: Credit** granted for the *production* of products and services is called '*commercial credit*'; credit to *purchase* consumer products and services is called '*consumer credit*'].

Although **credit** increases the costs of both **production** and **consumption**,
credit also *capitalizes* production and consumption
that wouldn't otherwise take place or be possible without it.
The overall effect **capitalizing production** and **consumption** through **credit**
is the creation of a powerful and positive economic *dynamic*.

Skillful handling of **credit** in today's economies is a vital aspect of successful **consumptive** practices. However, despite its benefits, poor handling of **credit** is the number one destroyer of **household** and **small business** economics.

Credit, Debt, and Basic Purpose – Capitalizing the Consumer

Establishing and advancing a viable level of **basic purpose** living standards *only through the use of one's own immediate productive gain* is usually a required standard in societies *not as developed* as ours. However, our society's standard of required living almost always also requires **capitalization** to achieve and maintain. Even our most minimal standard of living almost always requires an extension of **credit** for furniture, an automobile, professional or vocational tools, equipment, appliances, even renting an apartment.

All **credit** is a form of *capitalization*.

The extension of *consumer* **credit** to finance *expenditures* for acquisitions large and small is a form of *capitalizing that person on their **basic purpose** endeavors*. And that establishes an *application principle*:

The only proper use of credit is for *capitalization of business productivity*, or *actual* basic purpose *requirements*, *advancements*, or *improvements*.

Capitalization through credit is '*borrowing* **capital**' – i.e. '*borrowing other people's invested **gain**' for a fee*.

A good idea for **capitalizing** a *business*, but only in particular conditions is it appropriate in achieving *household* **basic purpose** objectives – i.e. only when the *extra cost* of **capitalizing basic purpose** pursuits with **credit** creates enough improvement to still be considered *gainful* – and within one's means:

- With the exceptions of house mortgages and automobile loans, average **loan** and **credit** card debt should not be more than *ten percent* of our yearly *after*-**tax**, take home pay – that's not *payments*, it's your *total debt*. [Financial experts say no more than fifteen to twenty percent, but that's for *credit rating* reasons not for **household** or **small business** *economic* (**basic purpose** or **budgeting**) reasons. (**Credit for credit's** sake is a really bad idea. When it comes to **credit**, stick to absolutely necessary **basic purpose** reasoning.)]

- Total monthly debt *payments* should be no more than *twenty five percent* of *disposable* monthly income. However, never charging anything on **credit** that you can't pay off at the end of one month is a much better economic policy.

Saving **productive gain** for future purchases is still the most valid **basic purpose** approach. Over the long term , the added costs of purchases on **credit** are as much as *thirty percent* more [mortgages as much as two hundred percent more] – therefore, *reducing* one's long term **basic purpose** success by as much as *thirty percent*. [More on **credit** and **capitalization** in **Derivative Operating Dynamics: Capitalization/Capitalizing**]

Producing Begins *All* Consumption

All consumption *starts* when resources are consumed in order to *produce*.

28

['*All things economic begin with **produce**.*']

Consuming is *always* a part of the **productive** process, even when **consuming** for non-economic **basic purpose** activities or pursuits [most *'pursuit of life dynamics'* are not, in their essence or intent, economic. They simply have a *material*, and therefore *economic*, aspect to them].

Taxes and 'Consume'

Taxes are **currency** collected by a **governing** body to be spent on providing *publicly* [collectively] utilized **products** and **services**, such as *infrastructure*, ***education**, defense, first response equipment and personnel, care for the infirmed*, the *costs of governing*, etc.

> When we pay our **taxes** *we are being collective **consumers** –* **consuming** *collectively* for the greater and shared good.

We are fronting the money for our elected officials to purchase the kinds of 'whole society' **products** and **services** that only a **governing** body can provide. (More in **Derivative Operating Dynamics: Government**)

About Consumption:

Characteristics and General Factors

Consumption Depletes Resources

The very moment you start utilizing **resources** you start *depleting* them. You have **consumed** a portion of them. Not much of a big deal if it's common **raw material resources** like most metals, water, silicon, etc., they're so abundant. Not much of a big deal if it's agricultural renewables, you can always grow more.

But it matters big time if your access to a **resource** is limited, or there is not enough of something *vital* for the size of your population. Then, everything you do with that **resource** to *deplete* it reduces the further **production** of **basic purpose** requirements from that **resource**. Without **trade** for more of that same **resource**, or clever shifts in **productivity** to provide for those same needs, decline of **basic purpose** conditions is the result. [A stagnant **resource** in a population that is growing has the same net effect as a diminishing **resource**.]

The same holds true with **financial resources**. Whenever you spend [expend] discretionary **income**, you have *depleted* the **gain** left over after you've met your current **basic purpose** requirements. You have depleted what was going to go to your *savings* or *investments*, your *reserves*, or your *cash on hand*. The measure of that is always the contribution to **basic purpose**. Was the **basic purpose gain** *worth* what was expended?

Effective Consumption Requires Education [Just as **producing**]

It makes poor sense to **educate** and **train** yourself to be a top **producer** while you *squander* any **gain** you make because you didn't **educate** yourself on the subject of **consumption**.

In an economy as sophisticated as ours, a fundamental **consumer education** on the subjects below, *and more*, is vitally important if you want to achieve success and stability on your **basic purpose** conditions throughout your lifetime:

- **Consumer contracts** [mortgages, home rental agreements, car loans, credit cards, furniture, appliance, electronics, home improvement financing, personal loans, leasing, and appliance rental agreements, etc.]

- **Pricing and spending** [appropriate expense savvy]. [balancing the *predetermined* **market value** placed on **products (prices)** with the *actual* **utility value** (what it's *actually* worth) and the actual contributive **value** to one's **basic purpose** requirements or intents.]

- **Distinguishing between** '*need*' **and** '*want*' [and balancing the two] **and between** '*quality*', '*mediocrity*', **and** '*shoddy*' before acquiring **products** and **services** [and when and how to choose between *levels* of quality. *You don't always want or need the best.*]

- **Organization** [How to establish and **organize** a gainful *household* and even a *basic one to five person* **small business**.]

If you are going to get out there and be able to **produce**, provide, and **gain** for yourself and your family, you have to be **educated** on effective **consumption** practices equally as much as your **specialized productivity**.

NOTICE: The following section on Economic Education is going to read as though it were a lot more complicated and difficult to understand than it really is. Read it slow and deliberate and if necessary several times. It's all very simple. It's just the writing that makes it seem difficult to understand.

THE PRINCIPLES of ECONOMIC EDUCATION

"Human history becomes more and more a race between education and catastrophe."
Author: H. G. Wells

Primary Axiom Two:

In order to actively PRODUCE what we need and want,
we humans EDUCATE ourselves
so to become *knowledgeable* and *skilled* in
the 'causation' and 'application' principles of PRODUCING
which requires as a precursor we
locate, obtain, and develop for use all possible RESOURCES.

Active, but limited, TRADE and concepts of ETHICS begin here.

About Economic Education:

Productivity Class Economic Theory Statement

Productivity requires, *at the very minimum, competence* in producing basic purpose needs and wants. Competence requires *education* and *training* to achieve.

The average person's innate *capacities* for knowledge and productivity are very high – possibly limitless. It is our level of economic education and training, however, that turns our innate *capacities* into actual productive *capabilities – potential* into actual *competent ability*.

Therefore, it is our level of economic education and training that determines our *actual productive capability* and, therefore, our *actual consumptive measure* or *scope* and consequently our *basic purpose living standards*.

The need for *competence* in order to *produce* establishes 'educate' as an elemental activity and primary operating dynamic in economic function.

Productivity Class® Learning/Education Axioms

ALERT: What comes next are a set of *highly effective* **basic purposes, axioms,** and 'elemental activities'/'**primary operating dynamics'** that are basic to **learning** and **education** and are highly effective to <u>*any learning*</u> circumstance.

PRODUCTIVITY CLASS DEFINITION of EDUCATION:

The process of *'informing through communication'*, and *'training through doing and practice'* – so as to educe* an individual's *capacities* and *potentials* into *capabilities, competence,* and *skills.*

EDUCE: (SOED) verb **2. Bring out or develop from [a] latent or rudimentary [condition or] existence;** [*For our purposes...* to develop *skillful capability* from innate *capacity*; or to bring out *useful ability* from latent *potential*]; The root word of **education** is 'educe' ['educe'+'-ation']

IMPORTANT:
Read these *Productivity Class Basic Purposes* and *Axioms* carefully.

They may seem complex, *but they are not.* They are actually quite *simple* and *observable, self-evident* facts about *very basic human faculties,* and clearly explain *highly useful* and *effective 'causation'* and *'application'* principles:

THE BASIC PURPOSE of *LEARNING*:

The basic purpose of the human ability to 'LEARN' is...
the acquisition of an accurate mental 'full sensory duplication',
of the world in which we live [*i.e. to acquire an accurate*
'live action mental duplicate' of the world around us using our senses];
and to develop the understanding and know-how
necessary to live in it successfully.

THE BASIC PURPOSE of *EDUCATION*:

The basic purpose for the existence of 'NATURAL EDUCATION' is
for *LIVING EXPERIENCES* to *'provide for*
the acquisition of the required knowledge and understanding of
our overall environment, its workings, its circumstances, and its conditions
and the corresponding skills and disciplines
necessary to succeed in living life'.

The basic purpose of 'FORMAL EDUCATION' is to
'provide PERSON[s]-to-PERSON[s] COMMUNICATION
– through a *proper format of appropriate 'input' and 'activities'* –
the knowledge, understanding, and successful skills and disciplines
necessary to succeed in any subject, circumstance, or aspect of living life.'

THE PRIMARY AXOMS of 'LEARNING' and 'EDUCATION'

'LEARNING' and 'EDUCATION' AXIOM ONE:

In order to acquire an accurate and *full sensory 'mental duplication'*
of the world in which we live,
with the understanding and know-how necessary to succeed in it,
we *'physically observe'** and *'mentally assimilate'**
sensory input communication.

[**Physically observe** here means: *to apply one's 'attention' to something
with the 'intention' to 'assimilate' information.*
*To **'mentally assimilate'** is to *'receive, duplicate, assess, and store for recall
information for future use'.*]

[i.e. We apply our **attention** to **sensory input communication** with the **intention'**
to *'receive, duplicate, assess,* and **store** it for **recall** *and future use'.*]
Elemental Activities [Primary Operating Dynamics] of Axiom One:
'OBSERVE' and *'ASSIMILATE'*
[*ATTENTION–INTENTION–RECEIVE–DUPLICATE–ASSESS–STORE for RECALL and USE*]
[sensory input communication]

'LEARNING' and 'EDUCATION' AXIOM TWO:

All *concepts* [*abstract, non-physical ideas*] held in the mind must have a
'matching real world physical image' of its function or its application
in order to be *correctly grasped and* to have a
mental reality that is *accurate, tangible*, and *useable** in the real world.

[**An *accurate* understanding or mental picture of how a thing *exists* and is
experienced or utilized *physically in the real world*. aka: A *substantive* reality** or a
physically understood *mental duplication* of the *real world* aspect of something.]

[***A substantive reality is a *'mental duplication or picture'* of *'actual* and *accurate*
sensory input'* of something in the real world of *actual physical substance*, with
enough *correlated understanding* so that **it can be utilized to translate something
in the mind into real world *physical use or doingness*. It** is an *accurate
substantive reality* that allows a person to *apply concepts or imaginings in the
mind to the real world*. See bracketed explanation of Axiom Five for additional
clarity.]

Elemental Activities [Primary Operating Dynamics] of Axiom Two:
Match ABSTRACT ideas with MENTAL DUPLICATIONS of the REAL WORLD
[Accurate mental duplication of real world physical, tangible reality.]

'LEARNING' and 'EDUCATION' AXIOM THREE:

Assimilated knowledge, understanding, and skills build upon each other on a
'sequential, supporting step-by-step process' –
i.e. gradiently on 'a structure of supporting earlier knowledge or steps'.

[All knowledge requiring earlier supporting knowledge to understand –
building from simple to complex, or elemental to advanced – *requires learning
in the proper sequence*. All necessary earlier understanding must be correctly
learned before learning further steps *requiring that earlier knowledge* to
understand.]

Elemental Activities [Primary Operating Dynamics] of Axiom Three:
'GRADIENT SEQUENTIAL LEARNING'
Building knowledge, understanding, and know-how
upon *earlier required* knowledge, understanding, and know-how.

'LEARNING' and 'EDUCATION' AXIOM FOUR:

'Learning' [or 'education'] can be both *random* and/or *deliberate*,
and is acquired through sensory input from:
○   *random* experience*,
○   *self-directed* experiences and study*, or
○   imparted, directed, and supervised *by others** through
    person-to-person communication and training.

Elemental Activities [Primary Operating Dynamics] of Axiom Four:
RANDOM and DIRECTED LEARNING

[**Random experience is* **Natural Education**; *Self or informally imparted by others is*
Informal Education; *Formally imparted, directed, and supervised by others is*
Formal Education.]

'LEARNING' and 'EDUCATION' AXIOM FIVE:

Humans share learning.
In order to *share* known and successful mental duplications, understanding,
skills, etc., learning is transferred from one person
to the next *through sensory input* by means of...
○   *verbal and written language,*
○   *graphic representation/illustration,* and
○   *physical demonstration.*

[**Educationally,** a previously acquired **substantive reality** *that can mentally be* *matched with current verbal or written communication can sometimes be drawn upon to substitute for 'illustration' or 'demonstration'.* However, in **educating**, it is vital to be sure to match *verbal* and *written* communication to physical reality with accurate, communicative *graphic representation* and/or *physical demonstration of the thing described in words*. It is the graphic illustration and physical demonstration that give 'physical reality' to what is being taught, communicated, or learned.]

Elemental Activities [Primary Operating Dynamics] of Axiom Five:
PERSON-to-PERSON COMMUNICATION via
Verbal and written language – Graphic representation/illustration
– Physical demonstration

'LEARNING' and 'EDUCATION' AXIOM SIX:

The Basic Purpose of learning is
'development of the understanding and know-how
necessary to *succeed in living life'*.
Therefore... *'the purpose of all learning is for real life application'*
of what was learned, applied toward living life successfully.

Elemental Activities [Primary Operating Dynamics] of Axiom Six:
REAL LIFE SUCCESSFUL APPLICATION of KNOWLEDGE and SKILLS

Creating from the Axioms a *Workable* and *Successful* Methodology

This is *a simple to follow but very powerful methodology*, for anyone of average intelligence [that would be you] to effectively apply the above **learning** and **education axioms** to whatever subject you choose to learn:

The Beginning of True Competence is
Understanding *Cause-and-Effect* and *Application Principles*

Actually understanding *cause-and-effect* means
knowing '*what*' happens when something happens,
and '*why*' it happens.

Knowing the 'application' of it means
knowing how to *use* the '*what*' and the '*why*' to '*cause*' one's own '*effects*'.

Only when one knows the *cause-and-effect* 'what's' and 'why's' can one
cause those effects efficaciously in any particular circumstance
and still get the proper and '*intended outcomes*'.

The 'Communicator's' Job:

[The one *imparting* information or skills – teacher, parent, instructor, trainer, etc.]

Required to ensure actual *functional* understanding by the **recipient**:

Imparting Communication Effectively [Information or Skills]:
As a **communicator** you have to make sure that **competence** is what it is you are **communicating** – and in *language, illustration,* and *physical demonstration* the recipient can understand, all integrated as one effective **communication** :

- o Ensure all words used to delineate are clearly understandable by the **recipient**. 'Plain speak' is always best, especially when defining technical terms for the *uninitiated*. [Remember, if he or she doesn't understand a sentence or paragraph, it is *always* because there is a word or words in it (*or earlier*) that they didn't get the correct or intended meaning of.]
- o Ensure all illustrations and demonstrations *show* what the words are *saying*, and that they together properly represent what you are trying to teach or impart to the **recipient** – make sure they all match *as one* **communication**.
- o **Communicate** within the recipient's current level of language and understanding, and build the **recipient** up **gradiently** to each next **communicative** level in 'nomenclature' and educationally;
- o Build from non-technical terms to technical terms, explaining technical terms and nomenclature in non-technical, plain speak, but accurate, terminology;

Gradients, Gradients, Gradients:

- o Don't just start easy and get tougher. Make each step *show openly what is needed to be known to do the next step*, and the next step, and the next step. Make each **gradient** a learning step for the next.
- o Work from the simple to the complex; from elementary fundamentals to the more advanced;
- o Require the **recipient** *demonstrate understanding and ability* at every step so that misunderstandings and lack of ability to *apply* can be caught and corrected before the next step or stage is undertaken.

Practice, Practice, Practice:

- o As much as possible, assign **practice** that allows the recipient to *see* the 'what', 'why', and 'how' of it all [*recognizing* and *understanding* the principles and workings of the whole thing] so they can learn to wield the subject *competently* with certainty and with confidence. **Practice** should *show* in *real life* [and in the **recipient's** *substantive reality*] everything **communicated** in *language, illustration,* and *demonstration* and that *what they now know, they can wield.*

Supervising and Directing –

- o Direct the **recipient's** training 'input' and 'activities' according to *required knowledge and type of practice that develops <u>real life competence</u>*; Grade progress according to his or her '<u>demonstration of understanding</u>', '*ability to <u>apply</u>*', and successful <u>outcomes</u>.

The Recipient's Job:

[The one *receiving* the information or skills – student, trainee, apprentice, etc.]

Required to ensure actual *functional* understanding by the **recipient**:

Receiving **Communication Effectively:**
As a <u>recipient</u> you have to make sure that you are ***observing and assimilating competence*** – you must apply your ***full sensory attention***, with all necessary *technique* and *focused diligence*, to the **communication** with the ***intention*** to ***receive, duplicate, assess,*** and ***store*** [competent *ability*] ***for recall*** and <u>***utility***</u>.
- o Ensure all misunderstood words are cleared up in a plain speak intermediate dictionary [Remember, if you don't understand a sentence or paragraph, it is *always* because there is a word or words in it (*or earlier*) that you don't get the correct or necessary meaning of].
- o Ensure all illustrations and demonstrations *show* what the words are *saying*, and they all together properly represent what you are trying to learn – make sure they all **communicate** the **competence** to you.

Demonstration [*by* the **recipient** *to* the **communicator**] of *Understanding* and *Ability to Apply*:
- o **a)** Answering relevant questions [verbally or in writing], **b)** doing pertinent tasks that *show understanding and ability to apply* the material at **c)** the expected ability level under *real life* circumstances, accomplishing **d)** successful outcomes.

Practice, Practice, Practice:
- o Under *supervision* and *direction* by a **supervisor** or **authority** that possesses the proven knowledge and skills in what is being taught, until you as **recipient** can demonstrate ***competence*** under *real life* conditions – or at least that **practice** without immediate or constant supervision is acceptable, and that working up the actual skill levels can begin [*student, novice, competence, expertise, authority*].
- o **Practice, practice, practice** – until you can *see* the 'what', 'why', and 'how' of it all, *understand* the principles and workings of the whole thing, and can wield it ***competently*** with *certainty* and *confidence*.

Get All That?
It is the responsibility of the **communicator** to
properly present and supply the knowledge, know-how, and practice
with the proper techniques.
*It is the responsibility of the **recipient** to also apply the proper techniques and
diligence of <u>educating</u> themselves in what is presented to them.*

'Minimum Technique':
*The above is your minimum 'workable learning methodology',
– for reading, studying , and skill developing in anything –
that you must become adept and successful with
if you are going to be able to self-educate throughout your life.*

Beware The Paradox of Language:

Verbal and written language is the primary reason for successful exchange of information, ideas, and **education** *of all knowledge and know-how* in *all* aspects of human culture – including economics. The paradox?... it is also the primary reason for *failure* in all **communication** – *especially **education***.

Here is where the paradox comes from:

Accurate and *effective* **communication** only occurs when **communicator** and **recipient** share the same meanings of **words** – *verbal* and *written* – including their method of delivery [symbols, inflections, punctuations, grammar, syntax, etc.], and what is **communicated** is *true* and *accurate*.

> 'Educational Axiom':
> You cannot correctly understand a verbal or written communication
> if you do not understand *exactly what the words mean*
> or how the words are used *for that specific communication!*

Accurate *education* only occurs when accurate and complete information is delineated in accurate *terms* that are understood by both communicator and recipient – i.e. the words, symbols, graphic illustrations, etc. used by the communicator to describe or delineate the information, and the information itself, *must be accurate* – and the recipient *must know* the accurate meanings of the words and symbols used in the communication.

If either is off, *accurate duplication* of the subject matter – and therefore *education* of the subject matter – *cannot occur*. Inaccurate communication and not understanding the accurate meanings of words – or their misuse – are the primary culprits of educational failure by both communicator and recipient.

> You really need to get the impact of this:
> In education, on this matter, "good enough!" is *not* good enough.

Hence, in so many ways, language is an educational 'paradox' – a 'godsend' to educate broadly, but also a 'trap' for **communicator** or **recipient** to *fail to communicate*, and therefore, *fail to educate*.

The solution to this paradox is:
   a) *Both parties accurately using 'common terms' and 'accurately defining subject nomenclature';* and
   b) *communicating in terms at the recipient's educational level of understanding, while gradiently progressing the recipient to more advanced terms.*

For the Communicator: *Complete, accurate descriptions or instructions* should be in the *simplest terms* possible or allowable in accurately delineating information – *all within the* **communication** *range of the* **recipient** [i.e. in the *terms, communication, existing education,* and *experiential reality* level of the **recipient**].

When instructing or teaching, from a text even slightly 'advanced of the **recipient'**, a **communicator** should *a)* explain the text in simpler terms more suited to the **recipient**, while *b)* ensuring the **recipient** learns accurately the advanced terms used by the text, industry, or profession so that they can complete the course of study at the level intended by that text.

For the Recipient: Diligent *'acquisition of the correct meanings and usage'* of the *words* [including *grammar, punctuations, symbols,* etc.] being used or delineated by the **communicator** – *plain speak dictionaries* or glossaries help. Also, diligence in the *application of techniques* of how to *accurately understand* verbal and written **communication** [see **axioms one, two,** and **four** above] – measured by the ability to *'put to use'* what was **communicated**.

The primary key to all of this is effective, accurate, plain speak dictionaries and access to *effective, accurate, and easy to understand graphic representations* and *physical demonstrations* [real life or video] *of what is communicated*. [See page ii Dictionaries Notice for recommended dictionaries and **productivityclass.*info*** for words defined exclusively for this text.]

About Economic Education:
an
Overview

The purpose of **education** is to turn human *capacity* [or *potential*] into human *capability* [actual ability to *do*] in any acquired human knowledge – from *study,* to *practice,* to *competence,* to *expertise,* to *authoritative mastery* [command and/or teaching mastery] – the skill levels.

Therefore, in order to competently execute the **five primary axioms**, skillfully implementing each of their **twelve elementary activities** – including every related and peripheral subject and skill necessary for their success – *education and **training** is required.* [*i.e.* **economic education.**]

Only an **economic education** *sufficient for success* across all **twelve elemental activities** can fully establish the necessary **productive** capability to successfully achieve any quality of **basic purpose** living standards for individuals, groups, or societies. And only by providing such an **education*** to *every individual in a society* can any **governing** body provide a *worthwhile quality of **basic purpose** living standards* for an entire society.

[*It is also vital, as a matter of **ethics** and social or societal responsibility, to include in one's **education** a full grasp of *'basic humanity'* – i.e. basic human responsibility toward the well-being of others. The lack of such an **education** can easily cause acceptance of **inverted** economic behaviors.]

> *Education [and general **learning**] is a fundamental to all human activity.*
> *It is an **elementary activity** – a **primary operating dynamic** – to everything.*

'Economic education', however, is not limited to **education** on the subject of 'general economics' alone – even **productivity class** economics. It must include at least a *basic* **education** on *the fundamentals of every subject related to successful performance of each of the* **twelve elemental activities** – enough to work each dynamic competently and in synergy with the others.

> *The ability to successfully apply and manage the whole clockwork of economic*
> ***primary operating dynamics*** *and* *their related* ***productive activities***
> is what we mean when we use the term *'economic* **education'**.

Each and every one of us is capable of learning, understanding, and effectively applying, at a fundamental level, *all* of those necessary requirements – which *minimally* requires the basic know-how of ***self*-education**. [Honestly, it sounds a lot more difficult and complicated than it really is].

In fact, no person should even graduate high school without having enough rudimentary capabilities to successfully **produce** and get effective results, *in real life conditions*, on every basic principle of the **twelve elementary activities** enough to *successfully* begin **employment** and maintain an effective, **organized household**. And, if necessary, even if with minimal coaching, to **organize**, begin, and operate a small one to five person **self-employed business**.

About Economic Education:

Characteristics and General Factors

[**Reminder:** In **education**, there are principles and phenomena, not covered here, that are neither self-evident nor observable without **specialized training**. However, such are *rarely* required in **economic education**. *Therefore, in this entire text, we are delineating only long known, easily self-evident and observable, and* <u>*patently effective*</u> **learning** *and* **training** *fundamentals and methods.*]

Final Educational Axiom [for this text]:
Practical application of *any* concept or activity
requires that <u>definitions</u> or <u>explanations</u> be worded
general enough to *understand conceptually and apply broadly,*
but at the same time
specific enough to *understand its real life functionality*

in order for the concepts or meanings to be translated
from 'mental understanding' to *'real life application'* or *use.*

The Two Primary Processes of Education: *'Communication'* and *'Practice'*

Education at its most basic is a simple process of
effective 'communication'
[on a particular subject, know-how, or skill],
then
effective 'practice'
[of what was communicated].

But first, *grasp this*: **In education, what is communicated it is not communication until the recipient** *receives* **it,** *understands* **it, and can** *utilize* **it.** Until then, it remains *uncommunicated. Therefore, for their part, the recipient must know how to ensure their own accurate duplication, understanding, and ability to utilize what is* **communicated.** *Both parties are responsible for effective* **communication.**

And get this fully:

If a **communication** is received and *truly* understood correctly [via verbal and/or written *language, graphic illustration,* and *physical demonstration*], the recipient will be able to *do it* or *put it to use* – even if poorly or sloppily at first. **Corollary:** *if one can't do the thing, then it wasn't effectively* **communicated,** *or correctly received, duplicated, and/or understood in the first place.*

Do not underestimate or take lightly this fundamental principle of education. This can be a hard principle to understand or believe, but it's observably and provably *true* – and lays responsibility hard upon *both* the **communicator** *and* the **recipient** to get the job effectively done of **educating** the **recipient** to any level of *competence.*

There is no *application principle* on the subject of **education** more important or *fundamental* than this. *Only successful tangible results will convince you of this.* Nothing else – no arguments, no explanations, no clinical studies – only *your own experienced results* with it.

The key to all this is *'effective'* **communication** by the **communicator,** and *'effective'* **study, observation, assimilation,** and **practice, practice, practice** by the **recipient.**

Educational Communication

*For our purposes…***Educational Communication is: 'to give or receive information necessary to** *successfully complete a task, acquire competence* *in an activity, abide by a behavior,* or *add to one's understanding – correctly* **duplicated** and **usable** by the recipient'.

Further...
All communication, *all* education
is '*receiving information through the senses'.*

That means, for **communication** to occur, there does not need to be any 'human giver of information'. No one has to be *giving* verbal, graphic, demonstrative **communication** to us for us to *receive* **communication**.

That's important to know. If we are '*receiving information*' about the world around us *through our senses* – even when we 'practice' – we are 'in **communication**' with the environment around us. And we are **learning** about its current status. This is how we learn by *observation*.

Practice, Practice, Practice

Practice is how we learn by *doing*. As we do something,
we '*observe*' and '*assimilate*' the effects our skills or activities
have upon what we are working with.
[Including any direct and indirect circumstances and conditions.]

This is how we learn by doing: we **observe** our own results, gain in understanding of *function* or *application* from those results, and make corrections necessary to get *better* results. Meanwhile we improve upon our knowledge and skills, and our ability to understand the subject matter practiced, so to **produce** more effectively upon it. It's all a part of the **educational communication** process. And that's why **practice** is an innate '*primary and fundamental principle of education*'. [This is what homework was for in school.]

*Observation of our own work is actually a '**communication**'*
of how well we know something and our skill levels in applying it –
*our ability to **produce** the proper results with what we know –*
*in **value** and in **volume** [in economics, but also in living life].*

Corollary Note:
Therefore, if it *wasn't* **communicated** or **demonstrated** or **observed** *correctly* or the **recipient** *just didn't grasp it* correctly, then
what the recipient is practicing is the wrong thing.

THE PRINCIPLES of RESOURCES

"We already have – thanks to technology, development, skills, the efficiency of our work – enough resources to satisfy all human needs. But we don't have, and we are unlikely to ever have, enough resources to satisfy human greed."
Zygmunt Bauman - Polish sociologist

Primary Axiom Two:

In order to actively PRODUCE what we need and want,
we humans EDUCATE ourselves
so to become *knowledgeable* and *skilled* in
the 'causation' and 'application' principles of PRODUCING
which requires as a precursor we
locate, obtain, and develop for use all possible RESOURCES.

Active, but limited, TRADE and concepts of ETHICS begin here.

NOTICE:
'Resource Types' is placed here in advance of 'Overview' to ensure understanding of all the *terms* and *principles* included in the **Economic Theory Statement**.

RESOURCES – *For our purposes...* anything that can be utilized to produce *products* or *services,* or to *cause effects.*

Productively speaking, there are three types of resources:

- **NATURAL RESOURCES** – are the raw materials we obtain from the earth and nature [also called '**material**', '**raw**', or '**land**' resources].
- **CAPITAL RESOURCES*** – also called '**capital assets**' or '**developed resources**' are man-made tools, equipment, mechanisms, or any type of fabrications used to **produce products** with, facilitate **production**, or **produce** an *end result* or *outcome.*
- **HUMAN RESOURCES** – any kind of labor, talent, know-how, or other skill or capability done or delivered by a person.

These three categories are not random. All three need to be *utilized together* in order for **production** to occur. i.e. All **consumables** are **produced** from...

- naturally originated *materials*... ['**material resources'**]
- using *tools, mechanisms,* or **productive** *fabrications* [called **capital***]... ['**capital* resources'**]
- by a *skilled* or *capable* **human** [or *group*] ['**human resources'**].

*Currency [money]: is actually a '**capital' resource** because it is a 'man made* *fabrication'* utilized to facilitate **trade** and **capitalize productivity** – aka *'financial capital'*. Although, in **productivity class** economics, we consider **'financial capital'** already included as a **'capital resource'**, we add **'financial capital'** as a *separate resource type* below in order *ensure that it is looked upon as a **capitalizing** resource*. [More about this in **Derivative Operating Dynamics: Capitalizing.**]

[***WHY THE TERM CAPITAL?** 'Capit' is Latin meaning *'head'* [in English, it's *'cap'*]. Figuratively: *'a thing that goes at the head of'*, or as in our case, *'a thing that comes first or before'*. The '-al' simply turns the *noun* 'capit' into the *adjective* 'capital': *a thing that comes first or before*, as in **'capital resource'** – *'before* you can **produce** something, you *first* need the *tools, equipment, mechanisms* [aka *fabricated* **resources**'] necessary for a skilled ***human* resource** to make a **product** out of a ***material* resource.**]

About Resources:

Productivity Class Economic Theory Statement

Producing consumptive needs and wants to meet even the most minimal of basic purpose requirements requires the resources to do so. Those resources always come in the forms of *material, capital,* and *human effort.*

Producing , by its nature, *requires the integrated use of all three types* of productive resources – material, capital, and human – in order for production to occur [also including *each* of the Primary Operating Dynamics – and *every* related and peripheral activity required for their success].

Therefore, in order to produce for basic purpose needs and wants, humans must *educate* themselves in *locating, obtaining,* and *developing for use* all possible resources, as well as the knowledge and skills to effectively produce with them.

About Resources:
an
Overview

'Productive' Classification of Economic Resources

At today's level of highly developed technological advancement, ***material, capital,*** and ***human* resources** are more complex than ever before in human history. And they are going to get even more and more complex as discoveries, technologies, and know-how forever continue to develop and advance.

The classification of *economic* **resources** can get simple, complex, or downright useless depending on whether it's being done for **productive** purposes, economic calculating and planning, or academically by a **productive** non-participant. As we are, in this text, dealing with basic fundamentals only, we will stick to **productive** classifications of **resources** only.

Productively, This Is How to Classify Resources:

Economists, and economics texts, teach that there are three types of **resources** – we [and they] actually also add a fourth:

- ○ **Natural Resources** – are the raw materials we obtain from the earth and nature [also called '**material**', '**raw**', or '**land**' **resources**].

- ○ **Capital Resources** – also called '**capital assets**' or '**developed resources**' are the man made *tools*, *mechanisms*, or *fabrications* used to **produce products** or **services**, facilitate **production**, or to **produce** any *end result* or *outcome*.

- ○ **Human Resources** – any kind of *labor*, *talent*, *know-how*, or other *skill*, *capability*, or *personal asset* done, delivered, or used by a person. [When spoken of collectively as the aggregate available human workforce, the term **human capital** or **labor** is normally used.] [**Intangible resources** such as literacy, certainty, personality, honesty, etc. may be **human resources** also, but are usually considered non-economically as an individual's **personal resources**.]

- ○ **Financial Resources** – '**money**', '**financial capital**', '**currency**', etc. is actually a '**capital resource**' as stated above. It is singled out here only because it is not utilized to *directly* **produce** a **product** or **service**, but rather *indirectly* by financing [i.e. **capitalizing**] **productivity**. [More on '**money**' or '**currency**' in the '**Currency**' section; more on **capitalizing** in **Derivative Operating Dynamics**, '**Capitalization**'.]

These four categories are not random: Note the *operating relationship* of the first three types of **resources**. *All three types of **resources** must be present and utilized together in any **productive** activity* in order for **production** to happen – in order to **produce** a **product**, **service**, or any type of **productive** result. *That's what makes understanding them so important:*

All **consumables** are **produced** from…
- ○ **naturally** originated *materials*…
- ○ using *tools*, *mechanisms*, or **productive** *fabrications* [called **capital resources**]…
- ○ by a *skilled* or otherwise *capable* **human** or group of **humans**.

Although **financial capital** does not *directly* participate in the **production** *process*, it is what '*finances*' the doing of it. **Currency**, when applied to the financing of **productivity**, is actually a '**capital**' type of **resource** because it is a 'man made fabrication' utilized to create **productivity**.

[**Note:** Due to the 'fluid nature' of **currency** serving as **'investment'**, 'stored **value**', 'measure of **gain**', and many other economic purposes, **financial capital** is treated as though it were something separate than, or really *more* than, a **resource**. However, for **productivity class productive** purposes, when used as 'stored **value**' or **'investment'**, **currency** , or for **trade**, it should be thought of as a **resource**.]

There Are 'Product Creating' and There Are 'Administrative' Capital Resources:

'**Product** *creation*' **capital recourses** are what economists are generally referring to when they use the term '**capital recourses**' – *machines, tools, equipment*, etc. created for the purpose of *manufacturing a **product** or **service***.

'*Administrative*' **capital resources** do not actually contribute *directly* to making a **product** or **service** but rather are necessary to **produce** the **administrative** work necessary for **organizing** the activity of **production** – *record keeping, goal planning, communications, accounting, marketing research, IT*, etc. These would include *desks and chairs, file cabinets, computers, mail carts, carrying and moving equipment,* even *office cleaning equipment*. It would *not* include *general supplies*. *General supplies* are considered more akin to **material resources** with their **end-products** as the *file records, communications, administrative **productivity***, etc. [Yeah, I know ...way over thought.]

Diversity of Resources

This is an economic concept – a 'condition' really – that isn't much of a problem for advanced economies anymore due to their world wide access to, and ability to wield **resources**, but certainly is for *lesser* advanced economies:

*The greater the diversity of **resources** an economic community can locate, obtain, develop, and wield, the greater that economy can grow and the more broadly it can serve the **basic purpose** needs and wants of its own economic populace and the populaces of its economic **trade** partners.*

That concept, of course, has its corollary:

*The lesser the diversity of **resources** an economic populace can locate, obtain, develop, and wield, the less that economy can serve the **basic purpose** needs and wants of its economic populace or grow and advance technologically.*

In the case of **resources** *in general*, it's obvious that any community with limited *basic life* **resources** is limited in its *population growth*. A particular **volume** of basic living **resources** supports a correlating specific **volume** of humans. When the population expands beyond that point, *suffering ensues*.

Therefore, *worthwhile* **basic purpose** *conditions are directly affected by the* **value** *and diversity of* **resources** *an economic populace has access to and can technologically wield.*

About Resources:

Characteristics and General Factors

'Allocation' of Resources vs. 'Flow' of Resources

Allocation of **resources** is connected to the concept of **'scarcity'**. If there is *never enough* **resources** to **produce** everything we can possibly think of, *all* **resources** are therefore **scarce** by comparison, and we must, then, decide *how* and *to what* to **allocate**, the **resources** we have.

In **productivity class** economics we do not think in terms of *'allocation'*, but of *'flows'*. In **productivity class** economics **resources** tend to *'flow'* toward **producing** those **products** or **services** most **valued** by **consumers**, as it does in any **market economy**. **Producing** only **products** and **services consumer's demand** naturally generates *only the necessary* **volume** *of 'flow'* of **resources** to wherever they need to be.

Adjustments to the *flow* of **resources** are made according to shifts in **consumer demand** for different **products** or **services** [more on this later in **'supply and demand'**]. When **consumer** desire for a **product** or **service** wanes and the **gainfulness** in **producing** it dwindles, **production** stops and **resources** are no longer utilized for that purpose. The *flow* of that **resource** shifts to some other **product** or **service** with strong enough **consumer demand** for **producers** to make a worthwhile **gain [profit]**.

Which also leads to thinking of, or categorizing, **resources** in one more way...

Two more classifications to help understand resources productively:

From a **producer's** point of view, there are two additional **production** 'categories' to think of when handling **resources**: *'finite'* and *'renewable'*. These are **producer** categories because they help determine present and future availability of a particular **resource** necessary to **produce** a **product** or **service**.

Finite Resources

Finite **resources** are just that -- **resources** the availability of which have a fixed, predetermined, definitive amount.
- They can be *plentiful* [iron, tin, or copper ore; oil, coal, or natural gas; top

soil; etc.]

- They can be *limited* [general quality gem stones or pearls; cable bandwidth; high quality hardwoods; etc.]
- Or they can be *scarce* [precious metals; high quality gem stones; rare earth minerals; etc.]

There are many factors to consider when determining the *finite* availability of a **resource**, and, therefore, **production** consistency, **production** costs, **end-product** price, as well as an end-**product's marketability**. Limited and scarce resources are most subject to 'depletion', which can mean higher costs or even unavailability as they become more and more depleted – less and less available.

Renewable Resources

This category is also self-explanatory. These are resources that can be 'renewed' indefinitely. There is no definite, fixed, or predetermined amount. As they deplete from use, we just **produce** more, indefinitely.

- They can come from an *organic* source [food; leather; paper; plastics; fabric; etc.]
- They can be *man-made* – a '*developed*' or '*invented*' source [wind or solar energy; financial capital (if created in an organic or digital form); intellectual property; artworks; etc.]
- They can be *human capabilities* [trades; unskilled, semi-skilled, and skilled white collar and blue collar labor; management; **inventiveness** and **innovativeness**; etc.]

Note the same **supply**-and-**demand** factors discussed above remain the primary drivers determining a **renewable resource's** economic **value**, its **price**, and **marketability**.

THE PRINCIPLES of TRADE

"The propensity to truck, barter and exchange one thing for another is *common to all men*, and to be found in no other race of animals.
Author: Adam Smith "The Wealth of Nations" [italics mine]

Primary Axiom Two:

In order to actively PRODUCE what we need and want,
we humans EDUCATE ourselves
so to become *knowledgeable* and *skilled* in
the 'causation' and 'application' principles of PRODUCING
which requires as a precursor we
locate, obtain, and develop for use all possible RESOURCES.

Active, but limited, TRADE and concepts of ETHICS begin here.

About Trade:

Productivity Class Economic Theory Statement

Basic purpose *needs* and *wants* generate *demand* for resources, products, services, and knowledge beyond that which individuals or groups can provide for themselves – even though what they do produce, they can produce in *excess*. This generates the concept and practice of 'exchange' between those that have something they can produce over and above their own needs, that others may *want* or *need*.

Trade is the *exchange* of productivity for productivity in the form of *products* and *services*. Trade itself is also a *productive activity* between two or more parties *exchanging* their own products and services in order to obtain more varied basic purpose *needs* and *wants*.

All those who *trade* are both producers *and* consumers – all who would trade must first produce in order to have something to trade; and a *producer* becomes *consumer* when *trading for resources* in order to produce, and then again when they trade what they have produced *for the products and services of others*.

As trade develops, and in order for *productivities* and *trade* and *societies* to advance, the use of a standardized currency naturally develops as a method to overcome the cumbersome and unwieldy practice of trading products and services only for other products and services.

In addition, currency also advances '*employment*', as employment is a '*trade of service for a standard tradable currency*' between the employer and the employed.

About Trade:
an
Overview

A Note About Trade and All Other 'Operating Dynamics'
The activity of *trade*, and its influence upon the other eleven **primary operating dynamics**, is the *primary generator* of most of the well-known **derivative operating dynamics** [**supply**, **demand**, and **pricing**; **market equilibrium**; **risk**; **capitalizing**; etc.]. The influence of the activity of **organizing** [**business**; **governance**; **infrastructure**; etc.] generates almost all of the rest. [More in Chapter Three: Derivative Operating Dynamics.]

General Economic Concepts of Trade:

The Activity of Trade Expands Productivity and Consumption

As human communities grow and extend outward – in *population* or in connection with *other communities* – so too do the **producers** of those communities expand their access to new **resource markets** and sell their **products** and **services** to serve the larger expanded **market of consumers**.

The **basic purpose** drive of *all* producers [**employed** and **employer**] impels them to exploit the entire range of expanding **resources** and **markets** of the various geographical locations, populaces, and income levels of **consumers**. Through **invention** and **innovation**, they utilize the increased access to **resources** and **markets** of **consumers** to expand the *diversity* and *utility* of their **products** and **services** in an attempt to take every advantage of the entire expanded society's **basic purpose** *needs* and *wants*.

It Is The Organization of Trade That Begins an Economic *System*

"... economic *systems* begin as
'organizing the *continuous cycle* of production and consumption'."
['Produce: Economic Theory Statement']

A economic *system*, then, is primarily a '**producers create products and services – trade that productivity to consumers – consumers apply that productivity to basic purpose fulfillment**' system. Therefore, with the advent of such a '*start-to-finish*' economic system, **trade** becomes different things to different economic 'entities' depending on their activity:

- ○ **For the overall system: trade** is the *exchange* or *purchase* and *sale* of a **product** or **service** [barter or exchange for **money**];
- ○ **For the producer: trade** is the final step of **business productivity** – the *sale* and *delivery* of the **product** or **service**; and,
- ○ **For the consumer: trade** is the whole point of **productive employment** – to **trade** their **productivity** for its **value** in **currency** so they may **trade** that **currency** for widely varied **products** and **services**.

The resource market works the same way [covered more fully in Chapter Three: The Cyclic Flows of Trade].

Trade *Extends* the Individual's Productive and Consumptive Activities and Benefits to Include The Productivity and Consumption of Others

Trade extends the **basic purpose productive** and **consumptive** options of one person or group to include the **productivity** and **consumption** of others. In serving their own **basic purpose** needs and wants, **trade** expands *one's own* material options to the **products** and **services** of others – while also serving the **basic purpose** *needs* and *wants* of those others.

Trade, therefore,
makes basic purpose success within a society *a group activity.*
Thanks to trade, people live better as a group.
Further, *specialization*, *currency*, and well **organized**, well **governed** *trade* expands and evolves a society into a full civilization.

Trade Expands 'Utility Value' [aka 'practical value'] to Include 'Market Value' [aka 'consumer demand value' or 'trade value']

The activity of **trade** generates *consumer demand* for **products** and **services**. **Consumer demand** generates a new kind of **'value'**. Beyond **utility value** [aka 'practical value'] is the **value** a **consumer** places on a **product** or **service** – what they are willing to **trade** [or pay] to have it.

Producers gain by creating **products** that will **trade** for more than it cost to produce them. By further adding *desirability* and the principles of **supply** and *demand* to **trading** their **products** and **services**, **producers** can increase the **tradable value** [**market value**] of their **products** and **services** *beyond* basic **utility value**, thus further increasing their **margins** for **gainful profit**.

There are Five Steps in the Trade Process:
- **Produce** [a *saleable, desirable* **product** or **service**]
- **Market** [place and present that **product** or **service** to the right **consumers** at the right **price**]
- **Advertise** [promote: advise of availability and create desire]

- **Sell** [convince to buy]
- **Transaction** [close the deal: complete the **trade** transaction]

All together these add up to the natural process of **trading** – the subject of **trade**. From rain forest tribes or primitive ancient cultures to modern day highly sophisticated global techniques, this is what you do when you **trade** your **products** or **services**, or you risk failure regardless of their actual **value**. Each of these steps is so important, in fact, each has become a **specialization**.

Specialization and Trade: [A complete section on **specialization** coming up.]

Trade is what makes **specialization** [and all the benefits of 'focused expertise'] such a powerful asset. If an individual makes or does one thing *needed* or *wanted* by **consumers** very well, and becomes a *master* at it, he or she can **trade** that **product** or **service** for everything else he or she needs or wants. Further, with **specialization**, *more expertly made **products** and **services** become more and more **valuable***, and in acquiring that **value** through **trade**, people begin to flourish.

About Trade:

Characteristics and General Factors

Trade Is Exchange [of Ownership]

You can overcomplicate **trade**, but you really can't oversimplify it. *'I'll give you what I've **produced** if you'll give me what you've **produced**'*, *'I'll give you what I have if you'll give me what you have'* is the essence of all that **trade** is. Yes **value**, **price**, **currency**, **ethics**, etc. all come into play at one point or another. And there is a clockwork of eleven other **elemental activities** that conflate with it, each having its effect, and each being effected by the others. So, **twelve elemental activities** conflating together can create very complex interactions.

Yet, underneath all that complexity, **trade** is simply *'exchange of ownership'*.

Trade *Generates* the *'Use of A Trade Medium'* – Currency

The cumbersome, inconvenient and, most importantly,
economically limiting practice of
trading products and services for other products or services
creates the need for an 'intermediate medium of exchange'
– a *'substitute item assigned an agreed upon equivalent value'*
tradable for *actual* productivity, products, or services – money currency.

Monetary currency [**money currency**] is *'a tangible object given [assigned] a tradable value*, the **value** of which is *commonly agreed upon*, and *officially supported'* to act as a 'substitute' for actual **productivity, products**, or **services** in a **trade** – instead of a **product** for **product** barter. Therefore,...

> *Spending 'currency' for a product or service is*
> *expending the '<u>value of one's productivity</u>'*
> *[in an alternate or substitute form]*
> *for a product or service.*

With the advent of **currency**, the cumbersome **bartering** of **product** for **product** becomes unnecessary and **trade** becomes more *smooth, fluid*, and *rapid*. **Specialization** and its *focused expertise* becomes a distinct advantage over **producing** all of one's own **basic purpose** needs.

Further, with any form of *monetary unit* that holds *'an assigned, agreed upon, and officially supported* **tradable value**', that monetary unit can be used as a method of *holding or storing* **value gained** from a **trade** to be used at any later date for any other **tradable** purpose or use.

An individual or **business** can deliver in **trade** an expertly made single type of **product** or **service** for **currency**, and the **gain** generated can expand so far over **basic purpose** *needs* or *wants* that an individual can *'hold in reserve [**save**] the **value** of that **gain** in **currency** form for future use'* or '***invest** it to generate more* **gain** '.

With the advantages of **currency, specialization**, and **organization, trade** can keep expanding *exponentially* and *indefinitely*. [More in the section on **Currency**.]

Trade *Generates* the Need for Economic Ethics

> The need for *symbiotic trade relationships*
> and *agreed upon standards of fairness*
> creates the subject of economic ethics.
> Without agreed upon standards of economic ethics,
> *conflict* instead of *cooperation, hindrance* instead of *conduciveness,*
> *harmful behaviors* instead of *symbiotic exchange* ensues.

Ethics develops naturally in **trade** because the consequences without it can be catastrophic, not only to **organized trade** and prosperity, but to the safety of human life.

Ethics, however, needs to have a *basis* for judgement – a *fundamental understanding* of *the essential purpose for economic existence* upon which to base our decisions. Unfair **trade** practices set people against each other, very often violently – *most especially when* **basic purpose** *is threatened*. Agreements must be made, **standards** must be set, harm must be made up for [justly], fairness must be abided.

Ethics further develops as **producers** without scruples cause recognizable harm of one kind or another through **productivity** or **product**. **Ethics** at this point extends beyond **basic purpose** *material* requirements to *general* quality of *survival*, *dynamics of living*, and *living conditions* – i.e. *general* ideas of right and wrong, not only economic gains and losses. [More in **Ethics** *next*.]

About Trade:

Principles and Concepts Important to Success

The Basics of Successful Trade

[The basics of successful **trade** are covered in **Derivative Operating Dynamics: Marketing**.]

Trading in Employment as an Individual or Business
[A complete section on **Employment** coming up later.]

As explained earlier, **employment** is a **trade agreement** – the **working producer's** *productivity* **for the organized producer's** *currency*. [This includes **management employees** that are *not* owners or part owners of a **business** as **'working producers'** – they are *selling* their **management** *knowledge* and *skills* as a **service** to the **organization**.] And in that **employment** is a *trade* agreement, and that **specializations** and labor are **services** offered in **trade**, it would be good to keep in mind that *all* **trade** *principles and* **ethics** *also apply to* **employment** *for both parties*.

THE PRINCIPLES of ECONOMIC ETHICS

"Would that the simple maxim, that honesty is the best policy, might be laid to heart; that a sense of the true aim of life might elevate the tone of politics and trade till public and private honor become identical."
Author: Margaret Fuller - May 23, 1810 – July 19, 1850 - American journalist

Primary Axiom Two:

In order to actively PRODUCE what we need and want,
we humans EDUCATE ourselves
so to become *knowledgeable* and *skilled* in
the 'causation' and 'application' principles of PRODUCING
which requires as a precursor we
locate, obtain, and develop for use all possible RESOURCES.

Active, but limited, TRADE and concepts of ETHICS begin here.

About Ethics:

Productivity Class Economic Theory Statement

The need for symbiotic trade relationships and agreed upon standards of fairness generates the subject of economic ethics.

The basis of <u>*general* economic ethics</u> is...
...long term well being
for all people, populaces, species, and environments
included in, contributing to, or *effected by* any economic activity.

The basis of economic ethics <u>*in a trade transaction*</u> is: *a fair and agreed upon 'value for value' exchange – wherein each party has access to know and understand all values involved*, and neither party is using the other's ignorance or circumstances to undermine or circumvent symbiotic exchange.

The basis of economic ethics <u>*by a governing body*</u> is '*long term well-being, and reasonable considerations to ensure basic purpose gainful opportunity*, for *all* members of the governed society' through fair and practical structural frameworking and judicial enforcement over any adverse effects of any of the twelve elemental activities upon consumers, populaces, life forms, and environments.

The structural basis for building a system of ethical basic purpose pursuit is 'symbiotic exchange' properly alloyed with the appropriate type of 'altruistic support structure', designed to empower every participant in the economic community to productively achieve basic purpose pursuits. Symbiotic exchange is the 'application mechanism' that implements the principles of economic ethics.

General altruistic support for those who, for mental or physical reasons, cannot productively support themselves applies.

Economic ethics is not philosophy. Economic ethics is how human life *inherently operates* on the subject of material pursuits within the social and natural environments in which we live.

About Ethics:
an
Overview

All human social drives extend *outward* from ourselves
into our living environment and its conditions – both natural and social.

The need for **symbiotic trade** relationships and *agreed upon standards of fairness* generates the subject of economic **ethics**. Without agreed upon standards of economic **ethics**, conflict instead of cooperation, hindrance instead of conduciveness, harmful behaviors instead of **symbiotic exchange** ensues.

Unfair **trade** practices set people against each other, often violently – most especially when a person or group feels their **basic purpose** drives are threatened. Agreements must be made, standards must be set, harm must be justly rectified, fairness must be abided. **Symbiotism** and fairness become the standard – agreed upon *benefit* for *benefit* and **value** for **value**.

There are Three Bases for Ethics Determinations in Economics

- *General* economic **ethics**
- *Trade transaction ethics*
- *Governing ethics*

And are as stated in the **producer class economics** theory statement.

Ethical Frameworks

To INVERT *economically...* To change the directional flow or activity so as to produce the opposite, reverse, or harmful effect. INVERSION – Perversion or corruption of the *innate* human intent to 'contribute to' others for reciprocal gain, into an *inverted* human intent to gain by '*drawing away from*' , '*taking from*' or '*depriving*' others.

Providing the *structure* for **ethical trade** requires application of the **fifth primary axiom**:

Humans are social, cooperative beings and therefore
survive and thrive only in symbiotic patterns and systems,
and suffer and decline in *inverted* or *over altruistic* patterns and systems.

However, properly *principled, structured, compatible*, and *applied*
altruistic support activities *strengthen* symbiotic systems and make
them more stable, resilient, and contributive to the basic purpose success
of an economic community.

Improperly principled, poorly structured, incompatible, misapplied, excessive, etc. **altruistic** patterns and systems tend over time to cause similar effects as **inverted** patterns and systems by [often] reducing **productive** capability levels of economic participants and drawing excessive **resources** from the **symbiotic** exchange system.

Symbiotic Exchange
[*properly* alloyed with the appropriate type of altruistic support structure]
designed to empower every participant in the economic community
for successful achievement of basic purpose pursuits
is the *mechanism* that *applies* the principles of economic ethics.

The Need for *Enforceable* Ethical Economic Frameworks

It is not uncommon for both **employers** and **employees** to try to take advantage of situations and conditions that give them the opportunity to exploit the other or **gain** for themselves by reducing the **basic purpose** conditions of others. Such ill intentions and behaviors are simply a factor of the human condition.

Further, when the proper **ethical** framework of a **market economy** is weakened or violated, such conditions will *always* eventually *empower the wealthy*. And those that are willing to use that empowerment to 'rig' the system to suit their greed at the expense of others [and *all else*] will do so.

Inverting or otherwise **corrupting** or deviating from *balanced benefit-for-benefit* exchange, reducing the **basic purpose** conditions of individuals, families, or communities, creating conditions conducive to harm or suffering, or cause the economic weakening or failure of communities, populations, or environments must be considered *criminal* in nature.

There must, therefore, exist *enforceable standards* of **ethical** behavior. And such standards must be *established upon our basic nature*: that *we survive and thrive as social, cooperative beings* – i.e. on the basis of principles fundamental to all of humanity. *Fairness,* **symbiotic exchange,** and *socially contributive behaviors* are standards fundamental to all of humanity.

Every *Life Dynamic* Has Its Fundamental Purpose ...Its Reason for Evolving Into Existence ...Its Contribution to Living Life Successfully

The most important thing you need to understand about any aspect or characteristic of life, including economics, is its fundamental *purpose – why has this basic human dynamic evolved into existence in human living?...what is its contribution to human life? ...what is it for?*

Answering those questions tells you its **ethics** – how to apply that human dynamic to proper outcomes. Which, in human life – in order to be harmoniously compatible with all other human dynamics – is always going be:

long term well-being for
self and all people, populaces, species, and environmental conditions
included in, contributing to, or effected by
any human activity on any subject or endeavor.

It is through economics that we address the *material* requirements that determine our *quality of survival, successful pursuit the dynamics of living,* and *improvement of our living conditions.* This is the reason human economics has evolved into existence – its '*most basic*' **purpose.** And therein lies the basis of economic **ethics.** If this '**basic purpose**' is the reason for the evolution of the **five primary axioms** and the **twelve elemental activities,** *then that is the basis for* **ethical** *application of them – the evolutionary basis of intended outcomes.*

Other Life Forms and Environmental Conditions?

In a nutshell, *economically speaking,* environmental conditions effect human *survival,* human *living dynamics,* and human *living conditions.* Imbalances of life forms and natural conditions *always* effect human life adversely. And that is why '*general economic ethics*' must include '*long term well-being*' for *other species,* and *environmental conditions. Living things and conditions should never be harmed or decline by human economic activities.* Economic activities should *symbiotically contribute* to their well-being –domesticated or other.

So What About 'Creative Destruction'?

In economics there is a principle called '*creative destruction*'**:** It means that when some **products** and **services** are *created and brought to* **market,** other **products** and **services** can get *destroyed, abandoned,* or *pushed out of existence* – along with their **employment** or **basic purpose** contributions.

Competition, invention, innovation, are part of economic *advancement.* It is not **unethical** behavior. As **working** or **organizational producers**, we are required to adjust to *ever advancing* economic circumstances and situations.

More or *Bigger* Is Not The Same As *Better*

Having '*more*' than is needed for **basic purpose** well-being – does not mean **basic purpose** conditions are '*better*'. Note that nowhere in the **basic purpose** statement does it say the purpose of economics is '*to secure more and bigger material assets*'. If a society misinterprets '*improved living conditions*' as '*having more and bigger stuff*' they will always find themselves quite lost, and miserable – never satisfied.

> '*Improved*' means '*better*'. Not 'more' or 'bigger'.
> '*Better*' means '*higher quality of contribution to well-being and happiness*'.

About Ethics:

Characteristics and General Factors

[**Ethics**: *For our purposes...* **the mores, rules, standards, and laws required to regulate human behaviors and interactions to non-harmful outcomes.**]

Human **ethics** comes from our *fundamental humanity – our innate fundamental drives as social beings to desire right behaviors from ourselves and those around us – concepts of rightness usually based on happiness and/or well-being*. And it is from our *fundamental humanity* that we develop intolerance of the suffering and conflict that arise when anyone causes harm or loss to others. It is this *fundamental humanity* that naturally generates the development of **ethical** standards in human behavior.

Economically, our innate social drives desiring well-being for others can often be *overridden* by our *also innate* material drive to **gain** for oneself. When **gain** becomes more important than the well-being of others, harm and suffering of those effected becomes a very real threat. It is innate to all human societies to adapt, apply, and enforce '*behavioral standards*' – *ethical behaviors and operating frameworks* – as a preventive and corrective measure.

On '*Fair*' Exchange:
FAIR: *For our purposes...* **The perception of '*balance*' of inflow and outflow between ourselves and others [and sometimes incorrectly between ourselves and life in general].**

'Fairness' is a matter of balance. The balance we are talking about economically is that of *inflow* verses *outflow* of **value**, or at least our perception of it. This applies in economics, but also in all human interactions. What you do for me should be '*equal*' to what I do for you [*equity*]. What you **trade** to me should be '*equal*' to what I **trade** to you [*equity*]. '*Inequity*' in **trade** is a sense of *loss* of having inflowed **value** *less* than what has been outflowed. And therein lies *imbalance – inequity*.

An *imbalance* of fair exchange in *any* human activity, under *any* circumstances, can create feelings of resentment at having been treated with *inequity* – an unequal *balance of exchange* [a *loss* in the exchange] in some human relationship. In the sense of loss lies the source of conflict – the indignant urge to correct the imbalance. Preventing such conflict is one of the primary purposes of the establishment of *any* **ethical** standards – in our case, *economic* **ethics**.

In Economics, *Symbiotic Exchange* Is The Primary Mechanism that Brings *Ethical* Outcomes In Trade

The basis for setting *mutual **basic purpose** benefit* in *economic* **ethical** standards is:
> *...long term well-being for all*
> *people, populaces, species, and environmental conditions*
> *included in, contributing to, or effected by any economic activity.*

One of the primary keys to **symbiotic exchange** is 'equity': e*qual balance in human interactions* – in economics that means a ***symbiotic 'exchange** of equal value'* in a **trade**. Equity in **trade** brings well-being to all **trading** parties.

About Economic Ethics:

Principles and Concepts Important to Success

The *broad-scope, overall* view of economic **ethics**, up to this point, has meant **producing products** and **services** with both *life* and *economic* **basic purpose value** and **trading** them in **symbiotic exchange** with **value** for **value** equity – *all **produced, consumed,** and **traded** in a manner contributive to long term well-being for all people, populaces, species, and environmental conditions included in, contributing to, or effected by any economic activity.* [Yeah, I know, that's a mouthful. But by now you should be used to it, and it should make perfect sense to you.]

At this point comes **Work Ethic** and **Employment Ethic**.

'**Work Ethic**' [for working producers – the employed] and '**Employment Ethic**' [for organized producers – the employer] *For our purposes...* the ethical disciplines and behaviors of *contributing to* a group productivity; and the ethical behavior and disciplines required in administrating a productive group.

We call ourselves **productivity class** because we earn our livings **productively** as **specialized producers** [**working producers**] or **organized producers** [**businesses** or **organization administrators**]. That means we are *productive contributors* and operate to the standards of **productivity class ethics**. In order to live up to that standard, we abide by '*codes of productivity and behavior*' called a '**work ethic**' and an '**employment ethic**' as defined above.

As this is a 'beta' version text
and is limited in the number of pages we can print to keep the price down,
Work Ethic and **Employment Ethic**
are presented on our web site at **productivityclass.*info*.**

THE PRINCIPLES of ECONOMIC GAIN

Your net worth to the world is usually determined by what remains after your bad habits are subtracted from your good ones. Author: Benjamin Franklin

GAIN *For our purposes...*To increase in amount, value, rate, development, etc.; To acquire profit, wages, or salary in business, through employment, or from investment over and above the costs of acquisition; To improve overall basic purpose conditions.

Primary Axiom Three:

As humans we are endowed with all the physical and mental capacities
necessary to PRODUCE and provide beyond our own
individual and family *essential* BASIC PURPOSE needs.

Thus material GAIN and
asset accumulation begins.

With GAIN and asset accumulation comes indefinite expansion of
TRADE and concepts of ETHICS.

Active, but limited, EMPLOYMENT begins here.

About Gain:

Productivity Class Economic Theory Statement

In order for something to be consumed, it must first be produced. Therefore, consumption cannot exceed production. Production, however, can far exceed consumption. And thus there can be *gain.*

Economic gain, then, is an *accumulation* and/or *improvement* of *material assets* that contribute to basic purpose success. *Accumulation or improvement of assets* is produced when the rate of consumption necessary to maintain our current standard of basic purpose is *less than* the volume or value of what we produce.

Once rudimentary 'basic purpose' needs are secured, the drive to *advance basic purpose standards* through *further accumulation or improvement of material assets – gain –* becomes the driving force of all further economic endeavor.

[*Corollary: if asset accumulation or asset improvement does *not* improve basic purpose conditions, it is *not* gain. It is useless excess or material waste.]

About Gain:
an
Overview

Achievement of *Essential* or *Rudimentary* Basic Purpose Drives *Always* Graduates to The Drive to *Gain* over *Current* Basic Purpose Conditions

However well or poorly worked out, straight and true or twisted and false, ethical or unethical, *all drives for* **gain** *are* **basic purpose** *drives.*

We are *required by our very nature to* **gain**. Every pursuit for **gain** is a pursuit for *increases* or *improvements* in the material prosperity that contributes to *'higher quality of survival, more successful pursuit of the dynamics of living,* and *better living conditions'* – the **basic purpose** of all that is economic.

Immediately after *'essential* or *rudimentary survival'* is achieved, **gain**, then, quickly becomes the main goal of all economic endeavors. Whether personal, business, or societal, the pursuit of **gain** becomes the driving force that advances of the quality of our **basic purpose** standards.

For the *well*-**educated**, life becomes a 'game' of **gainful** pursuit. For the *less* **educated**, life becomes a 'striving' for enough **gain** to create economic stability, safety, and security. For the **uneducated**, life becomes an 'arduous day to day, week to week, year to year struggle' for essential survival. *Gain for the* **uneducated***, therefore, is not a factor. Only after essential* or *rudimentary survival* is achieved, does **gain** become the primary economic pursuit.

Establishing the Gainful Condition:

In order ensure that our **productivity** actually produces **gain**, we must **consume** appropriate to our current **basic purpose** standards, which must be established at *less than* our **income produced**.

> *All personal economic security lies in the ability*
> *to* **produce** *and* **consume** *in a* **gainful** *manner.*

When *we* talk about economic **gain**, we are talking about **producing** beyond our **consumptive** needs and thereby *increasing* or *improving* material contribution to the dynamics of human life.

Gain is not actually an economic or **currency value** measurement. **Basic purpose gain** is *not* about **money** or materialism. True '**basic purpose gain**' is about material *contribution* to *success in living life*, and nothing else. We **gain** when our *quality of survival* is *better*. We **gain** when we more *successfully pursue the dynamics of living*. We **gain** when we *improve* our *living conditions*.

> *The basic purpose of any subject – the reason for its existence in life –*
> *is the only true standard by which its success can be measured.*

About Gain:

Characteristics and General Factors

"In life, there is advancing, there is staying the same, and there is declining. There are no other conditions. You are always either getting better, staying the same, or getting worse. However, life is a dynamic, ever changing activity. *Nothing, therefore, ever stays the 'same' for very long.* All human economic activity has to keep advancing, or suffer eventual decline – it is the nature of material existence. *We must ever strive to gain.* Staying the same is just awaiting eventual adverse decline." Author: Paul D. Ahearn

Economic Gain Occurs When Productivity Exceeds Consumption – *Period.*

Getting Productivity to Exceed Consumption is a Simple Twofold Activity:

a) Increase **productive income** while maintaining **consumption** at *less than* that **income**;
b) Utilize **gain** earned to create more **gain** through financial **investment**; or to increase **productive income** through **educational**, **capital**, or entrepreneurial **investment**.

Gains in How Well We Live Life:

However, **gains** in how well we live life and the quality of our living experience, occurs *only* when improvements in our **productivity** *improves our basic purpose conditions.*

Most people create **gain** by improving their ability to earn – through better jobs or promotions, increasing **education** and capabilities, **business** expansion, etc. 'Judicious spending' of that increased **income** on **basic purpose** needs and wants, *when materially applied to a better life experience*, is what creates *true* **gain**.

However, **basic purpose gain** also requires **savings** and **investments** that pay for 'large ticket' expenditures like *college tuition, houses,* or *retirement.* Therefore, prospering beyond current **basic purpose** conditions – actual **gain** – requires tough **productivity** in the **volume** and in the **value** that earns it.

Gain Can Be Interrupted by Stagnancy or Loss.

Consistent, uninterrupted **gain** is rarely possible. **Gain** can be interrupted by *stagnancy* or *loss* due to unforeseen or uncontrollable economic circumstances.

When our **consumption** is equal to our **productive** earnings
and our **productive** earnings are not increasing, we are *stagnant.*

Short term stagnancy is harmless if a comfortable level of **basic purpose** conditions are maintained. Life, however, is *a dynamic, ever changing* activity, *and nothing, therefore, ever stays the same for very long.* All human economic activity has to keep advancing, or suffer eventual decline – it is the nature of material existence. *You must **gain**.* Staying the same is just awaiting eventual decline.

Long term stagnancy, therefore, is a threat to **basic purpose** stability. *Our 'productivity in trade' and economic circumstances must continuously evolve forward, or the advancing economic conditions around us will leave us behind and unable to compete.*

About Gain:

Principles and Concepts Important to Success

A Little About *Gain* – From Its *Produce* and *Consume* Aspects

*The whole purpose of effective **consumption** is to be able to allocate our hard earned **productive income** to the fulfillment of our **basic purpose** objectives and pursuits.*

Half of the *trick* to **consumption**, of course, is to make sure that **consumption** is *well enough spent* to accomplish our **basic purpose** *needs* and *wants* and still amount to less than our **productive income** so as to still create **gain** – which is itself a **basic purpose** objective.

The first thing we learn about economics is that *consumption [costs] must always be less than income [revenues],* no matter how we work that out.

Wastefulness, extravagance, squandering, etc. can always outpace **productivity** – *but only if we let it*. If **money** is a **resource** [and it is], no matter how much of it we have, we can always think up more ways to spend **money** than there is **money** to spend. It's probably the only aspect of what economists call 'scarcity' that is actually true.

When applying this principle in **business**, we must not only create **gain** [**profit**] for the **business** itself, but we must create enough **gain** for the *owners*, *operators*, and *employees* to also create **gain** in their *household* economics [*their personal and family lives*]. We do this with three primary means…
- o Ramping up the *value* and *volume* of our **productivity***, and persistently pushing it upward throughout our lifetime;
- o Keeping **consumption** *well below* one's **productive income**; and
- o **Investing** *earned* **gain** to create *more* **gain**.

*Produce *'more'* and/or *'better'* – increasing *volume* or *value* of **productivity**

far *above* **consumptive** needs – is the *primary route* to producing **gain**. *Any* prosperity we *ever* get to achieve will only be in direct proportion to what we can **produce** – *in volume and in value*. **Frugality**, however, is the *operating principle* that ensures our **productivity** actually **produces** the **gain** we strive for.

Invest Gain to Create More Gain:

Gain *invested well* **produces** more **gain** – gradually, but exponentially.

Gain is '**invested**' through four primary methods:

- **Financial capital *investment* – capitalizing** other **productivity**
- **Human capital *investment*** – development of human capability – **education** and **training**
- **Capital resource *investment*** – development of more *efficient*, more **productive capital resources**
- Entrepreneurial ***investment*** – new **business productivity**

Every economic 'entity' [**household, business, government**, etc.] must understand and utilize the economic strategies of **saving** and **investing**. **Saving** is '*holding on to and accumulating*' what has been **gained**. While **investing**, although including some element of risk, is '*utilizing*' what has been **gained** to **produce** further **gain**. *A huge and very important difference.* Over time, '**saving** *only*' as a strategy can allow naturally occurring **inflation** [increases in prices] to *reduce* the **consumptive value** [spending power] of **saved currency**. Proper **investing** as a strategy *increases* **currency invested** and counters naturally occurring **inflation**. Further…

Investing rather than saving* also capitalizes productivity.
*Invested gain generates expanded **productivity** and **trade**, and therefore,*
*produces increased **prosperity** and further **gain** for*
the entire economic community.

[*If you **save** in a bank account, the bank **invests** that money anyway – and gets the benefit of that **investment** instead of you. Learn to **invest**.]

THE PRINCIPLES of ORGANIZE

Of all human inventions the organization, a machine constructed of people performing interdependent functions, is the most powerful.
Author: Robert Shea -- Former Associate Dir. U.S. Office of Management and Budget

Primary Axiom Four:

In order to be more *efficient*, *productive*, and most especially *consistent*,
in PRODUCING for 'BASIC PURPOSE' needs and wants,
we humans create *patterns* and *systems* of doing things.

Thus, concepts and methods of ORGANIZATION begin,
and therefore also, SPECIALIZATION, EMPLOYMENT, and CURRENCY.

With the development of ORGANIZATION,
all TWELVE ELEMENTAL ACTIVITIES
develop into full, expanded, and ever more sophisticated use,
and become more properly referred to as
the PRIMARY OPERATING DYNAMICS of economics.

About Organizing:

Productivity Class Economic Theory Statement

Organizing is *'the arranging into a single coordinated whole all the different activities necessary for the accomplishment of a purpose'*, and evolves from our capacity to create *patterns* and *systems* of doing things. Organizing creates *structure*, *streamlining*, and *coordinated effort*, therefore providing more *consistency*, better *efficiency*, and higher *productivity* in producing.

Organization is the formation of a *'pattern'* or *'system'* for operating the *'functions'* and *'flows'* required in the accomplishment of a productivity – the creation of a 'clockwork functioning whole of all of the functions' necessary to produce.

An organization is a 'dynamic productive *operating system*' made up of *'several* or *many* separate interrelated and coordinated specialized activities', some of which naturally become 'organs' of the whole [thus the term *organ*-ization].

All organizing at first *simplifies*. However, that original *'simplified organized operating base'* inevitably serves as a *foundation* to expand upward and outward into an *'ever more complicated and diverse application and operating structure'*.

Organization is the elemental activity that provides the twelve elemental activities with *limitless expansion capacity*, and therefore also, expansion to limitless basic purpose gain and accumulation of wealth.

About Organizing:
an
Overview

Understanding What 'Processes', 'Organization', 'Administration', and 'Management' Are

Processes

Processes are the first and simplest step in creating an **organized** activity. Our innate desire to be more ***productive***, *efficient*, and *consistent* drives us to ***'order the steps or actions'*** with which we **produce** a **product**, deliver a **service**, or put causing any effect into a *pattern* or *system* that works to deliver those three qualities. Any **process** is an **organized** activity.

Organization

Understanding **organizing** can seem daunting and confusing when one looks at all the myriad of process, procedures, and people to coordinate. However, it's actually not confusing at all if you understand these two things:

- *Each **specialized** function is an **'organ'*** as in a living **productive** 'body'; and
- Any **organized** structure, small or large, is simply a <u>well ordered system of *functions* and *flows*</u> – each **specialized** *function* [*task*] and the *directional lines <u>flowing</u>* input and output to and from it [completing a **productivity** and *flowing* it to its next step or end result].

i.e. Every *'function'* [organ] is *ordered and arranged through lines of inflows and outflows* 'to' and 'from' it into a single coordinated whole, designed for the accomplishment of the total purpose' – the **productivity** is 'organ'-ized.

Administration and Management

Every **organization**, in order to operate *consistently*, has to have **policies** – *'decided upon operating requirements needed to operate effectively'* based on *cause-and-effect* and *application principles* – all designed to achieve the goals and purposes of the **organization**. And someone has to **administer** those policies, **execute** planned strategies, and **manage** and **lead** the group. And that is what **administration**, **executives** [*execute* + *'ives'*], and **management** is for.

Organization Makes Building Communities and Civilizations Possible

Half of what holds a culture together is the *agreements* held by a society on social behaviors, human values, principles of humanity, and behaviors that affect others or the community at large. However, agreement on **governmental** and economic structures, technologies, material values, functional institutions, etc. are the other half of what holds a culture or a society together – and that is all **organization**.

The simplicity of organization is that, as complicated as it can get,
it is still only the formation of *patterns* and *systems* of *functions* and *flows*.

And the beauty of **organization** is that the creation of *patterns* and *systems* is limitless in design, limitless in scope, and limitless in size, expansion, or inclusion. It is upon this unlimited size, scope, and design that communities grow into civilizations, and civilizations grow indefinitely broad, large, and 'ever more sophisticated'.

Types of Economic Organization

The Difference Between an Economic *Entity* and an Economic *System*.

Economic 'entities' need other economic 'entities' to interact with –
some to 'inflow from' and others to 'outflow to'.

An economic 'system' is made up of economic 'entities'
*that all together **produce** and **consume** all the necessary*
***basic purpose** needs and wants of an economic community –*
*forming a <u>complete</u> and <u>continuous cycle</u> of **production** and **consumption**.*

Households, **businesses** [and other **organizations**], and **governments** are *inflow/outflow* economic *'entities'*.

Economic *systems* are whole societies or geographic populations of economic *'entities'* inter-**trading basic purpose** needs and wants in an **organized** *system* of *self-sustaining **productivity***.

There are Three Primary Forms of an Organizational *Entity*
○ **Household:**
In economic theory, a **household** is an economic 'entity'. It is **organized** economically; it *inflows* **currency** by *outflowing* **productivity** within the community; and **consumes** according to **basic purpose** *need* and *want* principles, thus *inflowing* needs and wants by *outflowing* [and further circulating] **productively** earned **currency**.
○ **Business:**
A **business** is an economic *'entity'*. It actually shares the same inflow/outflow characteristics as a **household** or a **government**. But

further, it is built and **organized** to *inflow* resources and *outflow* **products** and **services** so to generate **revenue** and create **profit** [**gain**].

○ **Government:**
Governance' is also an '**organized** earning [**taxing**] and spending [**service** providing] entity', similar to **households** and **businesses**. An economic **governing** body, however, is the **organization** that *administrates and manages* the complete economic system itself.

Infrastructure

*In **productivity class** economics, **infrastructure** is simply an application of economic **organization**. It is the **organization** of **capital resources** into a 'service structure base' upon which the economic entities of a society can operate, build, and expand, and accomplish their purposes.*

Infrastructure delivers the necessary **services** for an **organized** economic system or social system to *function*. Further, in any type of economic **organization** an *internal infra-structure* is a required aspect of **organizing**:

The **organization** of *functions* and *flows*
and the **capital resources** necessary to operate a **productivity**
is the establishment of internal **infra-structure**.

Free Market vs. Command vs. Oligarchies vs. Plutocracies as Organized Economic 'Systems' – as Economies

Free Market economies are regulated by a **governing** body providing **ethical** frameworks within which to operate, and are *free* to run on *market* **supply**, **demand**, and **pricing** equilibriums [all explained in chapter three] to determine how *needs* and *wants* are provided to the populace. When **ethical** frameworks are wisely designed and enforced, **free market** economies provide the highest level of **basic purpose gainful** prosperity to the overall populace.

Command economies [communism (socialism)] as an overall full cycle, self-contained economic system are all but gone from the world today, although some *combinations* of **command** and **market** economies do still exist [e.g. China]. Over burdened by bureaucracy, they could not effectively provide for their populaces, nor keep up with the **basic purpose** advances of the rest of the **free market** economic systems of the world.

Oligarchies and **plutocracies**, however, are on the rise. Although considered **governing** systems, *they are also very much economic systems*. The rich and economically powerful determine how a **market** economy gets 'frameworked' [rigged]. *And it is always for their own benefit at the expense of the broad populace and the very environmental conditions we all live under*. **Oligarchies** and **plutocracies** are *always* 'inverted economies', and in order to function, they must also *always* be **inverted** *governing* systems. [More in **Symbiotism**.]

About Organizing:

Characteristics and General Factors

'Functions and Flows'
The Coordination of Productive Functions Along Coordinated Flow Routes

Organiz-*ing* is the setting up of *functions* and *flows*. Each **function** has to have *flowed* to it: **administrative** or **managerial** direction, material **resources**, information **resources**, possibly other completed tasks to further add to, **currency** to operate, etc. When that *function* is complete, its completed work is *flowed* to a 'next function' or final destination.

All these *flows* to and from each *function* must have efficient predetermined *routes* ['lines'] by which each **resource** and finished work must *flow* to get to the next point. All of these *functions* must be interconnected and coordinated like 'organs' into a single efficient **productivity** *flowing* forward toward the intended result. Setting up or adjusting all these *functions* and *flows* is **organ-*izing***.

An **organization** is a **productive** *operating system* of *functions* and *flows* **producing** an intended result.

The Stages of 'Organ'-ization

Organization is not currently measured or thought of as developing in '**stages**'. However, it *does*. And it is better understood and learned one development '**stage**' at a time:

Stage One: The creation of a process:

Arranging the steps
**of producing a product, delivering a service, or doing a task
in the *sequence* most *efficient, productive*, and *consistent*.**

The first stage of **organization** is the simple construction of a **process**. This is the fundamental *everyone* seems to get. Take any type of task and order the steps to accomplish it in the most *efficient*, **productive**, and **productively** *consistent* sequence. *Voila*, **organized production**.

Stage Two: Coordinating a group of processes or a series of processes

'**Arranging a number of *different* processes,
each separate from the other, or in sequence one after the other,
to come together at a single point as a completed task'.**

In order to **produce a product** or complete a task, often several **processes** have to be done at the same time on separate but related parts and then compiled, fit, or assembled into a completed **product** or result once all **processes** are done and/or parts are ready. *Coordinating* them to be done separately but so that the end **product** or result is efficiently accomplished is **organizing** [each separate **process** being an **'organ'** of the whole **production** – **'organ'-ize**]. So too, would a number of different **processes** performed in a *series* or *sequence*, one after the other, completed in the order necessary to culminate into a completed **product**.

Stage Three: Forming complex interconnecting activities

There are many dissimilar tasks required in an **organization** – *accounting, information technology,* **marketing, product** *or* **service** *production,* **administration** and **management**, etc. Yet all are necessary and all are interconnected. Therefore, the third 'stage' of **organizing** is...

> **Forming a group of seemingly unrelated specialized tasks or operations,**
> [separated into divisions, departments, sections, etc. – 'organs' of the body]
> **each with their *own* arrangements of ordered and coordinated processes,**
> **and creating a system of *productive functions* and *flows***
> **that operate these seemingly unrelated tasks in a coordinated and**
> **cooperative manner causing the 'complete system' to operate**
> **efficiently and profitably as a 'whole'.**

That sounds a lot more difficult than it actually is for a **small business** or a **household**. For **corporations**, however, it can be just as complex and difficult as it sounds – even more so. *However, the simplicity of arranging 'functions and flows' as the basis of **organizing** still applies.*

*Most importantly, this is the level of **organization** that requires **managing** people – **managing** the actual **specialized producers** of each **productivity**.* Therefore, 'stage three' is that part of **economic organization** that separates the capable from the unsuccessful in *expanded* **productivity**.

Stage Four: Expanding the organization and the organized activity *outward* to participate in the *greater economic community*:

Up to **stage three**, **organizing** is *internal* to the activity being **organized**. It is all about laying out and arranging things *within* the activity. **Stage four** is expanding one's **organizing** *outward* and fitting one's own **organization** into the larger 'playing field' or 'game board' of the community of **organizations** and **governing authorities** one is operating in and under – which requires an understanding of how that system itself is **organized**, or of taking a leadership role and **organizing** it oneself.

> The purpose of **stage four** is *participation* and *managing influence* within
> the economic frameworks, circumstances, or conditions

of one's operating environment [**competitive, governing,** and **market**].

About Organizing:

Principles and Concepts Important to Success

A Successful *Economic* Organization Requires More Than Productive Mechanics

A successful **organization** must be built to accomplish a *worthwhile purpose* [yes, **ethical profit** is a worthwhile purpose]. A successful **organization** requires *more* than putting *functions* and *flow-lines* together – although, that is *how* it is done. To be successful, an **organization** must be aimed at the achievement of **basic purpose** pursuits for its **consumers**:

> "In order to be more *efficient, productive,* and most especially *consistent,*
> in producing for 'BASIC PURPOSE' ...
> ...concepts and methods of ORGANIZATION begin,..."

The purpose of *economic* **organization** is stated in **axiom four** itself. It is always **basic purpose** success that is the end goal of any economic activity – the actual well-being for self and others.

Important Notes to Remember:

- *Functions*, even those done by machines, are done, or overseen by **producers** – *people*. The success of an **organization** depends upon the quality and motivation of its **producers** – **specialized** and otherwise – its **productive** *people*.

- Don't let sophisticated or academic terminology, theories, buzz-words, and philosophies intimidate or confuse you or your **personnel**. Simplify everything to *plain speak* terminology. You must execute **administrative** and **management** plans and purposes in terms *non*-**management** personnel can *understand* and *do*.

The Most Common Economic 'Organs' of a Business

These **specialized** activities apply to *every* **business** activity, even a one person **business** wherein the owner/operator does everything themselves:

- o **Administration and Management** [running things]
- o **Human Resources** [people make it work (or fail)]

- o **Marketing and Sales** [**producing** something **tradeable**, and convincing **consumers** to **trade** their hard earned **currency** for it]
- o **Production** [**producing** in **volume** and **value**]
- o **Material Accounting** and **Warehousing** [account for everything]
- o **Financial Accounting, Money Management,** and **Payroll**
- o **Asset and Equipment Maintenance** [maintaining **capital resources**]

In a one person **business**, the above is simple and amounts to not much more than

- having something you can **produce** to offer;
- a **market** that needs or wants it;
- a method to **advertise**;
- a place to keep and account for **resources** and **supplies**;
- controlling **costs** of **resources** and **supplies**;
- **accounting** for **income revenues** through a **business** bank account;
- and **administrating** and **managing** the activity to a worthwhile **profit** [while keeping accurate records and paying your **taxes**].

As a **business** gets larger, or the **product** or **service** gets more complex, operating the above activities gets more and more complex and requiring of **specialized education** – including specific **education** of how each activity applies to that particular business. But *the fundamental set up is the same* – the *basic* '**organs**' are always the same.

THE PRINCIPLES of SPECIALIZE

Primary Axiom Four:

In order to be more *efficient, productive,* and most especially *consistent,*
in producing for 'basic purpose' needs and wants,
we humans create *patterns* and *systems* of doing things.

Thus, concepts and methods of ORGANIZATION begin,
and therefore also, SPECIALIZATION, EMPLOYMENT, and CURRENCY.

About Specialize:

Productivity Class Economic Theory Statement

Specialization begins when individuals or groups realize that by becoming highly skilled at a single needed or wanted product or service, or type of product or service, they can trade that one product or service for all other basic purpose needs and wants.

Specialization is the development of the *'specialized expertise'* necessary for producing in any *specific* field of endeavor, and in concert with education makes possible unlimited levels of *discovery, invention, innovation, expertise,* and *efficiency. Increased expertise* increases product or service *value,* while *increased efficiency* increases *volume* with decreased costs, together increasing potential for *gain.*

Organization utilizes 'specialization' by placing individuals or groups into specialized tasks, functions, or activities [e.g. accounting, marketing, administrative management, manufacturing, or some other *specific* activity or productivity] that act as productive 'organs' of the whole body of productivity – and sometimes for 'additionally needed Independent expertise'.

[In productivity class economics – productive economics – dividing up the functions of a process into 'single repetitive tasks' (production or assembly lines) – aka 'division of labor' – is *not* specialization.]

About Specializing:
an
Overview

Although it is never best to jump right into a list of bullet points of the benefits of any economic activity, **specialization** has such a great number of

productive benefits that, just for the sake of brevity, it is best to just list them out:

Productive Benefits of Specialization...

- **Specialization** expands the number of different **products and services**, and types of **products** and **services**, that can be **produced** and **consumed** *proportionally with the expansion of the size of the economic community*. Further, in *group* **production**, very complex things requiring many different **specialized** components can now be **produced** that could not otherwise be **produced** at all – *and is the single most effective way to include everyone in an economy*.

- **Specialization** expands **discovery**, **invention**, and **innovation** exponentially with the size of an economic community – the more people **discovering**, **inventing**, and **innovating** the better. This is especially true when **education** is inclusive of that need.

- **Specialization** is the primary cause of the evolution into a 'market system' of **trade**, wherein *everyone* **specializes** and **trades** for **currency**, then, in a **market** environment, **trades currency** for **basic purpose** needs and wants.

- **Specialization** allows for the development of *expertise* to *levels far beyond what would otherwise be possible* if every person had to **produce** for their own **basic purpose** needs or wants before they could **produce** for **trade**. This added *expertise* in turn increases **product** and **service values** adding to the 'trade value' of an individual's or group's **production** –which in turn increases **gain** for *everyone*.

- **Specialization** increases **productivity** of the individual by allowing that individual to focus and become more *expert, skilled,* and *adept* on one subject or category of **product**, and so also increasing their **value** to **employers** and communities of **consumers**.

- **Specialization** *reduces* the number of **products** and **services** that an individual or group has to be *expert* at in order to meet their **basic purpose** needs, wants, and goals.

- **Specialization** allows for better **organized**, more *productive, efficient,* and *consistent* **productivity** [most especially by groups]. Better *productivity, efficiency,* and *consistency* in **producing products** and **services** translates to increased **volumes** and **values**, and therefore, **gain** and prosperity.

- **Specialization** is *necessary* for any individual **employee** to become *highly* **productive** in an **organized** group effort **productivity.**

- The increased *expertise* and *efficiency* of **specialization** creates a **trade** [and **marketing**] advantage for both **producers** and **consumers.** [Increased **quality** of **products** and **services** from **specialized productivity** improves their 'trade value', while the increased *efficiency* of **production** increases the **volume** and decreases the **costs** of **products produced.** *Lower* **prices** with *higher* **profit margins** result, while the **products** and **services** available to **consumers** *increase* in **value** and **volume.**]

- **Specialization** *intensifies* economic **competition.** Increasing **utility value** through *expertise*, or decreasing **price** through *efficiency* are primary elements of **product** or **service** *competition.* Also, in the attempt to gain *competitive advantage*, **producers** also employ the *expertise* of **specialization** to advance the ***invention*** and ***innovation*** of their **products** and **services** – further advancing the **volume** and **value** of **products** and **services** available to the **consumer**, and the number of **producers** in the community working and **prospering**.

- **Specialization** expands general **employment** – *and therefore whole community* **basic purpose** *success* – by allowing all **productivity** to be parsed and divided into **specialized businesses competing** to **provide** the **products** or **services** *needed* and *wanted* by the community.

- **Specialization**, properly wielded, allows **employment** and **organization** to expand proportionally with the size of the economic community [as long as the *structure, objectives,* and *competence* of **education** and ***ethical governing*** *frameworks* provide for it].

- **A Cautionary Note on Over-Specialization:** *What* we **produce** and *how* we **produce** it is constantly evolving. Loss of **consumer** and **business demand** for jobs and **businesses** that are *too* highly **specialized** is now a constant. [See next for how to avoid this.]

About Specializing:

Characteristics and General Factors

Specialization Is Required to Expand an Organization

Expanding an **organization** beyond **stage two,** *demands* **specialization. Stage three** and **stage four organization** *demand* **specialization** in order to create the separate **organs** of the whole and maintain *expert* **productivity**, each coordinating *efficiently* and *effectively* with all the others. Only in this way can an **organization** expand indefinitely and remain *efficiently* **productive** and successful.

As an **organization** expands to increase its **production**, every other operational activity in the **organization** expands with it. The solution to expansion is dividing **specialized** tasks into even more **specialized** tasks – the task of '**accounting**' becomes the '**Accounting** Department' divided into the Payroll Unit, Budget Unit, Materials Control Unit, and General Accounting Unit – **specialization** down to *each separate activity* of accounting is inevitable as the **organization** grows. And so it goes for *all* **specialized** operational activities – **production**, **marketing**, even **management**. *With this simple tactic, an organization can expand indefinitely.*

Specialization Accelerates the Development of Higher Technologies

Increases in *expertise* alone advances technological development. *Focused expertise* on *any subject* can by itself accelerate **invention** and **innovation** on that subject.

In addition, making our living in a single line of work requires that we ***compete*** with others in the same line of work. If we get *out*-**produced** by another expert, we can lose our **consumer's** [or **employer's**] **business** and fail to meet even our minimum **basic purpose** requirements. So, **competition** with other **specialists** requires **competitive productivity**, in **volume** and in **value**, but also requires the use of new **inventions** and **innovations** as a **competitive** tact.

About Specializing:

Principles and Concepts Important to Success

One is not '**specialized**' until they
achieve some level of expertise *well beyond* a 'functionary' skill level.

General Specialization vs. Specific Specialization

General specialization is **specializing** in a *general subject*, say interior designer or electrician, for example. **Specific specialization** is **specializing** in a *single specific type* of task, like drapery hanging or house wiring. **General specialization** has the benefit of a far more broad range of skills allowing more varied types of work and a broad spectrum of **employment**. A fully trained electrician, for example can wire or repair any or all electrical work in homes, buildings, machinery, construction equipment, automobiles, etc., sometimes even small boats or aircraft. A **house wiring** specialist only works when a house needs wiring, rewiring, or electrical repairs.

Therefore, An Important Note:

The more *specific* one's **specialization**, the more likely one will lose work during economic slowdowns or shifts in **productive** technologies. The more *general* one's **specialization**, the more likely they can find *or even create* work on their own terms under such conditions. *General* **specialization**, however, requires more depth of **education** – *a much more broad expertise* in order to succeed in these circumstances. A broad, but superficial knowledge is not enough.

In an Organization

A **manager** or **administrator** worth their salt
employs the **specialized** expertise
required for *only* those **specialized** activities necessary to operate
an effectively ***gainful*** enterprise – *and no more*.
Specialized expertise is *expensive* – as in '*expense*'.

He or she *also establishes enough **specialized** expertise
to provide for the **organizational** capacity to expand
as opportunities present themselves.*

A **manager** or **administrator** hires **specialists** in every aspect of **organizational** operations [**production, marketing, accounting,** etc.] in order to establish the highest **productivity** and **quality** of **products** or **services** achievable in the most *efficient* manner, thereby in turn establishing the highest possible, most consistent, monetary ***gains*** and **competitive** advantage.

In Government

In **governing** an economic community, we promote **specialization** by supporting **higher education** and **educational** facilities, along with **incentivizing small business** and **corporate** research and development to also train **employees** who demonstrate potential. We do this as a means to advance *expertise,* ***discovery****, ingenuity,* ***invention****,* and ***innovation*** in order to **produce** *more* and *better paying* **employment**. The resultant increases in **tax revenues** from more **profitable business** and better paid **employed working producers** allows for improved 'public good' programs, while reducing the need for public assistance, which also further provides for increases in support for **higher education, educational** facilities, and **small business** and **corporate** *research* and *development* – a self-perpetuating economic advancement. [At least that's how it's done when done *correctly*.]

The subsequent advancing, **gainful** upward-spiral in the amount of **production** and the number of **products** and **services** available in a community ensures a higher level of **prosperity** and higher **basic purpose standards** for everyone.

Critical to Economies... Specialized Education

In real world practice, **specializing** in any **productive** endeavor, usually requires **specialized** and even *advanced* **education**, *even before we are allowed to begin working as a novice* or take any entry level **employment** in our chosen field.

The effect of such a **specialized**, advanced **education** is usually a **specialty**, or *specialist*, that will earn a substantially higher **income** than without it. With such **education** and **training** we expect to **produce** enough **gain** to pay for kids **educations**, our own retirements, still have enough to also consistently improve our current **basic purpose** conditions.

Generally, that level of *expertise* is not easy or inexpensive to accomplish. It takes a dedicated, **organized**, and focused effort that takes much longer to accomplish.

THE PRINCIPLES of EMPLOYMENT

"Will capitalist economies operate at full employment in the absence of routine intervention? Certainly not. Are deviations from full employment a social problem? Obviously."
Author: Janet Yellen – Economist; Federal Reserve Chairman 2014–2018; Vice Chairman 2010 to 2014

Primary Axiom Four:

In order to be more *efficient, productive,* and most especially *consistent,*
in producing for 'basic purpose' needs and wants,
we humans create *patterns* and *systems* of doing things.

Thus, concepts and methods of ORGANIZATION begin,
and therefore also, SPECIALIZATION, EMPLOYMENT, and CURRENCY.

About Employment:

Productivity Class Economic Theory Statement

When one producer employs the resource of another producer for an agreed upon value in return, it is a 'trade agreement' between the two – primarily a symbiotic trade of skills, knowledge, and service for currency.

Trading for [and thereby 'employing'] the specialized services and productivity of others is one of the fundamentals that allows organization to expand beyond a single individual or partnership group into an organized productive system that can continue to expand to *any* size and indefinitely [*specialization* and *currency* are the others]. Employment therefore broadens into an *organizational* activity as well as a *trade* activity.

The activity, by organizing producers, of employing others allows working [employed] producers to focus on furthering their expertise in their specializations – which also furthers the value of their specialized *skills, knowledge,* and *services* to the organizations that need them.

[1 Organizing Producers – producers operating *organizations* – businesses]
[2 Working Producers – the *employed* work force – management, specialists, workers]

Paying the employed in currency unencumbers employers from the need to provide basic purpose needs and wants in order to maintain permanent, highly skilled, highly specialized employees. In equal benefit, being paid in currency gives the employed expanded basic purpose choices in the

economic environment.

Therefore, specialization and currency allows both parties *improved, far reaching benefits*, increased gain from the transaction, and accelerates and expands the effectiveness of *all* organizational activities, as well as organization itself in general.

About Employment:
an
Overview

In many circles it is believed that *conflict* and *war* is mankind's defining factor. That is a shortsighted, superficial, and most assuredly a very wrong view of humanity. Mankind's defining factor is '*cooperative and creative **productivity***'.

> *Cooperative and creative **productivity*** are the cornerstones upon which all civilization and human flourishing are built.

Employing The Capacities and Capabilities of Others

The *activity* of **organizing** begins when one person, or group of persons, begins creating *patterns* and *systems* of doing something, which in the case of economics is **producing** for **basic purpose** needs and wants. However, in order to create a fully functioning, physical **organization** that can actually *do* the **organizational** activities, even in lesser economically developed societies, **specialization, employment,** and **currency** *all* tend to be required.

Like economics itself, an **organization** is a 'clockwork' of **specialized** activities all functioning in concert to achieve a single desired result. If something in the clockwork doesn't operate properly or fully, it effects the results of the entire operation. **Employing** the right **working producers, specialized** in the skills necessary to perform all of the required tasks of an **organized** activity, and disciplined in the **work ethic** necessary to accomplish them, is *required* for successful achievement of any **organization's** purposes.

Paying for Employment in Currency Expands Organized Productivity Exponentially and Without Limit

Before a **currency** develops in an economy, while it is still **trading products** and **services** for **products** and **services**, non-permanent workers are usually paid in goods **produced** by the **employer**. Permanent **workers** or *apprentices* often stay with the **employing** family as an extended family member, or in some trades, as a **tradesmen's** apprentice. In either case, **specialized tradesman** or extended family, they also work as 'general helpers' in the 'economic **household**' and have their **basic purpose** *needs* provided for as extended family members [not so much '*wants*'].

Currency allows **employment** to eventually evolve past live-in arrangements, and for the **employer** to hire highly skilled **specialists** in their fields. In order for the '**trade agreement**' of **employment** to operate most *efficiently*, and for **organizations** to expand without limit, *employees must be remunerated in currency*.

Payment in **currency**, and **training** in a *needed* and *wanted* [in **demand**] field of expertise, provides the **working producer** the freedom and expanded choices necessary for *both* **employment** with **organizations** [advancing from **employer** to **employer** in **gainful** career advancement] and in *self*-**employment**.

The *efficiency* of paying **employees** in **currency** rather than **products** or **services**, not only streamlines an **organization's** payment for **employment** services, it also lifts all limitation on the *volume of* **working producers** *employed*. With the advent of **currency** in an economy, an **organization** can grow in size without limits.

Employment and *Indefinite Expansion* of Productive Organizations:

These four **elemental activities** – organization, employment, specialization, and **currency** [i.e. 'patterning' **productive** tasks into **organ-ized** 'systems', **employing** a **specialized** workforce to accomplish all tasks in coordination with one another, and paying them in **currency**] – work naturally together to create the *most efficient operating basis for* **productivity** and, therefore, the highest **volume** of **gain** in any type of **organized** activity. **Employment** of **specialized producers** further allows an **organization** to expand *indefinitely* by providing the **productive** and **administrative** capacities necessary to operate effectively at *any size*.

About Employment:

Characteristics and General Factors

Using 'Humans' as 'Resources'

Organized productivity requires a recognition of the *functional* aspect of **human resources** as '**working** [or *functioning*] **capital**' – meaning *an organizational need for '***productive*** *capacities of the type or in a form only humans can do*'. Usually the most *expensive* of **resources**.

When thinking in terms of '**monetary** economics' alone, from an **accounting** point of view, **human resources** appear the same as **capital resources**. It is just another **resource**, just another **expense**. That viewpoint is actually *half* true, as indicated in the term itself **'human *resource*'**.

There is, however, the other half of the nature of **'*human* resources'**. This half requires the recognition that the 'hiring of a *human* as a **resource**' is not the same as acquiring a **capital resource**. **Employment** is a '*trade agreement*' between *human beings* in which both parties are in pursuit of the **basic purpose** of economics. Therefore, the very nature of **ethics** enters into the relationship – both *economic* and basic *human* **ethics**, which is based on fair treatment and equitable **symbiotic exchange**.

The human aspect is also why laws exist requiring **employers** to live up to minimum wage, safety, and social and personal treatment standards of **employees**, usually based on what is considered 'decent' for human needs and conditions and culture at the time.

There is a *functional* aspect of using a human as a **resource**; and there is a *human* aspect of using a human as a **resource**. *And the two cannot be **ethically** separated.*

Capital Resources vs. Human Resources?
Technology, Education, and Employment vs. Unemployment

Advances in **productive technologies** in any existing field usually increases *mechanical* **productivity** [*capital* **resource productivity**], which in the immediate reduces the need for ***human*** **resources** in that field in the short term. So technology, then, creates what appears to be a *competition* between the two types of **productivity**. And people react to that accordingly.

There is, however, no *actual* competition. The **organization** or **organization's administrators** are doing exactly what they should do – *increasing* **productive volume** and **value**, while *decreasing* **expense**. In the short term, however, the **employed** are now the ***un*employed**.

The **unemployment**, however, is usually only temporary. New **employment** also develops as other fields of endeavor also advance. The process is called '**creative destruction**'.

But **specializations** and certain types of jobs can *permanently* pass away with each **capital resource** advancement. And therein lies the problem. There is, however, a solution… ***mass availability*** of technological advances.

'Availability to the Masses' of Technological Advances

The real economically expansive effect comes later when those technologies discussed above are further developed and advanced to the point of *availability to the masses*, which creates far more opportunities for **specialized working**

producers to contribute to a larger number of **organizations, self-employ,** and sometimes **organize** and expand into **employers** themselves.

In order for this to happen, however, the new **productive technologies** have to *advance enough to become available* to **specialized working producers** – common middle class and working class individuals. All advancing technologies *must* reach *'mass available utility'*. The longer it takes, the longer the economic harm of **unemployment**. **Governments** should **incentivize** this.

About Employment:

Principles and Concepts Important to Success

Government Incentives to Encourage Technologically Advanced Capital Resources to Advance to Mass Use

When a *technological advance* of a **capital resource** is designed and created to improve *productivity*, *efficiency*, and *consistency* for **organizations**, that is likely to reduce **employment** of **working producers**, **governments** must offer *tax incentives* and promote *production contracts* to **capital resource** *designers* and *manufacturers* to develop **specialized working producer** versions that effectively mitigate the **unemployment** that will come along with the advancement. [More in **Incentivizing** and **Governing** in Chapter Three.]

Work Ethic and Employment Ethic

In **productivity class** economics we categorize an 'organization's and personnel's productive ethics' under 'Work Ethic' and 'Employment Ethic'.

General **'work ethic'** and a **business's 'employment ethic'** are each a set of simple behavioral disciplines that maintain the proper standards of both *life* and *economic* **ethics** in **employee** and **employer** *relationship* and *conditions*.

'Work ethic' up until recently had been a simple code of *'be punctual'*, *'work hard and well'*, *'be worthy of your pay'*, *'work well with others'*, and *'serve the best interests of the company'* or **business**. **Employment ethic** was to reciprocate with favored status toward those whose **work ethic** was of the highest standards and who performed admirably in their **productivity**.

Nowadays things have gotten a little more developed. As before, since this is a beta version of this text, and we are limited in space, we have placed a codified, *suggested* common sense set of principles and policies, for **work ethic** and **employment ethic** at **productivityclass.*info*.**

The Employer/Employee 'Trade Agreement': Considerations of Primary Importance

These can be considered *principles of primary importance* regarding any agreement between an **employer** and **employee:** [The most basic requirements each should have toward the other.]

- **Symbiotic Exchange**
  [*Cooperative*, agreed upon *'mutual contribution'* each to the other's **basic purpose** goals and purposes – the **employee produces** in **volume** and in **value** at a rate commensurate with reasonable **productivity** demands of the **employer;** the **employer** pays the **employee** (in **currency** and other 'benefits') commensurate with delivered **productivity.**]

- **Competence**
  [Each party must fully understand, and be **competent** in, the requirements for success in the **organization's** endeavors, maintaining the highest level of successful **ethical operating** and **productive** effectiveness – a competent and successful **employee** contributing to a competent and successful **organization.**]

- **Relationships**
  [An **employee** must be **competent** in 'teamwork **productivity'** and the **employer** must provide a *true team* to be a part of and to work within (much easier said than done); both must share in the understanding of, and cooperation in, the **productivity** and social roles of oneself and others (including **administrative management**), and the **organization's** culture as a whole.]

- **Contributiveness**
  [An **employee** must be willing to contribute to the **organization's** *purposes* and *stated mission* in addition to **symbiotic exchange** – again, a successful **employee** contributing to a successful **organization.** The **organization,** however, must have a purpose and mission conducive to motivate contributive drive in employees – and it must *live up* to that purpose and mission. Such contributive effect from **employees** must be rewarded with extra consideration toward a **working producer's** pursuits for additional responsibility, **productivity,** higher positions, and therefore, **pay.**]

Each of these could be a 'how-to' text unto itself. But usually, just understanding what they are is all that is necessary for **administrator** and **working producers** to operate successfully as a single group unit toward a common purpose.

THE PRINCIPLES of CURRENCY

**The value of a currency is, ultimately, what someone will give you for it –
whether in food, fuel, assets, or labor.** Author: James Surowiecki: 'The New Yorker'
magazine.

Fourth Primary Axiom:

In order to be more *efficient, productive*, and most especially *consistent*,
in producing for 'basic purpose' needs and wants,
we humans create *patterns* and *systems* of doing things.

Thus, concepts and methods of ORGANIZATION begin,
and therefore also, SPECIALIZATION, EMPLOYMENT, and CURRENCY.

About Currency:

Productivity Class Economic Theory Statement

The cumbersome, inconvenient and, most importantly, *economically limiting*
practice of trading products and services for other products or services
generates the need for an 'intermediate medium of exchange' – a '*substitute
item assigned an agreed upon tradable value*' equivalent to an *equal value*
of *actual* productivity, products, or services.

The *purpose* of an 'intermediate medium of exchange' [standardized
currency] is to...
   a)   facilitate trade by making it easier and more efficient; and to
   b)   establish the benefits of *acquiring, accumulating*, or *manipulating*
        earned but unspent 'trade value'.

The primary function of currency is to act as an item of 'standard trade
value' that is *universally accepted* in trade for actual productivity, products,
or services – making trade *easier* and more *fluid, efficient*, and *expandable* –
and can be held in retention until ready to trade for anything else.

The secondary, but just as important, function of currency is to be utilized
for the *acquiring, accumulating*, and *manipulating* of earned but unspent
'trade value', and therefore, to...
   o   allow 'saving' for higher expense products and services,
   o   provide for a privately owned 'currency form of wealth',
   o   and promote economic expansion through 'investment' in further
        productivity.

About Currency:
an
Overview

Monetary currency [minted or otherwise fabricated **money**] is: any item adapted for use as a *'medium of reserved trade value'* that *represents*, is *equivalent to*, and is *tradable for* **productivity, products, or services**.

Monetary currency possesses the *'value of one's productivity, products, or services in an alternate or substitute form'* until one is ready to utilize it for **trade**. So the actual *flow* in a **trade** is still of 'products and services' for 'products and services', it is simply that the latter 'products or services' are 'replaced' with ' a *substitute – an intermediate* **tradable** item *assigned an equal tradable value* to serve 'in the stead' for the* **products** or **services**' – **money**.

The creation of a **standardized currency** is an **organizational** action *supported* and *controlled* by an *authority of public confidence* that *guarantees* the **currency** through any acceptable means in order to ensure it is accepted *universally* and functions effectively as a *medium of exchange*.

Standardized currency allows **trade** to become more *developed* and *sophisticated*:

Fluidity of Use:
  o   The problem of the gross limitations of **trading products** and **services** for other **products** and **services** is resolved with a 'standardized currency'. The **organized producer** can now **trade** his **products** to *anyone* who wants them. **Working producers** obtain the **trade value** of their **productivity** in a much more *efficient* and *fluid* form. For their **products** and **services** they take a *'standard, universally accepted* **currency**' that they can **trade** for *anything else*, with *anyone else, anywhere else* – because it is *universally accepted* – and there is better *facilitation of* and more *efficient* **trade**.

  o   Also, a **standardized currency** eliminates *uneven* **trades**. **Trading products** and **services** for other **products** and **services** generates *uneven* **trades** where the **products** or **services** one has to **trade** *are not equal in* **value** to the **products** or **services** to be **traded** for.

  o   Finally, an agreed upon form of **standardized monetary currency** allows the for *accumulation of wealth* in the form of **currency value**. Wealth no longer depends upon land, personal property, agricultural produce, or livestock holdings. Wealth can now be created through the *accumulation* of **currency** [**money**] because it holds **trade value**,

Investment:
  The accumulation of wealth in the form of currency allows for the use of currency to *capitalize* **more productivity.**
  o   **Investment** is using *'earned, unspent* **currency**' to *capitalize*

additional **productivity**, and thereby earn additional *gain*. The primary purpose is to utilize one's earned, unspent **currency** to *a)* cause it to *grow* more rapidly than the natural increase of **prices** can *reduce* its **trade value**; *b)* increase the **value** of one's wealth by the **value** of one's **investments**; and *c)* promote the **capitalization** of **productivity** in the economic community one lives in.

This opens up everything. The common man can now **produce** personal *wealth* in the form of the **currency value** of his or her *now possible* **investments**. With this *newly generated dynamic* of '*monetary capitalization of productivity*', mankind sends its capacity to **produce** into high gear through **investment**.

About Currency:

Characteristics and General Factors

What Can Be Used as a Currency

All **tradable** things carry a '**currency value**' because they have **value** in **trade** and can *flow* from one person to another.

But such '**tradables**' cannot be used as a '**standardized currency**' because when each **tradable product** gets into the hands of the person who wants it, they will keep it and **utilize** it. It therefore stops *flowing* from person to person, **trade** to **trade**. A **currency** has to be an item that *flows continuously* in order to work – as in a *current – [current-cy]*. Anything that will eventually be '*held on to*' for *utility* purposes, even if only ornamental, will not work as a **currency**.

The best **currency** items are *a)* in a primitive economy, moderately rare or difficult to obtain products of nature, *b)* in a more advanced economy, items that can be manufactured only under a supervising authority.

'The Currency Must Flow'

In a **currency** based economic **market**:
*one party trades their **productivity**, **products**, or **services***
*while the other party trades their **monetary currency**.*
Currency flows in one direction,
productivity, products, or services flow in the *opposite* direction – *always*.
[Productivity→ ←Currency]

This is most vital to grasp when
managing or governing an entire economic system.

As long as the **currency** flows, the '*continuous cycle of production and consumption*' continues – and serves the **basic purpose** needs and wants of the populace. If the **currency** stops *flowing* [or there is not enough of it], the populace must return to **barter** – an impossibility for a technologically advanced society of **specialized productivity** to do. *The* **currency** *must flow – and in the proper amounts.*

Flowing **money investments** *from the top to the bottom and back again* is how an economic system creates the flow of **productivity, products,** or **services** throughout the society and stays healthy for *everyone*. When it does, **trade** and **productivity** expands and continues to improve – and **basic purpose** standards continue to improve along with it.

When an economic system is 'rigged' to incentivize **investment** that does not create **productivity** [e.g. investing in **money** *manipulation*, buying and selling **stocks** and **bonds**, etc.], then **currency invested** does not *circulate sufficiently* back to *the* **working producer** *base of the economic society*. When **money** *does not flow* [circulate] *back to the bottom in* **investment** that part of the society cannot **produce** or **consume** and degrades into *impoverishment and suffering*.

Currency Requires Confidence

The basic requirement for **currency** to work is '**confidence**' – *the trust that the* **currency** *offered will be universally accepted in the* **trade** *system in which the recipient is going to use it*. It is that **confidence** that allows for the agreement of universal acceptance. If there is no public confidence in the currency, and no one will take it in **trade** for **products** and **services**, the **currency** goes defunct. If there is *confidence* in the **currency**, it is *universally accepted* and stable.

The creation of a **standardized currency** is an **organizational** action taken by *a supporting authority* that *guarantees* the **currency** through any acceptable means. Usually that guarantee, in the beginning, is supported by the governing authority by promising to redeem the **currency** 'on demand' with something of tangible, stable, and universal **value** [gold, silver, etc.]. Confidence that the **government** will keep such a promise, *establishes confidence in the* **currency**.

As economies develop, however, such a promise gets unwieldy and laws establishing the **currency** as '*legal tender* in **trade**' and backing it up with 'stable economic **productivity**' tends to replace guarantees of 'redemption' for some other tangible thing.

Monetary Currency Is... *Retained, Unspent 'Value Produced'*

'**All things economic begin with produce.**' **Trade** is the exchange of **productivity** for **productivity** – 'something **produced**' for 'something **produced**'. **Currency** represents the '**value of productivity**' – the '**value** of something **produced**'. Therefore, spending '**currency**' for a **product** or **service** is expending the 'value of one's productivity' – the 'value of what one has produced' – to obtain the products or services of others.

Therefore further, and in corollary, in order to acquire the currency necessary to achieve basic purpose pursuits, *everyone must produce* – and will succeed in basic purpose pursuits in proportion to the *trade value of their productivity*.

Monetary Currency Is A Capital Resource

Monetary currency is actually best thought of as a resource'– a *financial resource* – which is a type of capital resource – utilized by consumer and producer alike.

Capital resources – also called capital assets or *developed* resources – are the man made *tools, mechanisms,* or *fabrications* used to produce products with, facilitate production, or produce any end result. Money currency is a *fabrication* that facilitates trade and generates investment. Understand money in this way, and you are more likely to be successful in wielding it.

Setting The Volume and Value of The Currency

The volume of currency – the amount of currency in circulation in an economic community – must be enough to allow production, trade, consumption, and *growth* to occur, *plus enough extra so that people will be willing to 'spend' and not 'hold on to' too much in reserve.* Holding on to money *inhibits* its *free flow.* Enough extra allows people to feel free to use it, which *promotes* its *free flow,* which *circulates* the money and therefore advances gainful productivity. The amount of currency in circulation must then continue to increase in proper proportion with productive economic activity.

However, too much volume of currency in relation to economic activity creates 'inflation', a condition in which there is so much extra currency in circulation that prices, but not always wages, rise to equal the amount of currency in circulation – they become 'inflated' – *without the appropriate productivity,* economic growth, or gain for the society [sometimes causing economic activity to *recede* – a *recession*]. Too *little* volume means there is *too little circulating.*

So the volume of currency in an economic community must be properly balanced: "We issue it in *proper proportion* to the demands of trade and industry to make the products pass easily from the producers to the consumers." [Benjamin Franklin on 'colonial script', the colony's first currency.]

The value of currency is set by determining the *denominations* necessary for trade to *flow freely,* while maintaining *convenience of handling,* and dividing the volume up by those denominations. Controlling the stability and value of a

currency can get quite complicated and responsibility for it falls to the **government** and **central banks**.

About Currency:

Principles and Concepts Important to Success
Individuals or Small Business

True Standards vs. False Standards

By this time, the **value** of **productivity** is measured in *monetary currency*. When a *thing* or a *person*, is measured in this way, it is a **false standard**! Beware of measuring **gain** entirely in **monetary** or *material* terms. There is *economic* **gain** – i.e. *'material'* **gain** – and there is *true* **gain** – i.e. *'quality of life'* **gain**. And while *'material'* **gain** contributes to the success of *'quality of life'* **gain**, they are substantially different. A *'worthwhile quality of survival, successful pursuit of the dynamics of living,* and *improved living conditions'* are *'quality of life'* measures. Material success only *contributes* to that – and then only if wielded to *cause* that.

Household or Small Business *Money Management* and *Utility*:

The basic principles of **money management** for **households** and **small businesses** are always the same: **Produce** high – **Consume** low – Create **gain** – **Invest gain** for more **gain**.

There are entire texts on how to handle *personal* and **small business** finances: setting goals; spending; credit and debt; renting vs. purchasing [**household** *and* **business** equipment]; *needs* vs. *wants*; **investing**; **taxes**; personal **accounting** and banking; state and federal government benefits; etc.

Most of what you need to learn about **money management** is beyond a primer text like this. Although the *fundamental principles and activities* are the same for everyone, the *specific actions* one takes vary according to *circumstance, conditions,* **education,** **household,** **small business,** and *specialized productivity*. That's a lot of variances.

In the case of the ultra-small, one or two persons **business**, the *basics* are the same as above. However, only one step up, to the manufacturing, storefront, five or more person business level, things begin to require an ever broader understanding of **business** finance – **accounting** and financial structuring, accepted methods of record keeping and **money** handling, **cost** controls and **pricing**, planning and **investment**, research and development, etc. You guys have got a lot of further study to do.

Investment of Gain:

A Note About Compound Interest:

Compound interest is adding the interest one has earned on an investment back into the principle amount invested, so that one collects the next round of interest on the now increased principle amount.

Let's say we put $1000 **principle amount invested** in an **investment account** that pays 10% interest per year. That means we will earn $100 on our investment by the end of one year. Let's say we never take the $100 in **profit**, we just leave it in the **investment account** to become a part of the **principle amount invested**. Now we are collecting 10% interest on $1100. That's now $110 in interest. Now let's just do that year in and year out from 20 years old to 65 years old, collecting 10% per year compounding on each previous year. That's $72, 890 after 45 years with your investment of only $1000.

Now add $2500 more *every* year – that's putting up $136,500 by age 65 compounding to over $2,000,000 for retirement. Does **investing** seem so far-fetched now?

However, there are many different ways of **investing**: **education** and **training** in a **skill** or **trade**; buying and selling **products**; **producing** your own *unique* artisan **product**; learning how to **innovate** existing **products**, obtain simple Provisional Patents on your ideas, and then sell the ideas to manufacturers; learn how to evaluate companies and **invest** in growth probability; etc.

All these, and many more, are ways to take any amount of **gain**, large or small, and work it into ever increasing and larger **gains** – this is **investing**.

[There are a great deal of books on how to do any of these. *Read more than a few* and *get good at what you intend to do , before* you **invest**.]

THE PRINCIPLES of SYMBIOTIC EXCHANGE
[Including **ALTRUISTIC** Support Systems and **INVERSION**]

PRODUCTIVITY CLASS DEFINITIONS you will need to fully understand this section. These are all *'For our purposes'* definitions:

ECONOMIC SYMBIOSIS: Production and trade activities mutually beneficial to the basic purpose pursuits of trade participants, all other effected parties, environment, and ecological life.

ALTRUISM: The innate human desire to *'contribute to the well-being of others'* while *'serving the greater good'* – actively employed *'as one's guiding principle'* in living life.

INVERT: To reverse or alter the aspect, direction of flow, or activity causing it to produce the opposite or reverse effect.

INVERSION: Perversion or corruption of the innate human desire to 'contribute to' others in order to earn 'reciprocal gain', into an inverted human intent to gain by *'drawing away from'* , *'taking from'* or *'depriving'* others – *regardless of any adverse effects* upon others or living conditions.

Fifth Primary Axiom:

Humans are social, cooperative beings and therefore
survive and thrive only in **SYMBIOTIC** patterns and systems,
and suffer and decline in **INVERTED** or *primarily* **ALTRUISTIC**
patterns and systems.

However,
properly principled and applied **ALTRUISTIC** *remedial* and *support* activities
strengthen **SYMBIOTIC** systems and make them more stable and resilient.

About Symbiotic Exchange and Altruistic Principles:

Productivity Class Economic Theory Statement

The primary basis for cooperative economic structure is 'symbiotic exchange'. Symbiotic exchange is: *an agreed upon exchange of mutual benefit to the basic purpose pursuits of each participant* in a transaction.

What constitutes a *'benefit'*, and *'fair exchange'* for it, is most often determined by the economic culture and/or each participant for themselves.

However, equally required, in order to fully meet the standards of symbiotic exchange principles, *all effects beyond* those limited to transactions between trading parties must also be considered: all direct and indirect effects of *production, products, services* and *application of elemental activities* – prior to and following any exchange – must additionally cause *no significant harm* – *short or long term* – *to individuals, groups, populaces, or ecological conditions*. Economic activities cannot commit harm to people's lives or ecological conditions and still by definition qualify as symbiotic.

Any aspect of populaces, life, or environmental conditions that contributes to any aspect of economic productivity must receive '*mutual benefit without harm*' – must receive '*symbiotic mutual benefit*' in exchange.

In order to define and set standards for what constitutes '*exchange of mutual benefit*', and '*no significant harm*' to individuals, groups, populaces, environmental conditions, or life forms', *basic purpose benefit* and *long term survival concepts* must be the required standard.

Symbiotic principles of exchange and effect, therefore, becomes the elemental activity upon which basic purpose endeavors are carried out and the primary mechanism with which economic ethics is achieved. 'Properly alloyed altruism' being the remedial and supporting '*mechanism*' with which economic ethics is made complete.

A *primarily* ALTRUISTIC economic system tends to over burden itself over time and eventually must revert back to a SYMBIOTIC system *alloyed* with ALTRUISTIC *remedial* and *support* activities to be stably successful.

SYMBIOTIC principles properly alloyed with ALTRUISTIC *remedial* and *support* structure – when *specifically designed to provide routes to successful participation in SYMBIOTIC EXCHANGE for the entire populace** – completes the '*basis*' and '*structural principles*' for economic ETHICS. [*Altruistic support *must* also include that part of every populace truly unable to participate.]

About Symbiotic Exchange and Altruistic Principles:
an
Overview

Note the two equally important requirements in a **symbiotic trade**:
- o '*exchange of agreed upon equivalent value*' between participants in a trade, and
- o '*contributes to all* participants **basic purpose** needs and wants', both decided by the economic culture and the participants themselves.

However, there are two more requirements to *fully* qualify as economically **symbiotic**:

o   Humans are by nature social, cooperative beings and therefore survive and thrive in social, cooperative cultures and systems. Therefore, **symbiosis**, for humans, applies to *the whole of a human society*, not just participants in a **trade**.

o   Further, economic activities cannot commit harm to *other* individuals, groups, populaces, or the *ecological conditions* they live in, and by definition still qualify as **symbiotic** behavior. *Humans and all other living things flourish only in very specific environmental conditions, and suffer and decline if they are only mildly altered.*

Therefore, **symbiosis** requires that *creatures and ecosystems must gain survival from the provision of their resources, not suffer or decline from it.*

Finally, each participant in a transaction trusts that every other participant knows whether or not their **basic purpose** pursuits are being benefited in a **trade**. However, basic human **ethics** still rules out deceptive practices, knowing unfairness, and shoddy **products, services,** or **resources**.

Therefore, *cultural standards must be set* for what constitutes *'agreed upon equivalent value'*, *'no harm to others'*, and *'no significant environmental harm'*, along with rules *that must be enforced by a governing authority*. The basis of such standards must be **'basic purpose** benefit or opportunity' and 'long term survival concepts' [per economic **ethics**] for *all* others, populaces, environments, or life forms effected by **productive** and **trade** activities. There is no room for 'parasitic behavior' in human material **gain** – in economic **ethics**.

The Concept of Symbiosis

Activities of '*Mutual Benefit*' Determine Symbiotic Relationships

Originally **'symbiosis'** came from ancient Greek and simply meant **'living together'** [syn - 'together' + bios - 'life' / syn-bios = 'life together' or 'living together']. In 1876 botanist A.B. Frank made it a biological term meaning, **'union for life of two different organisms based on mutual benefit'** . *'Mutual benefit'* becoming the new key defining factor for **symbiotic** relationships.

We have therefore created a **productivity class** definition for economic **symbiosis**. And we base our definition on innate natural principles of '*trade*', '*mutual benefit*', and '*human social dynamics*':

ECONOMIC SYMBIOSIS – *production* and *trade* activities mutually beneficial to the basic purpose pursuits of trade participants, and at minimum unharmful to all other effected parties, populaces, species, environmental, and ecological conditions ['*beneficial* creative destruction' excluded].
Symbiotic standards for humans, as socially contributive beings, are served when one *contributes to others in exchange for their own needs or wants in*

return. The more contributors, and the more varied the contributions, the better off the community or society. Economically, this contribution manifests in the form of '*needed or wanted* **products** *or* **services**'.

If *harm*, other than 'beneficial creative destruction', to participants, non-participants, or environmental conditions occurs, **symbiotic**, and therefore **ethical**, standards are violated.

Balancing Inversion with Altruism *Doesn't Work*

> Inverted economic activity, *left to commit its offense*, but 'balanced'
> with altruistic activities that *handle the inversion's ill effects*,
> does not lead to a good economic outcome.
> Altruism, applied as a 'balance' to inversion, *subsidizes* the inversion.

Altruism is Necessary

Altruism *is necessary*, but it must be alloyed to **symbiotism** much the same as carbon is alloyed to iron to make steel. Iron remains the main ingredient. Carbon strengthens the iron, and the combination becomes much tougher, harder, and longer lasting – steel. **Altruism** is the secondary 'carbon-like' alloy in strengthening and improving **symbiotic exchange** – the 'iron' of economic structure. But, as in the making of steel, *only when properly done , of the right type, and in the right amounts. Too much, badly structured,* or *poorly conceived* **altruism** makes for *weaker, poorer* economic structures and conditions.

INVERSION *For our purposes... short version*: **Perversion or corruption of the** *innate* **human intent to 'contribute to' others into an** *inverted* **human intent to** '*draw away*' , '*take from*' **or** '*deprive*' **others for self-serving gain.**

In most advanced societies today, **symbiotic** exchange is the primary basis for economic structure. Most toxic economic situations come from **inverted** economic policies, practices, and behaviors. The adverse *human* effects of **inverted** economic activities can be mitigated by **altruistic** activities, but the *economic* effects are only exacerbated by attempts to '*balance*' them with the application of **altruistic** social programs.

Between the oppressive business and economic practices, and the over-burdening taxes necessary to balance their ill effects with social programs, the two, *allowed to get out of control*, can overwhelm an entire economic system. Each perpetuates the growth of the other until economic stall or collapse is inevitable.

Altruistic welfare, social, and 'safety net' programs are necessary, *but must not be a 'balance'* to continued **inverted** economic policies, practices, and behaviors. Leaving the adverse **inverted** activities in place, and taxing the populace to create **altruistic** programs to counter the adverse *effects*, simply *subsidizes* the **inverted** activity.

The solution is **ethical** frameworks that *resolve the inverted policies, practices, or behaviors* – and an **altruistic** support structure that includes, promotes, and incentivizes the *successful* **productive** *participation of every citizen* in the **symbiotic exchange** system. [See **Derivative Operating Dynamics – Governance**]

There Is No 'Pie'

There are those that believe that there is an economic 'pie' that is just so big and no bigger, and that for one person to **gain**, someone else has to *lose*. All things economic, however, are actually based on **productivity** – continuous and diverse **production–trade–consumption**. There is no *'pie'*. There is only **productivity administrated** to *'basic purpose success'* for all.

People who believe in the win-lose 'pie theory' tend to operate **inversely**. They believe that the only way to create economic **gain** for themselves is to *'take from'*, *'draw away from'* or *'deprive'* someone else. [All economic criminal acts are themselves acts of **inverted** economic intent.]

The Adverse Effects of Inversion

The adverse effects of **inverted** economic behaviors and practices need not be restricted to economic effects alone. The adverse effects of non-performing or adversely performing **products** and **services** that actively cause harm, hardship, or even destroy lives or the quality of lives of those effected can be far reaching. A list of examples of such brutal, adverse effects of **inverted** economic behaviors in today's society could actually be endless.

[**Note:** There are, of course, **inverted** economic conditions caused by poor economic **governance** or **administration**. This is not true **inversion**. They are **inverted** *conditions* derived of *incompetence.*]

Government and Economics
[More in Chapter Three, **Derivative Operating Dynamics: 'Governance'**.]

The purpose of government is to *unite the populace under a single set of agreed upon successful socio-political principles,* and to pattern and systematize that unity into an *efficient, productive,* and *consistently successful* way of life.

And further, to manage and administrate the required activities necessary for collective *survival* and *success* of the whole populace that makes up the community or society [infrastructure, defense, education, lawmaking, etc.].

These responsibilities mandate that government 'serve' the public, and that service be for the greater good of the whole and all aggregate segments thereof.

Under that mandate, wherever human *irresponsibility* creates irreconcilable adverse conditions in a society, that area of activity *must be governed*.

Inversion [and incompetence] require the need for *enforceable* **ethical** frameworks to **govern** *all* economic activities and economic **ethical** standards. **Government**, however, also opens the door for the entry of *politically based decision making* in economics – rather than decision making based on *fundamental economic principles and ethics*. Through politics, **inversion** often enters into the decision making process and *corrupts* it for the purpose of *contorting* laws, regulations, and policies to suit **inverted** interests.

Symbiosis must be enforced by a *strong, well educated, ethical governing authority*. **Market** response to adverse effects of economic activities is almost always too weak to stop truly powerful economic forces. Further, misinforming and deceiving a **consuming** public is an easy to do and powerfully effective **inverted** economic tactic. Against any truly powerful economic force, people are most often easily kept weak, confused, out maneuvered, and ignorant. *Without a strong, well educated, ethical governing authority*, the **consuming** public and **working producers** are easily overwhelmed and kept in harm's way or impoverished by **inverted** economic forces.

All *oligarchies* and *plutocracies* are **inverted governing** and economic structures.

About Symbiotic Exchange and Altruistic Principles:

Characteristics and General Factors

Mutual Advantage and the Incentive to Trade

The underlying concept of **symbiotic exchange** is *'mutual advantage'* – and *mutual advantage* is the fundamental that underlies all further development of the subject. In fact, the very nature of **trade** *incentive* requires that one must supply something of **basic purpose** advantage to others in order to get them to **trade** something of **basic purpose** advantage in return. It is this fundamental principle that makes **symbiotic exchange** in **trade** an **elemental activity**.

Therefore, when we **educate**, we **educate** in **specializations** that contribute *benefit*; when we **produce**, we **produce products** and **services** that contribute *benefit*. This is the very basis of **trade** itself. We **trade** our labor [**specializations**], our **products**, and our **services** for exchange of something of *mutual benefit* and *advantage* to our own **basic purpose** pursuits.

The 'Fifth Primary Axiom Imperative' and Economic Ethics

'Humans are social, cooperative beings and therefore survive and thrive only in symbiotic patterns and systems, and suffer and decline in inverted or antagonistic patterns and systems.'

The survival and growth of societies can only occur in economic systems of **basic purpose** *mutual advantage*, **symbiotic exchange** systems. **Inverted** behaviors cause lives, populaces, and societies to suffer and decline. Therefore, **symbiotic exchange** systems become an *'imperative'* of the **ethical** aspect of the **second primary axiom** – the **ethics** of requiring *well-being* and *long term survival* of all people and ecosystems effected by an economic activity.

The **basic purpose** of economics is to provide for the *material requirements* necessary for *survival, pursuit of the dynamics of living*, and *improvement of living conditions*. Therefore, *'genuine opportunity for **basic purpose** success'* for all people, populaces, environments, and ecological systems effected by any economic activity is the basis for economic **ethics** and the primary purpose of economic **governance**.

Symbiotic exchange, then, becomes the only *application principle* upon which can be built an economic system of **ethical trade**, and **trade** *outcomes*.

Therefore, *providing for mutual **basic purpose** benefit in all **trade** activities* becomes the *operating basis* or *functioning structure* upon which economic **ethics** is actually *carried out*.

Enforcement of **symbiotic** application of *all* **elemental activities** is the single applicative *device* by which the application of economic **ethics**, moral codes, and **trade** regulations are put into real life practical application.

CHAPTER THREE

The
DERIVATIVE OPERATING DYNAMICS
of Economics

also known as
The
SUBORDINATE or SUPPORTING
OPERATING DYNAMICS
of Economics

INTRODUCTORY STATEMENT

Basic purpose *drives* call into action the **five primary** *capacities* humans employ to achieve all material *needs* and *wants*. As expressed in the **five primary axioms,** those capacities create the first level of material **operating dynamics** – the **twelve elemental** *activities* of economics.

> **All human material pursuits are based upon these
> base fundamental *drives*, *capacities*, and *activities*.
> Their *activity* is what is meant by the term '*economics*'.**

> *The activities of these 'primary operating dynamics' generate into existence
> the next set of economic dynamic phenomena and forces.*

However, no matter how high above the original founding principles a new economic dynamic develops, no matter how large, complex, or sophisticated an economic system becomes...

> **...all things economic are *based upon, subject to*, and *must subordinate to*
> serving the success of these base original *founding* principles:
> basic purpose, the five primary axioms, and
> the twelve elemental – and *primary* – activities of economics.**

In this chapter we will present those known principles *that are newly created* when the **twelve elemental activities** are put into active operation and economic activity actually begins.

THE PRINCIPLES of
DERIVATIVE OPERATING DYNAMICS

About Derivative Operating Dynamics:

Productivity Class Economic Theory Statement

When the 'primary operating dynamics' are in operation, their activity generates a whole *new* set of dynamic operating phenomena. These newly generated dynamic phenomena are employed in economics for '*measuring, calculating,* and *reasoning*' or for '*driving, manipulating,* and *managing*' the primary operating dynamics whether they are structured as economic institutions [business or household 'entities'] or as whole economies.

Because these newly generated *dynamics* are *derived* from of the *primary operating dynamics* in operation, and are utilized to more successfully *operate* them, we call them the '*derivative operating dynamics*'.

These 'derivative operating dynamics' are broken into two categories: 'operating phenomena' the *manifestations* of which provide for economic *measuring, calculating, and reasoning*; and 'operating controls' the *causative principles* of which provide for *driving, manipulating,* and *managing* economically.

Subordinate Operating Dynamics: 'Derivative operating dynamics', *when in productivity*, are called '*subordinate* operating dynamics' because their usage must be *subordinated* to serve the successful operations of the *primary operating dynamics* [*twelve elemental activities*].

About Derivative Operating Dynamics:
an
Overview

Derivative Operating Dynamics are Divided into Two Types:

Operating Phenomena:
- o   *'Observable and measurable economic effects or manifestations'* that are utilized to *measure, calculate,* and *reason* more successful strategies, tactics, and management of the **twelve elemental activities** as the **primary operating dynamics** of an economic system or entity.
  [**Micro-economic examples** would include: margins; supply and demand;

102

market equilibrium; absolute and comparative advantage; risk; etc.; **Macro-economic examples** would include: employment rates; GDP; balance of trade; stock market trading; etc.]

Operating Controls:

o *'Economic cause-and-effect principles, and their corresponding application principles'*, utilized as controls for *driving, manipulating,* and *managing* the successful operation of the **twelve elemental activities** as the **primary operating dynamics** of an economic system or entity.

[**Micro-economic examples** would include: credit; investment; marketing; insurance; etc.; **Macro-economic examples** would include: manipulation of taxes; ethics regulation; fiscal policy; printing of currency; currency valuations; credit and control of interest rates; etc.]

To the degree these newly generated dynamics do *not* abide by and serve the success of **basic purpose** and the **twelve primary operating dynamics**, economics will go awry and take any effected portion of an economy awry with them.

The Derivative Operating Dynamics Charted:

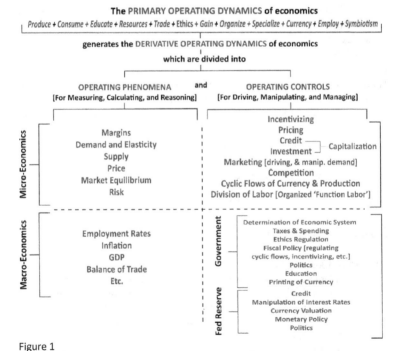

Figure 1

THE PRINCIPLES of
MICRO- and MACRO- ECONOMICS

About Micro- and Macro- Economics:

Productivity Class Economic Theory Statement

Every economic *participant* is both a producer and a consumer – a complete economic '*entity*' – but not necessarily a complete *basic purpose provider* unto themselves. Each 'producer-consumer entity' *must* interact in trade with other producer-consumer entities in order to acquire the full gamut of products and services required for basic purpose success.

As economic entities 'specialize' in producing and providing *continuously* '*needed but expended'* products and services, a *self-perpetuating system* of sustained productivity of *continuously needed but expended* products and services forms – with further additions as time goes on of more lasting '*durable'* products and services – and provides for *all basic purpose needs and wants for an entire economic community.*

Thus forms an overall economic *system*
made up of the interactive elemental activities of its *entity* participants.

Because the 'derivative operating dynamics' of the *entities* and those of the *system* are *different...*

The total aggregate of principles, activities, and generated phenomena
applicable to trading economic *entities within* the larger system
is called *micro*-economics –
'*micro-'* because the *'entities'* are the *smaller parts*
that *make up* the *larger organized whole;*

The total aggregate of principles, activities, and generated phenomena
applicable to the *complete operating system* is called *macro*-economics:
'*macro-'* because the system is the *larger organized whole*
made up of the smaller economic entities.

About Micro- and Macro- Economics:
an
Overview

In fulfilling **basic purpose** drives, we use up – **consume** – what we **produce**.

Continuous **production**, then, is required to fulfill continuously used up **consumptive** needs and wants. The 'cycle of **production** and **consumption**', then, first manifests itself on *constantly expended, continuously needed basic purpose needs and wants.*

As we begin to **produce** longer lasting, more durable **products** and **services**, these 'durable goods' are added to **trade** activities. Henceforth, we **produce** and **consume** a more and more broad spectrum of **products** and **services**.

In the accomplishment of all this, every economic participant is a complete **producing-consuming** economic '*entity*' – but not a complete *basic purpose* '*provider*' unto themselves. *Through* **trade**, each **producer-consumer** *must* interact with other **producer-consumer** '*entities*' in order to acquire the full gamut of **products** and **services** required for **basic purpose** success.

Since no individual can by themselves long fulfill basic purpose needs for even the most essential survival, the first level of *systemic* **activity is** *the productive and trade activity between economic* <u>*entities.*</u>

Further, there are newly generated phenomena – newly generated <u>*dynamics*</u> to <u>*operate*</u> with – that are <u>*derived*</u> from the **twelve elemental activities** in action between economic <u>*entities,*</u> and so are called the ***derivative* operating dynamics** of economics.

The total aggregate of *newly generated* ***dynamics*** that function <u>*between interacting economic entities*</u> are collectively called ***micro-economics.***

Micro- *because these economic 'entities' are the* <u>*smaller parts*</u> *which taken together form an emerging larger* <u>*self-sustaining system*</u> *of fulfilling* **consumptive** *needs and wants through* **productivity** *and* **trade.**

As the 'cycle of **production** and **consumption** and **trade**' starts to coalesce into *patterns* of *many* continuous 'cycles of **production** and **consumption**', planned **organization** of these patterns is applied. The result is the formation of a *complete, fully* **organized***, self-sustaining, system of 'cycles of* **production** *and consumption'* – *a* <u>*complete economic system.*</u>

The second level of true economic activity establishes itself as *the activity of the 'self-sustaining system' made up of the 'entities'.*

The activities of this system generates a *completely different set* of **derivative operating dynamics** for the <u>*reasoning* and *management of the overall system itself.*</u>

The total aggregate of *principles, activities,* and *generated phenomena applicable to this complete operating system* is called ***macro-economics.***

Macro- *because it is the* <u>*larger organized system whole*</u>

*made up of the smaller **producing-consuming** economic entities.*

Productivity class economics does not consider the concept of **micro-** or **macro-economics** applicable until *dividing up* **derivative operating dynamics** into their four categories [see Figure 1, page 102]. The **twelve primary operating dynamics** [elementary activities] are neither **micro-** or **macro-economic.** They are simply the *primary operative forces* of all economic activity.

Basic purpose, the five primary axioms, and
the **twelve elementary activities**
are the same no matter what aspect you look at them from.

They are the *base,* the *derivative source,* and the *operating purpose*
of all that come after them.

Productivity class economics is only concerned with *subordinating* **all**
derivative operating dynamics to *directly supporting* **or** *serving*
the primary operating dynamics
from whence they come and
for which they exist only to serve the success of.

The following will be the most common *micro*-economic and *micro*-economic **derivative operating dynamics** worthy of a decent primer on **productivity class** economics. Those shown here are essential to understanding the true **productive** usage of a **subordinate operating dynamic** for *measuring, calculating,* and *reasoning,* and *driving, manipulating,* and *managing* the success of the **twelve elemental activities** as *primary operating dynamics.*

THE PRINCIPLES of MARGINS

Percentage margins don't matter. What matters always is dollar margins: the actual dollar amount. Companies are valued not on their percentage margins, but on how many dollars they actually make...Author: Jeff Bezos, Founder, Amazon.com

FIELD *For our purposes...* noun **A space or range within which something is inserted, something occurs, or something is shown.**

MARGIN *For our purposes...* noun **The space or 'field' between the boundary of one part of a thing and a further boundary of its farthest edge [example below];**

PROFIT MARGIN *For our purposes...* noun **The *difference* between the '*cost of production, distribution, etc.*' and the '*highest price that can be obtained*' for a product or service; That *range* of 'total revenues projected' that is left over after projected costs are subtracted – within which there is actual potential for gain [profit] from any economic activity.**

Revenues possible from maximum obtainable price...

$100

$

$60	$40
...less total costs...	...leaves the 'Margin'
[invesrment; projected]	for 'Profit'

About Margins:

Productivity Class Economic Theory Statement

[The 'field' created by...] The difference between the *total cost* to produce and deliver a product or service and the *price* one can obtain for it creates the first economic 'margin': the 'profit margin' [optimal price – less total costs = equals profit]. A producer only produces a product or service so long as it provides an acceptable margin for profit, or future potential for it.

Consumers are also producers and therefore operate off of a 'household profit margin'.

All further *producer* margins are variations or derivative of the profit margin.

[The 'field' created by...] The difference between the *price* of a product or service [consumer's cost] and the consumer's *perceived basic purpose gain* ['utility' or 'benefit'] from purchasing that product or service creates the second economic 'margin': the 'consumer's margin of benefit' [or 'utility'].

A consumer expends currency or productive resources on a product or service only so long as the margin for benefit is perceived to be favorable or advantageous to basic purpose drives [i.e. personally gainful] and the expenditure falls within the household profit margin.

The consumer's perception of basic purpose gain is usually determined by *reasoning based upon their 'personal life dynamics'*, but can also be determined by *reasoning based upon the 'household profit margin'*.

Producers also consume when producing and therefore operate off of the 'consumer's margin of *utility*' *when consuming productive resources* – the determining factor in the producer's consumption [measured as 'costs'] is the profit margin – using *'business economic'* reasoning, not *'personal life dynamics'* reasoning.

All further *consumer* margins are variations or derivative of the 'consumer margin of benefit'.

About Margins:
an
Overview

Margins Are a Derivative Operating *Phenomena*

Use of the concept of **margins** is *vital* to all economic and **business** *measurement, calculation,* and *reasoning.* All measure of **profit** or **gain** is determined at the **margins**, both **consumptive** and **productive** [both for **consumer** and **producer**].

Understanding **margins** may be simple, but the ability to *measure, calculate,* and *reason* with **margins** in economics and **business** is equal to understanding the use of a *tape measure* in carpentry or a *sextant* in navigating – *you just can't do the job correctly without it.*

Margins Measure Projected [estimated] Gain and Potential Gain

Every **productive** and **consumptive** decision, **organizationally**, or even personally, is determined at the **'profit'** and **'consumer benefit'** margins – because *margins measure projected [estimated] **gain** or potential for **gain**.* All **margins** are *'calculated estimates'* of *'projected'* results.

'Margins' are a **derivative operating phenomenon** used to 'subordinate' **supply, demand**, and **pricing** to successful outcomes on the **twelve primary operating dynamics**.

Margins are what a **producer** uses to *measure, calculate,* and *reason* the **gainfulness** of economic ventures and activities. It is also how economists and **administrators** 'crunch the numbers' on *all* ventures of commercial activity. **Margins** are about *arithmetic.* **Margin** models or graphs are nothing more than *visual arithmetic: potential* or *projected* **revenues** minus the total **costs** equals the *visual* '**margin**' within which one can achieve **profit** [See Fig. 1 below].

About Margins:
the
Characteristics and General Factors

The Profit Margin

The first **margin** is the **profit margin**. The **profit margin** is the **producer's** primary **administrative** *measure* or *calculation* of potential for **gain**.

The **profit margin** is that *field* created by the difference between the costs of **producing** a **product** or **service** and the maximum obtainable **price** for it – anywhere within which **profits** can be realized even if the maximum **price** is not obtained or the total *volume* of **products produced** are not **sold** [**traded**]. That's why it's called a '**margin**' for **profit** and not a '*computation*' of **profit**.

After the **products** or **services** are sold, when the total **revenue** *actually collected* is known, and the total **costs** *actually expended* are subtracted from it, what is left equals *actual* **profit** or *loss*.

Margin graphs [or 'models'] simply show the arithmetic 'visually'. For example:
- o   **$100** [total expected **revenues** at optimum **price**]
- o   **-$60** [less planned **costs** of **production** and distribution]
- o   **=$40** [what remains is the *margin* in which *profit* can be made]
…visually looks like this ['*Figure 1.*' shows the actual '**margin**']:

Figure 1:

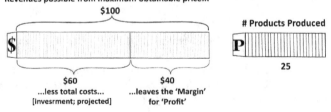

Revenues possible from maximum obtainable price…

$100

Products Produced

$

P

25

$60
…less total costs…
[invesrment; projected]

$40
…leaves the 'Margin'
for 'Profit'

Working the Calculations:
Dividing the total projected **revenues, costs,** or **profits**
by the total number of **products produced**
gives the projected **revenues, costs,** or **profits**
per unit [*each*] of **products produced.**

Per Unit [for each *item* **produced**]:
Revenues $4.00 each [**$100 in revenues ÷ 25 products produced**];
Costs $2.40 each [**$60 total costs ÷ 25 products produced**];
Profit Margin $1.60 each [**$40 total profit margin ÷ 25 products produced**]

Some Business Calculations:
1.   15 **products** must be sold to break even [**$60** total costs ÷ **$4** revenue per unit sold = **15** units]; all additional **sales** *beyond* 15 are **profit.**
2.   **Prices** can be dropped as low as **$2.40** before losses if all **25 products** can be **sold** [**$2.40** per unit **production** cost]; all higher **prices** are **profitable.**

So total **costs** and well estimated **sales** at *varied* **prices** must be worked out just to get this one vital economic factor worked out: the **profit margin** – that **margin** within which an economic 'entity' [**business, household, government,** or other institution] must work in order to ensure maximum **gain** [**profit**] and secure economic strength and stability.

Every Additional Production Run Creates A New Set of Margins:

When **producing,** working 'at the margins' means a more than working with **profit margins** alone:

Each additional expansion in productivity,
creates a new additional set of margins *added* to the previous set.

These are the new fields beyond the fields created by last productivity run. In other words, the difference between the current level of **costs, production,** and **revenues** and the *added* **costs, production,** and **revenues** generates a *new* set of **margins** for each. Therefore, they are called '**marginal revenues**', '**marginal costs**', and '**marginal product**', because they create *new **margins*** in the **costs, production,** and **revenues** amounts [See Figure 3 next page].

And they are *also* measured by their *totals* and by *units* just as the amounts in the original **profit margin** in 'Figure 1' above.

Important Productivity Class Note:
Economists currently measure additional '**marginal**' *inputs* [**resources**] and *outputs* [**products produced**] in terms of **costs** to **produce** *each* – one by one – calculating the *exact unit* where break-even point happens – when **producing** more *individual units* would produce *loss*, not **profit.**

However, in **productivity class** economics, we measure **marginals** by both totals *and* units. We must think in terms of *real life* **production**, not *theoretical accounting*. In real life **production**, **products** are generally **produced** in a 'production run' of a *bulk* **volume** [hence the need to know *total* **marginal** figures of the entire additional **production run** (see *Figure 3*)], but are then **sold** *one at a time* [and the need to know *individual unit* figures (*Figure 3 calculations*)].

Also, producers never produce to 'break even' point! **Producers** *only* **produce** for **gain**. **Producers** do not **produce** beyond the point of *acceptable* **gainful** **profit** – acceptable **R**eturn **o**n **I**nvestment [ROI]. [There are fascinating exceptions to this rule, but they are beyond the scope of any primer.]

This all may sound a little confusing, but it is really quite simple…

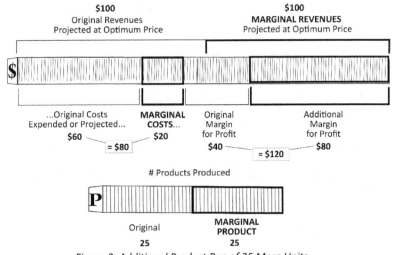

Figure 3: Additional Product Run of 25 More Units

The light lines show the original figures and **margins** from Figure 1 above. The darker, heavier lines show the *new, additional* **marginal costs**, **marginal revenues**, **marginal product**, and **profit margins** created by the *added* **production**. The difference in costs in the new production run is explained in '**Fixed Costs vs. Variable [Marginal] Costs**' next page.

Dividing the total projected *marginal* revenues, *marginal* costs,
or *marginal* profits by the total *marginal* product
gives the projected **marginal revenues, marginal costs,** and **marginal profit**
per unit [for *each*] of the *marginal* products produced.

Per Unit [for each *item* **produced**]:
marginal product 25 *total*;

marginal revenues $4.00 *per unit* [$100 ÷ 25];
marginal costs $.80 *per unit* [$20 ÷ 25];
profit margin $3.20 *per unit* [$80 ÷ 25]

Some Business Calculations:
1. **Producing** the same number of additional **products** cost only *one third* the original **cost**, increasing the **profit margin** per unit from **$2.40** to **$3.20** per each additional unit sold, or from **$40.00** *total* to **$120.00** *total* for the *additional* **production cost** of only **$20.00**. Note the need to use **marginal** *totals* in order to effectively **administrate** a true *projected* **profit**.
2. **Prices** can be dropped as low as **$.80** per unit before losses for all *additional* **25** products if they can all be **sold** [**$.80** per unit cost of additional **25** units]; all higher **prices** are **profit**. Note that using *unit* figures allows for effectively **administrating** *sales* to the best outcome '*within the* ***margin***' for **profit**.

Important points to get here:
a) After the first original **production run**, *all* additional **production runs** and growth cycles are called **_marginal_**.
b) The use of **margins** are for *measuring, calculating,* and *reasoning* in **trade**, make **margins** a **derivative operating** *phenomenon*.
c) **Marginal costs** almost always start out *lower* than the original costs because the *setup* and some other **costs** for the **production** are already done and do not apply to an *additional run* of **production**. [Up to a point. Below we will discuss *Diminishing* **Marginal Returns**.]

Fixed Costs vs. Variable [Marginal] Costs

For **management** *and economic purposes*, there are only two all-encompassing categories of costs: *fixed costs* and *variable costs*.

Fixed costs are costs that *stay the same* during the **production** run or cycle: loan or rental payments on **capital** assets, building or property rent or mortgage payments, insurance payments, salaried and non-overtime **employment costs**, etc. – and, for **management** purposes, *production set-up costs* [the costs of setting up a **production** run of a **product** or **service**].

Once equipment is set up for a **production** run, *set-up costs* are the same if **producing** one hundred units of a **product**, or one thousand units, or one hundred thousand units of that same **product** or **service**. They are *fixed costs* regardless of number of units **produced** – unless a set-up has to be *re*-set.

So fixed costs, *in totals* and *per unit produced*, help increase the **profit margin** *if one* **produces** *in higher* **volume** *and can sell the additional units* **produced**.

Variable costs, however, are costs that *vary* according to **volume produced**: **material resources**, *overtime* or temporary help **wages**, shipping and delivery costs, extra **marketing**, etc.

All *marginal* costs are *variable costs* because the *additional* costs *vary according to the additional volume.* The fixed costs are already accounted for in the original calculations. There are no additions to these costs on the additional run – they are *fixed*.

Diminishing Marginal Returns

Whether you are **consuming, investing,** or **producing,** you *invest a sum*, and from that *investment* obtain *utility* or **profit** from the **investment.** [In **business**, both are called '*return on investment*' – aka ROI.]

When continually increasing **productivity**, we discover another **operating phenomena**: after a point, **marginal returns**, that at first *increased* [as discussed above], begin now to *diminish*.

[And so we also have... **diminishing marginal product; diminishing marginal revenues;** and **diminishing consumer marginal utility.** (I know, way over-naming.)]

Diminishing marginal returns means that when you increase **production** over and over again, you always reach a point of diminished **productivity** in comparison to **costs.** The **volume** of **product produced** – *outputs* – *will diminish in relation to inputs* [**labor** and **materials**].

Increased **production** brings *stress* and *wear and tear* on *human* and *capital* **resources**, *adding* to **variable costs**, reducing [diminishing] returns on **investment** [aka ROI].

However, the *primary* reason for **diminished marginal returns** is diminished **volume** and **quality** of **productivity** *due to stress on human resources*: acquiring and **training** *new people*; **employees** spending time to **train** them; overtime; **reorganizing**; people wear out, tire, flub, or get sick; expansion can require adding **administrative producers** and **capital resources. Productivity** generally suffers during all of these processes, and the **costs** of it diminish ROI.

The Consumer Margin of Utility

The second **margin** in economics is the **consumer margin of utility** – that *perception* of **basic purpose gain** [*benefit*] a **consumer** compares against the *perceived* **value** of the **resources** they have to *expend* in **trade** to get it.

Diminishing Marginal *Utility* [This is *not* an absolute.]

Diminishing marginal utility is an **operating phenomenon** that operates on the same principle as **diminishing marginal returns**. The original purchase of a **product** or **service** is not **marginal**, it is the original *utility* or *benefit*, the original *measure of value* to the **consumer**. However, the more *often* one purchases and uses that same **product** or **service**, the less *utility* or *benefit* one gets from it – over the short term or over the long term.

It is easiest to recognize this concept in **services** or in food purchases: a **consumer** buys a dish of ice cream for $3.00. The first dish is so satisfying that the **consumer** buys another *additional* dish of ice cream for another $3.00 – *but the level of pleasure for each additional dish of ice cream is not as much as the last*. The *benefit* is *diminished* – '**diminished *marginal* utility**'.

About Margins:
the
Principles and Concepts Important to Success

Margins for Maximizing Profits [aka: '**Profit Maximization**']

> '**Maximizing profits' is nothing more than
> controlling costs, prices, and marketing
> to '*expand the profit margin to its maximum*'.**

'**Profit maximization**' is far more simple than the very important sounding term makes it sound:

- **Control costs**: Keeping costs as low as possible keeps the **margin** for **profit** as large as possible – it creates the largest 'field of difference' between **costs** and **revenues**.
- **Control price**: next, *market* the **product** or **service** so as to create the highest possible **demand** at the highest possible **price** – this includes the *designing* and *manufacturing* process as it includes **producing** the most desirable **product** possible.
- **Sell in volume**: when the **market** is ready to buy at the **prices** set, *sell* at the highest possible **volume** at the highest possible **price** to that **market** of **consumers**.

i.e.
*'Create a high **quality** and **consumer** desirable **product** or **service**
at the lowest possible **production costs**
marketed to the most willing and able to pay **consumers**'.*

THE PRINCIPLES of THE DIVISION of LABOR

About Division of Labor:

Productivity Class Economic Theory Statement

Organizing productive activity necessitates separating and dividing work activities. Organized divisions of work activity fall into *two very different categories*:

- o dividing the *types* of productivities to be done [accounting, marketing, administrative management, customer service, manufacturing, research and development, engineering, etc.]
- o dividing the *steps* *to be taken in a productive process or other unskilled or semi-skilled routine labor* [production and assembly lines, or necessary custodial, clerical, table or counter service, etc.]

When employing human resources to perform these two types of activities, they are divided respectively into...

- o productivities requiring *'specialized human expertise'* – i.e. specialization; and
- o *processing steps* requiring *labor only* – *'semi-skilled or unskilled labor'* or *'mechanical- or function-like labor'*

Division of Labor: *For our purposes...* 'Dividing among human resources the processing steps or separate functions of producing a product, service, result, or outcome; or to separate and distribute unskilled or semi-skilled tasks to human resources' – including any use of human resource labor where mechanistic capital resources are unavailable, unrealistic for the circumstances, or too expensive.

True 'division of labor' begins when organizers realize that by *dividing the actions or steps required to produce any productive result* among *human* resources, that activity can be done more *productively*, *efficiently*, and with better *consistency*. In productivity class economics, *'division of labor'* is not *'specialization'*. It is considered a *'derivative operating dynamic control'*.

About Division of Labor:

Overview

'Division of Labor' Does *Not* Include 'Specialization' in Productivity Class Economics

Specialization is *not* the same as being assigned a single task or function by an **organization** or by doing a *task-labor* work in **trade** for an **income**. **Task labor** is actually *'function labor'* – not *'specialized labor'* – and is utilized to accomplish necessary chores of every kind, or is utilized in the same way *'mechanical function'* is used.

> **In productivity class economics, organizationally,**
> **'dividing up labor' for *'mechanistic or function-like labor tasks'*,**
> ***of any kind, in any manner***
> **among human resources is called 'division of labor'.**

Although **specializing** is an **organizational** type of activity, it actually begins long before **organized employment** when *'dividing up labor functions'* actually begins. That difference makes **specialization** a *primary* **operating dynamic**, and **division of labor** a *derivative* **operating dynamic**, *derived* from actions of **organizing producers**. [Still, yes, a good amount of overlap is likely to occur.]

About Division of Labor:

Characteristics and General Factors

Always an Organizing Action

True **division of labor**, then, is always an action by an **organizing producer** utilizing **human resources**. Even *'dividing up processing steps'* is not what is meant by **division of labor**. **Division of labor** only occurs when an **organizer** divides the unskilled or semi-skilled processing steps or functional tasks of **productivity** among *more than one* **human resource**.

Therefore, in **productivity class** economics, there are only two ways for an **organized producer** to apply the principle of **division of labor**:

- divide among more than one employee the processing steps or separate functions of producing a product, service, result, or outcome; or
- separate and distribute unskilled or semi-skilled general tasks to human resources.

The Benefits and Adverse Effects of Actual 'Division of Labor'

Actual **division of** *'drone-like'* **labor** can breed 'helplessness, dependence, and ignorance' and usually undermines responsibility. Adam Smith called this the "mental mutilation" of **division of labor**, which he described as "*single repetitive tasks*" [i.e. production and assembly lines, etc.]. Alexis de Tocqueville called the assignment of *single repetitive tasks*, "*extreme* **division of labor**".

Specialization *does not usually* produce such an adverse human result.
The *benefits* of **division of labor** on **productivity** are obvious – *the **producer** benefits big.* For the **working producer,** the benefits are the availability of unskilled or semi-skilled labor which can provide a living while the laborer pursues **education** in a more lucrative skill set – a **specialization**. That can be a big benefit, too, *if one can pull it off.*

However, in the near future, '**production**' and 'assembly line' **division of labor** will become rare. 'Robotics *operators*' will remain but will need to be **production** *specialists* on their type of computerized robotics operations in order to keep up with advancing computer and machine technology. And they must be at any time ready to switch back and forth from **producing** for **organizations** [companies] to directly for **consumers** [self-employment], in a days' notice, at any sudden shift in economic conditions. Thinking like a '***worker bee* producer**' isn't going to work in the very near future.

THE PRINCIPLES of
SUPPLY, DEMAND, PRICING,
and MARKET EQUILIBRIUM

INTRODUCTION:

Demand, supply, pricing, and **market equilibrium** are all **derivative operating dynamics** so interconnected and interwoven **productively** that they cannot be discussed individually without explaining, in each discussion, the *inter-dynamic effects* each has on the other three and vice versa. So although it may seem that principles are being explained repetitively in each of these sections, the seemingly repeated principles are actually presented in each section from an understanding of the inter-dynamic and balancing forces *upon* and *from* the **operating dynamic** *being discussed.*

Presenting these principles in this way, we can take up each **operating dynamic** individually from its own unique cause-and-effect perspective.

Complexities of Interrelationships:

Every **product** is a combination of many **resources** and **sub-products.** Every **service** is a **product** unto itself – something **produced** – and every **service** requires **products** to deliver it. Every **resource** and **sub-product** is also a **product** unto itself. And every **service, product, resource,** and **sub-product** is a **productive specialization** of some individual or group and is **traded** for **wages** or a monetary **price.**

And every one of the above **products, services,** and **productivities** is subject to the principles of '**supply, demand, and pricing**'. Therefore, every **cost** factor in a **profit margin** when **producing** a **product** or **service** is individually subject to **supply, demand, pricing,** and achieves its own **equilibrium** in the **market** for them. Did **productivity** suddenly just get complex? Fear not –

Every complexity can be broken down into its component simplicities and thereby understood.

Let's get started.

THE PRINCIPLES of DEMAND and 'ELASTICITY'

About Demand:

Productivity Class Economic Theory Statement

The basic purpose drives of a consuming public create needs and wants for a wide variety of both necessary and desirable products and services. The *aggregate drive by a consuming public to acquire such products and services* is what we mean by 'demand'.

'Demand' is the elemental activity of 'consume' manifested as '*the aggregate basic purpose drive of a whole populace, or a market of people therein, to acquire products or services*'. It is the drive to 'consume' manifested as 'demand' for specific products or services, or specific types of products or services, that creates a buying 'market'.

The demand for any type of product or service is variable. It is influenced and regulated by specific factors [listed further below].

Demand correlates interactively with Supply and Price. When any one of the three are altered or adjusted, the other two alter and adjust in accordance with and in specific proportion to it. No other influences or regulating factors upon demand are necessarily correlative.

About Demand:
an
Overview

'Demand' is the **elementary activity** of '**consume**' manifested as the *aggregate basic purpose* drive of a populace or *'market* of people' to acquire a **product** *or service*, or type of **product** or **service**. Therefore, until a **product** or **service**, or type of **product** or **service**, is *recognized* as needed or wanted, there is no 'demand' for it. Conversely, **demand** can exist for something whether or not a **product** or **service** yet exists to fulfill it.

All Demand [Aggregate Consumptive Drive] Is Basic Purpose Driven

Consume is a **basic purpose** driven **primary operating dynamic**. We **consume** *when* we **produce**, and **consume** *what* we **produce**. All further **primary operating dynamics**, directly or indirectly, exist only to serve the success of **producing** and **consuming** for **basic purpose** requirements.

'**Produce** and **consume**' is how we achieve material **basic purpose** needs and wants. **Demand**, therefore, is the **basic purpose** driven need to **consume** in any *aggregate* form.

About Demand:

Characteristics and General Factors

Demand is Measured in 'Volume', 'Potency', and 'Elasticity'

- o   **Volume** [volume of **products** and **services** needed or wanted];
- o   **Potency** [tenacity, hardiness, stamina, or strength of **consumptive** *drive* for the **products** and **services**]; and
- o   **Elasticity** [the degree of fluctuation in **demand** in response to a change in **price** or other influences].

These are *not separate*, but three aspects to fully measure the *condition* of **demand**.

The Demand for Needs and Wants Vary

Needs and *wants* vary from **market** to **market**, from populace to populace, culture to culture. Although **demand** can *fluctuate*, *shift*, *change*, and *vary*, and be influenced and regulated by a number of specific factors, it has three **operating dynamics** that are *primarily* used to *regulate* and *control* it:

The Derivative Operating *Controls* of Demand: The *primary* factors that control the measure of *intensity, volume, flexibility,* etc. of **demand** are:

- •   **Pricing**: **pricing** effects **demand** *primarily* by making a **product** or **service** more, or less, *affordable* and/or *desirable* when comparing **price** to perceived **value** or **competitors prices**.
- •   **Marketing**: **marketing** effects **demand** by making a **product** or **service** *known* and presenting it as *needed* or *desirable*.
- •   **Supply**: **supply** effects **demand** by making a **product** or **service** more, or less, *tangibly available* to the **consumer** – which further effects increases or decreases in **price**.

[Each '**control factor**' is discussed in more depth in their own section.]

Law [Rule] of Demand: In academic and analytic economics, the '**law**' of **demand** is:
- •   *If **price** goes up or down, **demand** fluctuates in the opposite direction.*
- •   If **price** goes *up*, less people are willing to or can afford to expend their

currency resources for that product or service – demand for it goes *down.*

- If price goes *down*, more people are willing to and can afford to expend their currency resources for that product or service – demand for it goes *up.*

[Except when it doesn't, due to other modifying influences. Hence, more a *'rule'.*]

However, the derivative operating phenomenon of elasticity, in productivity class economics, is the *true determining factor* of rises and falls in demand:

'ELASTICITY' of Demand noun *For our purposes...*The measure of rises or falls in consumer demand in response to corresponding rises and falls in the opposite direction of *prices [or other influences].*

IMPORTANT NOTE: The current academic term 'price elasticity demand' implies that elasticity refers to price. 'Demand flexibility' or 'elasticity of demand' are less confusing and more appropriately descriptive terms. In other words, 'flexibility of demand' is called elasticity, or more descriptively: *how far demand for a product or service will increase or decrease [i.e. 'stretch'], or not, in the opposite direction when its price is increased or decreased – or under some other influence.* Get that? Elasticity is not the *actual* rise or fall in consumer demand when prices change, but the *measure* of how far it *can* rise or fall.

DEMAND IS ELASTIC IF: consumers have *flexibility of choice* for or against a product or service or type of product or service. If a consumer can *go without* a product or service, *shift to a competitor*, or *shift to an alternative* product or service, then demand for the current product or service is going to be elastic – *flexible* – and will *fluctuate* according to rises and falls in price, and other influences.

DEMAND IS *NOT* ELASTIC IF: consumers do *not* have *flexibility of choice* to go without a product or service, to *shift to a competitor*, or *shift to an alternative* product or service. Demand for that product or service is going to be *in*elastic – *not flexible* – and will remain *stationary* regardless of rises or falls in price or other influences.

Now it's time to 'crunch the numbers'…

The Productivity Class Economist *Always* 'Crunches the Numbers':

In *real life* – in productivity class economics – *one must measure the actual projected dollars and cents to be gained or lost* in taking any action on price – elasticity or not. *If the increase in demand from a lowered price does not produce total revenues equal to the total revenues from the original price and demand, the venture produces a loss not a gain.*

Example:

Demand   100 customers
Price $20 per customer
Revenues $2000

New **Price** $10   50% drop in **price**
Old + New **Customers** 160   60% increase in **demand**
Total **Revenues** $1600   *Loss* in **revenues** of $400

Elasticity of the **demand** for one's **products** or **services** does *not* always mean lowering *price* will increase **revenues**. **Productivity class** economists – the actual **producers** themselves – always 'crunch the numbers' [*do the math*], research and survey their **market,** and determine the actual **profitability** of their actions – all the way back to **marginal** calculations.

In **productivity class** economics there is no thinking in academic terms of '*all things being equal*'. When doing '*real life*' economic calculating or reasoning, there is only 'real life math' [just arithmetic, don't panic]. The **productivity class** economist works out the math of the *actual situation and **marketing** intent**. If that shows an *increase* in **revenue**, *short* or *long term*, it's a 'go'.

***Marketing Intent:** Sometimes **losses** are acceptable to liquidate a **product** not selling so the **value** of it [**money**] can be re-invested into a more **profitable product**; or to introduce new **consumers** to a **product** ['introductory **price**']; or to introduce **consumers** to a larger line of overall **profitable products** or **services.**

'Other' Determining Factors of Demand and Elasticity of Demand

The **demand** for a **product** or **service** is *variable*. It *fluctuates* in volume of **consumers**, *shifts* away from one **market** and toward another, *changes* with technology and culture, and *varies* in intensity of need and desirability. And it is influenced by specific factors [also see '**Controls** 'above]:

- **Substitutes for products, services, or sellers:**
    - Other available **products** and **services** the **consumer** can shift to and avoid an increase in **price.**
- **Income available for expenditure:**
    - The **consumer's** *ability* as a **producer** to pay the new **price.**
- **Value to consumers of products or services vs. price:**
    - **Consumer** perception of **value** or benefit vs. the new **price.**
- **Product necessity vs. desirability** [need vs. want]:
    - **Price** vs. **consumer's** actual *need* or level of *desire.*
- **Time [for consumers] to adjust to increases in price:**
    - The *time* it takes for **consumers** to change their *habits,* find or develop solutions or alternatives *to do the same thing.*
- **Linked product prices** and **profitability:**
    - The **prices** and **profitability** of linked or associated **products**

and **services** that can be sold at a **profit** if an **unprofitable product** or **service** is used as a *starter* or *lead-in*.

- **Consumer tastes** [cultural and personal]:
    - Styles, flavors, atmosphere, design, etc. all effect a **consumer's** *willingness to pay* when **prices** change.
- **Expectations**:
    - **Consumer's** expectations of *better quality, better usability, better performance, and better results* for a higher **price**, or the opposite for a lower **price**.
- **Cultural changes**:
    - In attitudes, perceived **value**, utility, style, beliefs, etc. [including technology advancements, **product** development, etc.]

About Demand:

Principles and Concepts Important to Success

If demand is 'elastic', that means it rises and falls when **prices**, or other influences, make it rise and fall. This is directly related to the 'law'/'rule' of demand: *if price goes up or down*, **demand** *is driven in the opposite direction*. Except, of course, we also know that sometimes that doesn't happen. For many different reasons, *sometimes* **demand** *remains unchanged* – it is **in**elastic.

If **demand** is **in**elastic, that means it does not rise and fall when **prices** go up or down nor is it significantly affected by other influences.

So why do we want to know this? Why is 'demand elasticity' an *operating* **phenomenon**? Because, if demand is **elastic**, *raising* **prices** *could lose a* **business customers** – **demand** would shift *away* from the higher **price**. But *lowering* **prices** *could raise* **demand** and *gain* a **business** customers – **demand** would shift *toward* the lower **price**. Therefore, *if properly done, lowering* **prices** *should gain* **customers**, *raise* **revenues**, *and therefore* **profit** when demand is **elastic**. *Raising* **prices**, however, should lose **customers** and therefore lower **revenues** and **profit**.

However, if **demand** is **in**elastic, raising **prices** should *not lose* **customers** – as **demand** remains *un*changed. And lowering **prices** will *not gain* **customers** – as **demand** still remains *un*changed. Therefore, *if properly done, when prices are* **inelastic**, *raising* **prices** *should not lose* **customers**, *but will still raise* **revenues**, *and therefore* **profit**.

Therefore again, in **productivity class** economics, we consider the **derivative operating phenomenon** of *elasticity* the *true determining factor* of rises and falls in **demand**.

THE PRINCIPLES of SUPPLY

"Like any business, the oil industry runs on the basic premise of supply and demand. The more supply - the lower the price. The higher the demand - the higher the price. Author: Ron Wyden, Senator (D)-Oregon

About Supply:

Productivity Class Economic Theory Statement

'Supply' is the elemental activity of 'produce' when referring to...
   a. The aggregate [or cumulative] *products and services provided to the consumers* of a market, geographical area, or economic system; or
   b. *The total volume of any single, or single type of, product or service provided* to consumers [or consuming producers] by producers.

The basic purpose drives of a consuming public create *needs* and *wants* [demand] for a wide variety of both necessary and desirable products and services. The *products and services produced and provided to meet those needs and wants* is the 'supply' available to the consuming public.

Supply is provided by a producer only when a particular product or service, or type of product or service, is *recognized as needed or wanted, or potentially needed or wanted,* by the consuming public. [The exception to this rule is marketing – producers can *persuade* a buying public that they *need* or should *want* a product or service and to buy it.]

The supply of any type of product or service is *variable.* It *fluctuates* in volume and availability, *shifts* away from one market and toward another, and *changes* with technology and culture. It is influenced and regulated by specific factors: *profit margin*; *competition*; *demand*; and *resource availability.*

Supply correlates interactively with Demand and Price. When any one of the three are altered or adjusted, the other two alter and adjust in accordance with and proportional to it. No other influences or regulating factors of supply are necessarily correlative.

About Supply:
an
Overview

As indicated in the quote above, **supply** is the other side of the **supply-and-**

demand operating phenomenon. If the current supply for a product or service is *less* than the demand for it, prices go *up* [because consumers, competing for the existing supply, will pay the higher prices, and producers will charge them]. If the current supply for a product or service is *more* than the demand for it, prices come down [it's the suppliers that now compete – via price – with each other for the consumer's business].

Think of supply as the sum total of producing, marketing, distributing, and selling a product or service to the consuming public – all of which come under the heading of 'produce'. In order to meet our basic purpose needs, and also to further our gain, we produce for – that is, we 'supply' – the consuming public what it *needs* and *wants*. Therefore, we produce and supply pretty much *anything* the consumer will trade for.

In addition, if we are skillful at marketing and sales, we can *convince* the consumer of the *need* or *desirability* of the products or services we supply, and *persuade* them to buy. Therefore,...

> Producers 'supply' what the consumer *needs* and/or *wants*
> or what the producer can *convince* the consumer they *need* or *to want*.

Demand *alone* does not determine supply, nor does price *alone*. In productivity class economics, *__demand plus profit margin__* determines whether or not a product or service will be *__supplied__*. [The assumption in general economics is that price determines profit margin. In real life, 'price *less costs*' determines profit margin, and price affects demand.]

Profit margin determines productivity, and, therefore, supply. Total profit margin is determined by...
- O   actual obtainable price minus total production and operating costs
- O   likely demand volume
- O   marketing and sales capabilities [more later in ' Marketing']

In academic economics texts, fluctuations in price indicate corresponding fluctuations in demand. In productivity class economics, only actual sales reports are *indicators* of fluctuations in demand. [More below in 'Characteristics'.]

Other Determining Factors of Supply

As stated above, the supply of any type of product or service is *variable*. It *fluctuates* in volume and availability, *shifts* away from one market and toward another, and *changes* with technology and culture. It is influenced and regulated by specific factors:
- O   **Profit Margin** [the gainfulness of providing the product or service]
- O   **Competition** [other producers and/or competing alternative products and services]
- O   **Elasticity of Demand**

○ **Resources Availability** [of material, capital, and **human resources**, technology, etc.]

In addition, all the factors of *productivity* are also the factors of *supply*. What is *produced* is what is *supplied*.

About Supply:

Characteristics and General Factors

The '*Law* of Supply'

In academic and analytical economics, the '*law* of supply' says that, *all other factors discounted*, if the **price** of a **product** or **service** increases, the increase in **price** indicates that **demand** must be up, and that **producers** will be increasing their **volume** of **production** to sell at the increased **price**, thus increasing **profits**. And often enough, it does work out that way.

Lowered **price**, to an academic economist, means **demand** has gone down and **prices** have been lowered to entice **consumers** with a better, however less **profitable**, deal [or to clear out excess or unsold stock]. Therefore, **producers** will believe that their **investment** could be better spent elsewhere.

But to an *actual* **producer**, **prices** can go up or down for a lot of reasons. **Prices** can go up or down because **production costs** have gone up or down. **Prices** can go down because the **demand** is so *high*, **competition** for business is so *intense* that **profits** can only be made by selling in **volume**. **Prices** can go up because **consumers** are **demanding** *higher end* **products** or **services** with no actual increase of the **volume** of **consumers** to sell to. *To a producer, prices are no indication to increase or decrease production.*

To a **producer**, changing **prices** are an indicator that the **market** is *fluctuating*, and if he or she wants their **business** to continue to flourish, they better catch up with the **producers** that are changing their **prices** – *as they are already on to whatever is whatever is happening.*

In **productivity class** economics, one investigates the **market** and works *not by competitors increasing or decreasing price, but by increases and decreases in actual verified consumer demand, product or production advancement, and properly worked out profit margins.* There is **marketing** *homework* to do.

Prices are a '*Late Indicator*' for a Producer

In **productivity class** economics, a **producer** does not wait to see if **prices** are going up or down as an indicator of **demand** unless they want to be forever late in the game and woefully uninformed about the **market** of **consumers** they sell to. Using **price** as an indicator is for economic academics and analysts to do. *It is the **producers** themselves that raise or lower the **prices**. The academics and analysts observe and study the actions of **producers** and **consumers** – the actual participants. You are an actual participant.* The **producers** raise their **prices** according to **productivity** and **consumption** trends that they and their **competitors** are experiencing in *real time*.

So, in academic and analytical economics, the '**rule** of **supply**' only *assumes* an increase in **price** equals an increase in '**volume** of **consumers** willing to buy', and therefore, indicating a subsequent increase in **competitive supply**. **Consumers** willing to *pay more*, however, does not necessarily translate to *more* **consumers**. It could translate only to current **consumer** *enthusiasm* increasing in *intensity* enough for **producers** to raise **prices** – or it could just be **producers** just taking advantage of *inelastic* **consumer demand**.

To an academic or analytical economist,
a change in **price** is an *indicator* that the **market** is *fluctuating*
and that an appropriate change in **supply** will follow.

Producers and consumers *are* the market, and are *doing* the fluctuating.
*A **producer** determines actual **demand** trends,
determines their probable duration,
calculates the **profit margins**,
and takes the most **profitable** action.*

An increase in **price** in the **market** really means they've got **marketing** and **profit margin** homework to do – *and they're late*.

Remember also, that **price** can remain the same and **profit margins** *increase* if **costs** of **production** *decline* and **producers** decide to just take the increase in **profits** instead of **competitively** passing the savings on to the **consumer**. The **market** becomes more **profitable**, academically appearing to stay the same.

The variations are almost endless. But a **producer** *paying attention* eventually gets to know all of them. The thing to keep in mind is that if you are a **producer**, and you judge whether or not to increase **supply** by **prices**, you are forever **operating** from *behind* and playing 'catch up'.

Competition

Competition is the other way **productivity**, and therefore **supply**, goes up. **Competitors**, entering the **market** vying for **profits**, increase the **supply** of that **product** or **service** to the **consuming** public. **Competition** entering that **market** to compete for those **profits**, however, tend to **compete** via **price** – causing **prices** to go back down.

Additionally, *related alternative* **products** and **services** can also **compete** against any other **product** or **service**. For example, there are many different kinds of sport vehicles from ATVs to snowmobiles to jet skis, all competing for the business of the outdoor sport enthusiast **consumer**. Each is a *related* [outdoor motor sports] **product competing** as an *alternative* to the other.

Resources and Education

As explained in the Chapter 2, **The Twelve Elemental Activities**, the two primary requirements for **productivity** are **education** and **resources**. That also makes them two of the *primary requirements*, and *determining factors*, for **supply [demand, competition,** and **profit margin** being three more]. If there is no **education** or **resources**, then there is no **production**, and therefore, no **supply** of what might have been **produced**.

This subject has been covered, and necessary points made, in chapter two, so we will assume it sufficient to reiterate here only that without **resources** and the **education** to utilize them, there is no **production** and, therefore, no **supply** of anything at all. Simple, but highly impactful.

Therefore, in **productivity class** economics, the *primary determining factors* of **supply** must also include **resources** and **education**.

About Supply:

Principles and Concepts Important to Success

Productivity Turnover

TURNOVER: *the speed or rate at which it takes to complete a task or routine, accomplish a goal, replace something or someone, etc. – especially repetitively.*

i.e. **In business**, getting a **'production** to **profit'** cycle done quickly, and doing it again, and again, and again – the more times done in a physical year, the more **profits** made. **Turnover** is one area where the saying '*time is money*' comes from.

The most commonly known use of the term **turnover** is **employee turnover** in business – the number of **employees** that *leave and have to be replaced* in a period of time. But there are many types of **turnover** in business, and all work off of the same basic concept.

On the subject of **supply** we are concerned with only five types of **productivity turnover**. These are most the common **turnover** rates that effect **productivity** and, therefore, **supply**:

- o   The number of times you can **produce** a **product** or **service**, sell out the inventory, and **produce** that **product** or **service** again and sell it again, over and over, in a designated period of time [usually a fiscal year, monthly or weekly goal plan, or a promotional period].

o Client or customer **turnover** – the number of **clients** or **consumers** one can spend time with, complete the **service**, and move on to the next **client** or **consumer** in a designated period of time [usually used by professionals, tradesmen, restaurants, retail stores, etc.].

o Also, the number of **clients** or **customers** that patronize a **product** or **service** and move on to some other **product** or **service** and are replaced with new **clients** or **customers** – instead of 'employee **turnover**', it's client or **consumer turnover**.

o The speed at which an individual or group can accomplish any task, goal, or routine and move on to the next.

o The *quickness* with which one can invest **resources** and get a **return on investment** [especially the *rate* of *repetition* of a repetitive investment] – and usually move on to the next **investment**.

The point of measuring **turnover** is to measure, *and improve upon*,
the **volume** or *rate* of **productivity** and, therefore,
the accumulation of **profit** over a given period of time.

Get the **supply** connection? **Turnover** rates effect *volume* of **productivity**, and therefore the *volume* of **supply** of the **products** and **services** provided to a **consuming** public. **Turnover** *incentive* is increased **profits**. [Also, note the 'operating control' factor? Although turnover *rate* is 'measured', turnover as a productive tactic is actually *used* to *drive* **productivity** and **profits**, and to *manipulate* or *manage* **supply**.]

THE PRINCIPLES of PRICE and PRICING

People of the same trade seldom meet together, even for merriment and diversion, but the conversation ends in a conspiracy against the public, or in some contrivance to raise prices.
Adam Smith, Economist -- author of 'The Wealth of Nations' [1776]

About Price and Pricing:

Productivity Class Economic Theory Statement

A 'price' for a product or service is by definition simply the *value* of currency or barter *'asked for'* or *'agreed upon'* by a producer in *trade* for a product or service. That price can be in the form of other tradeable products and services [called barter] or it can be in the form of currency [money].

Price and *pricing* manifest naturally as a consequence *trade* and is both a 'derivative operating dynamic *phenomenon*' and a 'derivative operating dynamic *control*' [and is therefore only properly applied when subordinated to serving the success of the primary operating dynamics].

The influence of pricing as a derivative operating *control* is *tempered* by the forces of 'supply' and 'demand'. Further, pricing is a causative agent or factor effecting consumer's *'willingness to pay'* for a product or service, and therefore, influences both supply and demand in return.

Therefore also, the dynamic forces of supply, demand, and pricing, each directly effecting the other, inevitably become balanced into an equilibrium – called 'market equilibrium'. Market equilibrium is a balance in which the supply of a product or service is in sync with consumer demand for it at the price commanding the highest obtainable profit in the marketplace.

About Price and Pricing:
an
Overview

Price is a Derivative Operating Dynamic *Phenomenon*

In **trade**, **values** required for an acceptable **trade** must be determined. Therefore, **price** is a *naturally occurring* **operating dynamic phenomenon** generated by the **elemental activity** of **trade**.

Price is used to *measure, calculate,* and *reason,* by **consumers** and **producers** alike, on **trades** and **trade values** of **products** and **services**. Further, utilizing **prices,** one can *calculate* the projected return on any **product's** or **service's** **investment [profit margin]**. On a larger scale, **market prices** can be used to analyze **market** conditions, determine trends, and forecast economic 'futures'.

Price-*ing* is a Derivative Operating Dynamic *Control*

Price-*ing* is the 'action of utilizing **prices**' to *manage* **supply, demand,** and **profitability.** Therefore also, **pricing** is determined by a **producer** after observing and calculating **supply** and **demand** conditions, and using **profit margin** calculations to determine potential for **profitability.**

Pri**cing** is partially controlled by **supply** and **demand,** but it is also *itself* a **dynamic operating *control*,** and it is therefore also used to *manipulate* both **supply** and **demand** in return. In addition, **pricing** is used to *control,* and is *controlled by,* **competition,** another **derivative operating dynamic *control.***

Therefore, there are only four *primary* determining factors of **price:**
- **Demand**
- **Supply**
- **Profit margin,** and
- **Competition [competing producers, products, or services]**

Determining Price

Pricing is determined by **supply** and **demand,** and by the **profit margin** – i.e. '*asking price*' chosen through **supply** and **demand** analysis, less total **costs,** will determine potential for **profitability.** A *marketing* study of the **supply** and **demand** circumstances for the **product** or **service** is used to determine the *maximum obtainable* '*asking price*'. Then, when calculated into a **profit margin,** which also shows **costs,** the *range* of **profitability** is determined.

Skill in **marketing** and **selling** determines where within that 'range of profitability' a **producer** will exact an *actual* 'price paid', and **profit** earned.

Producers Set 'Price' – Consumers Decide Whether or not To Pay It:

As stated in chapter one, "**All economic forces are manifestations of basic purpose drive**". **Basic purpose drive** motivates a **producer** to **price** their **products** and **services** to *maximize* **profits.** They do this by observing **supply, demand,** and **competitors** **prices** and assert their own **competitiveness** accordingly.

Producers tend to follow the **consumer's** '*willingness or ability to pay*' [**elasticity**] as a *determining factor* for raising or lowering **prices**. [However, sometimes a **producer** will take an *opposite or differing approach* as a **marketing** tactic, a strategy against **competitors,** to 'corner a **market**', etc.]

Supply, demand, and **price** will exert their own **producer** and **consumer basic purpose** forces each upon the other until a *balance* is achieved – an *equilibrium* called **market equilibrium**.

About Price and Pricing:

Characteristics and General Factors

Supply, Demand, Pricing and *Resource Efficiency*

According to standard economic theory, it is **supply, demand,** and **prices** together, *left to work freely against each other*, that best allocates **resources** toward efficient use, and *not* 'waste' [based on the false assumption that what is 'wanted' is not itself 'wasteful']. i.e. A **producer** will not *make* what **consumers** will not *buy*. **Consumers** will not buy what they do not *need* or *want*, or pay too high a **price** for what they do. **Prices** must conform to what **consumers** *can* and are *willing* to pay [requiring **producers** to utilize **resources** most efficiently]. Thus, in **free trade** economies, **resources** get utilized [and, therefore, **allocated**] most *efficiently*, and only at the actual level of *needs* and *wants* of **consumers**.

Economists consider that this 'natural efficiency' is the '*primary role*' of **prices**. However, *resource efficiency* is really more of an *incidental* phenomenon.

> **The primarily 'role' of prices is for producers and consumers to achieve a basic purpose driven mutually gainful 'trade agreement'.**

That it also contributes to the most efficient use of **resources** is an incidental, useful *phenomenon*, but it is definitely *not* the actual economic *role* of **prices**.

The Resource Efficiency of Basic Purpose Drives

Producers: **Producers** operate off of **profit margins**. They use **resources** most frugally and efficiently in order to keep **costs** [the ***price*** of **resources**] down. That way, when requiring the highest obtainable **price** for their **products** or **services**, the **profit margin** is at its largest – they **gain** the most. They also only **produce products** and **services consumers** *need* and *want*, and *only* in *volumes* consistent with **demand** – unsold **products** and **services** would be waste – and *waste* in economics is *loss*. In this manner, the **basic purpose drives** of the **producer** causes **resources** to go only to where they are *needed* and *wanted* by the economic populace – the **consumer**.

Competition: **Competition** for the **consumer's** business requires a **producer** to be an *efficient employer* and *competent utilizer* of **resources** – absolute necessities in keeping **costs** down and thereby keeping **price competitive** and still **profitable**. Therefore, if **competitive marketing** requires it, a *decrease* in costs [**resources**] can translate to a decrease in **prices** without losing **profit margin** per unit. Therefore, **competitive** *pricing* for the **consumer's** business reinforces the **producer's** *incentives* to ensure that **resources** are used most *efficiently and profitably* – that no **resources** go to *waste* causing *loss* of **profit**.

<u>Consumers:</u> **Price** is of primary concern to the **basic purpose drives** of the consumer, who wants to expend his or her limited **currency resources** as *efficiently as possible*. Doing so means *more* **currency** *to expend on other basic purpose* needs and wants – of which there are so many.

Consumers want *good results* in the *utility* of **products** and **services** purchased. And they want their purchased **products** and **services** to *last*. This **demand** for a *lasting* level of **quality**, a *good result* in **utility**, at an acceptable **price** becomes the **ethical producer's** incentive – all requiring *efficiency* of **resources** by both.

In the end, at the heart of the *most efficient* **resource** *allocation* and *utility* is the drive for the best **basic purpose** outcomes by **producers** and **consumers**. **Ethically** frameworked **free trade** economic systems ['**symbiotic exchange'** frameworked economic systems], and **basic purpose drives** compel the most *efficient* and best *allocated* use of available **resources** through the fundamental *principles* and *behaviors* of **supply**, **demand**, and **price**.

[This efficiency theory only applies to <u>economically</u> efficient use of **resources**, not necessarily *actual best use and most efficient management* of overall **resources** for the best long term **basic purpose** outcomes for a whole society. (Think fossil fuels.)]

About Price and Pricing:

Principles and Concepts Important to Success

- *Academics...* and *analysts* use *observation* of **prices** as an '**operating phenomena**' for *measuring, calculating,* and *reasoning* economic conditions, trends, and predictions.

- *Consumers...* use **prices** as an '**operating phenomena**' for *measuring, calculating,* and *reasoning* **trade value** of **products** and **services**, determining **consumptive** practices.

- *Producers...* use the *act* of **pricing** as an '**operating control**' for *driving, manipulating,* and *managing* maximization of **profit margins** and actual **profit** outcomes.

THE PRINCIPLES of MARKET EQUILIBRIUM

About Market Equilibrium:

Productivity Class Economic Theory Statement

Market equilibrium is a balance in which the supply of a product or service is in sync with consumer demand for it – while also at the highest *consumer acceptable* price that commands the highest obtainable profit.

Producers, in their basic purpose drive to maximize gain, generally push to get the *highest* price for their products or services. Consumers, in their own basic purpose drive to expend their currency as efficiently as possible, generally seek out the *lowest* prices that will still get them the basic purpose outcomes they desire.

These two basic purpose forces push and pull against each other until price reaches an agreeable point for producer and consumer – a *balance* [*equilibrium*] in the *marketplace* between the maximum the consumer *demanding* something is willing to pay for it and a profit gainful enough for the producer to *supply* it – a supply-and-demand balance in the market, called '*market equilibrium*'.

About Market Equilibrium:
an
Overview

It's All Basic Purpose Drive

It is the **basic purpose** drive for *maximum gain* that drives the **producer** to get the highest price for their **products** and **services**.

Consumers, in their own **basic purpose** drive, *generally* seek out the *lowest* **prices** that will still get them the **basic purpose** outcomes they desire.

It is the drive for **basic purpose** outcomes
that drive both **producer** and **consumer**.

These two forces push and pull against each other until **price** reaches an agreeable point for both – a '*stable price range*' where the two agree.

The true **equilibrium** is the ***producer*** and ***consumer basic purpose*** *drives,*

manifested in the activities of *supply, demand, and price*
– in the *marketplace*: a 'market equilibrium'.

Therefore, **market equilibrium** is a balance in which the **supply** of a **product** or **service** is in sync with **consumer demand** for it – at the highest *consumer acceptable* price that commands the highest obtainable **profit.**

Derivative operating dynamics properly applied always serve the success of the **primary operating dynamics** – in this case, **produce, consume,** and **trade** in the drive to *gainfully* achieve **basic purpose.**

Dynamic Forces

Even though **supply** and **demand** are manifestations of two *primary* operating dynamics [**produce** and **consume**] and **price** is a *derivative* operating dynamic [derived from **trade**] *each of these three dynamic activities exerts equally its forces and effects upon the other two.*

As an inevitable result, the dynamic forces of **supply, demand,** and **pricing** each causatively effecting each other in the **marketplace** become balanced into an **equilibrium.**

About Market Equilibrium:

Characteristics and General Factors

Cooperation vs. Opposition

At the lowest levels of economic development – at the primitive or aboriginal level – **production** and **consumption** is almost a single activity completed by individuals in a family. A family at this economic level **produces** what is *needed* and *wanted* and **consumes** it through *expenditure* and *utility.* A family **gains** by **producing** *more* than they **consume** cooperatively.

In the economics of **trade,** however, the **producer** is no longer the **consumer** of what they themselves have **produced.** When **produce** and **consume** are represented by *different economic entities,* their interests come into a state of *opposition* instead of *cooperation.* The **basic purpose** intentions of each *pushes back* against the **basic purpose** intentions of the other.

Equilibrium is achieved when, manifested as a *balance* of **supply** [**producer**] and **demand** [**consumer**] agree upon a **price** that *serves the producer's and the consumer's basic purpose drives for gain* – i.e. a stable *counterbalance* of **supply, demand,** and **price.**

About Market Equilibrium:

Principals and Concepts Important to Success

To an academic 'theory' based economist, the key word in 'market equilibrium' is 'equilibrium' – whether or not the consumer's demand, producer's supply, and market price factors have yet been *balanced* in a particular market.

To a productivity class economist – a real world producer – the key word in 'market equilibrium' is 'market'. This is about markets, not balancing acts. And there are *many* markets. There are markets *within* markets. There is a market, not only for *types* of products and services, but for each *specific* product and service within each type, for every quality and *utility* level for each product and service, for a singular producer's products and services, and even for consumer's *tastes, locations, income levels*, etc. all within *each* of those other markets.

And every single one of those markets has a point of equilibrium, where the price *holds* at a profitable – gainful – position, where the demand and the supply for it at that price is profitably sustained.

> A real world producer sees themselves *as a 'player' in that 'market'*
> *– the supplier.*

And a producer learns how to take advantage of that. A producer is *focused* on...
- marketing within the range of the consumer's *'willingness to pay'*;
- competing for their particular niche or share in their *own* target market [more on 'target' markets in Marketing]; and
- how to *disrupt* the market ...and create a *new* more profitable equilibrium, with *themselves* at the top of the competitive totem.

THE PRINCIPLES of RISK

Investments take many forms, whether the investment is in human beings, steel mills, or transmission lines for electricity. Risk is an inseparable part of these investments and others.
Author: Thomas Sowell: Sanford University; 'Basic Economics' - Basic Books Pub.,

About Risk:

Productivity Class Economic Theory Statement

All things economic involve some degree of *'exposure to the possibility of financial loss or other harm'* – economic *'risk'*. Risk, therefore, is a *derivative operating phenomenon* inherent to *all* economic activity.

'Degree of risk' is *variable per undertaking or venture* and can *always* be mitigated.

'Variance from normal' is the standard by which *'degree* of risk' is determined. And, per the nature of our basic purpose drive for gain, the greater the risk of loss – *the greater the variance from normal economic risk* – the greater the return on investment [ROI] must be in order to induce a producer or productive investor to attempt any economic undertaking.

There are no corresponding 'derivative operating controls' that *handle* or *mitigate* risk. Therefore, all solutions to *handle* and *mitigate* risk come from *organizational operating tactics*.

About This Section:
The number of economic **risks** are as many as there are types of **productivity**, and there are *counter measures* for every type of **risk**. Those **risks** and *counter measures* that will be presented here are chosen as thought to be the best for introducing the *concept* of **risk** in an economic *primer*, and those most commonly needed to be *known* and *understood* by both **organizing** and **working producers**.

About Risk:
an
Overview

IMPORTANT:
'All things economic begin with productivity.'
When properly utilized, these 'organizational operating tactics' for handling or mitigating risk allow many productivities to exist that, due to the risk, might not otherwise be able

**to survive at all and play their contributive role
in the economic strength of a culture.**

Due to the unpredictability of human wants and needs, human skills and disciplines, human judgements, capabilities, and intentions, the unpredictability of economic **competition**, the unpredictability of **resource** development, and of natural occurrences, *all things economic involve some degree of exposure to the possibility of economic loss or harm – risk*. **Risk**, therefore, is inherent to *all* economic undertakings or ventures.

'Degree of **risk**' from one undertaking to the next, even from one *type* of undertaking to the next, is *variable* and can be *mitigated*. However, there are no corresponding **derivative operating controls** that *handle* or *mitigate* risk. Therefore, all solutions to *handle* and *mitigate* risk come from **organizational operating tactics**, and skillful **risk management**.

'*Variance from normal*' is the standard by which '*degree* of **risk**' is determined. Since all economic undertakings have at least a '*normal*' amount of **risk**, economic **risk** is measured by the '*variance*' from whatever is considered 'normal business **risk**' for the undertaking. And the greater the **risk** of loss – the greater the *variance from normal business risk* – the greater the return on investment must be to induce a **producer** or **investor** to attempt any venture.

There are as many types of **risk** as there are **productivities**. A full discussion of all or most of them is beyond the scope an economic primer. All of these **risks** have a broad spectrum of **investment** methods and **organizational** tactical mitigators – each of which can become a **specialized business** that handles or protects against each type of **risk**.

Working producers also have their own sets of **risks** [employment risks] including *risks of injury, job loss, loss of household breadwinner, health and life risks*, **unethical employer management** *tactics, shifting skills markets*, etc. All of which have methods of mitigation.

About Risk:

Characteristics and General Factors

Risk is a Derivative Operating Phenomenon

At the **basic purpose** level, human *wants* and *needs* can be quite predictable. People are always going to need food, clothing, shelter, etc. And people will always *want, need*, and be *drawn to* gimmicky devices, entertainment, sports, etc. in following their drive to *pursue the dynamics of living* and *improve their living conditions*. Very predictable.

However, *which* particular **products** and **services consumers** are drawn to, or *types* of **products** and **services**, or even *which **producers** **consumers*** are drawn to, are always shifting and advancing through time in one *unpredictable* direction or another.

Further, there is also the unpredictability of economic **competition** and **competitive** *discovery* and *development*. The latest **discovery**, latest **invention**, the latest **innovation** is always a heartbeat away. And with them a shift in **consumer** and sometimes even economic direction can send into a tailspin any **investment** in what is suddenly 'yesterday's **productivity**'.

Therefore, in *all* material endeavors, *all things economic involve some degree of exposure to the possibility of economic loss or harm – **risk**.*

About Risk:

Principles and Concepts Important to Success

General Risk Management

Risk management is far more complex than a primer can fully cover. However, below are the *general concepts* of the process of **risk** management:

   o   Assess the **risk**: determine the *type* of **risk**; the *probability ratio* of actual **risk** occurrence; probable **profits** of the endeavor; possible **losses** from the **risks**;

   o   Determine the **administrative** steps and amount of **management** control possible over the undertaking itself, including the **management** and **productivity** requirements necessary for success, and… *what mitigations of the **risks** are available to you and their costs;? is an outside source required?; can it be handled in house **administratively**?, etc.*

   o   Skillful **management** of the venture itself and the mitigations of the determined **risks**.

It may sound simple, but it can get quite involved and complicated. Most institutions that are in the **business** of mitigating each different type of **risk**, however, have the entire process down to a finely tuned science.

Organizational Operating Tactics for Handling Risk…
[***business** practices that handle or mitigate **risk**]*

There are no corresponding ***derivative* operating controls** that *handle* or *mitigate* risk. Therefore, all solutions to *handle* and *mitigate* risk come from ***organizational* operating tactics** – the *primary* methods of which are:

   o   '**sharing risk between multiple investors**' [*insurance, stocks and bonds, etc.*],

- o 'spreading risk over multiple investments' [called 'diversifying' risk],
- o 'requiring larger profits for investing in risk' [called 'speculation'], and
- o 'selling risk to a speculator or other type of investor' [called 'hedging'].

The above are all *organizational* operating tactics. These means by which to *handle* and *mitigate* risk are *created, organized*, and *operated* by **administrative producers** in order to **manage** each type of **risk** in their particular circumstances and **productivities**. And if you examine them closely, you will notice that each of the four *primary* means of mitigating **risk** listed above are simply means of '*diluting*' the **risk** and nothing more…

There Is '*Diluting Risk*' and There Is '*Real World Risk Mitigation*' All Else Are Variations of The Two

Dilution of Risk – Spreading, Sharing, Diversifying The Risk

Anything that *spreads* or *shares* **risk** is actually applying the **organizational tactic** of *diluting the risk*. '*Diluting*' spreads out or shares the **risk** among multiple **consumers** or *investors*, thus *diluting* impact on any one person: *Health insurance* policy holders *share* the **costs** of the entire groups health difficulties – *reducing* the **risk** to any one individual or family [*insurance* is also a 'hedge' – see below]; *Diversification* of a portfolio spreads out the *investments* of any individual or fund – *reducing* the **risk** of loss by any one investment; *Stocks* and *bonds*, intended to *raise financial capital* or liquidate the **value** of a business into **profit**, also serves to *dilute* **risk** by the spreading the number of 'shares' of the company among a larger number of owners.

Speculators, although it may not appear so on the surface, also *dilute* **risk** by *diversifying*. *Speculators* invest in *multiple* high **risk**, high **profit** investments. By investing in multiple ventures at a time, a speculator *diversifies* his or her portfolio [at the same time 'hedging' their risks – see below]. In addition, speculators *calculate* the **risks**, they do not actually *gamble*. That way the *aggregate of investments* in a portfolio are, overall, likely to **profit**, at least modestly. In this way the investments don't all need to pay off big. A *few* well paying high **risk**, high **profit investments** can sometimes make an **investor** wealthy enough to make up for all other losses.

Hedging – in the simplest case, selling a **risky** investment to a speculator so that a *lesser amount* of *guaranteed* **profit** can be ensured – actually helps *diversify* and thereby *dilute* **risk**.

Entrepreneurial Investments

Investment in **entrepreneurial** enterprises can be the most **risky**, especially when the undertaking is a new *type* of **product** or **service**. But those who **invest** in such enterprises are no more gamblers than speculators [and many *are* speculators]. They are skilled in assessing all the various aspects of entrepreneurial economic **risks** and potential for actual **profits**: determining which **products** and **services** have merit, and **skilled** in **administration** and **management** themselves, they know when they have a sufficiently **educated** and **skilled entrepreneur** in front of them. They crunch the numbers and all the necessary factors, and only when all the figures and factors 'add up' do they invest. ...and then, they also *diversify*.

And therein lies the final two, also vital factors in **managing** and *mitigating* risk:

- *'accurate risk assessment'*, and
- *'skilled administration of risk management'*

Also, *'return on investment' has to be commensurate with the degree of risk* in order to entice a **producer** and **productive investor** to attempt the venture.

Real World Mitigation – Actual Reduction of The Risk Itself

So what do we mean by *real world mitigation*? All of the above are *mitigations* of possible financial loss on **investments** that are by their nature, or can become, at **risk** for some *loss*. However, the *best* way to handle **risk** is to, if possible, handle the *actual source of the risk itself* – determine what makes an investment **risky**, and *eliminate that*.

Adverse situations in **productivity**, **education**, **resources**, **trade**, etc. are actually better *mitigated* with better **administration** [including **governance**]. Intelligent, well thought out **management** of **people**, **resources**, and **productive** activities is the best *real world mitigation* of the **risks** of economic **productivity** and **trade**.

For other types of **risk** eliminations, there are **inventions** and **innovations**. **Inventions** and **innovations** are often created *for the specific purpose of mitigating or even eliminating 'real world' life, economic, and **productivity** risks*. [Examples: seat belts and anti-lock braking systems, on the whole, reduce auto accident injury **risks** and, therefore, time out of work, loss of bread winner, or insurance and disability payouts; Robotics, besides reducing **costs** and speeding up **production**, also reduces or eliminates the kinds of human errors that can ruin the **quality** or **quantity** of an entire day's **production line** output; etc.]

THE PRINCIPLES of CAPITALIZATION

Capital flows to incentives. **If you disrupt the incentives, you disrupt the flows of capital.**
Author: Anthony Scaramucci, UP w/David Gura, 9 Nov. 2019 [italics mine (second sentence paraphrased)]

TERMINOLOGY NOTICE: *Do not confuse* the two usages of the term '**capital**':
- '**Capital**' as a single type of **resource** – *fabricated tools, equipment, etc.* necessary for **productivity**.
- '**Capital**' as a general term for *all* **resources** – *material, capital* (including *'financial'*), and *human*.

About Capitalization / Capitalizing:

Productivity Class Economic Theory Statement

Capitalizing is: *'providing or acquiring the resources necessary to produce or consume'.* **Capitalizing** *productivity*, **and capitalizing** *consumption* **is each slightly different from the other, but interactive and supportive of the other as inter-dependent operating dynamics:**

Productivity requires the investment *of all three types* **of resources: material, capital, and human.** *Providing or acquiring those resources – the total 'capital' – or the currency to obtain them, is the 'capitalizing' of productivity.*

Consumption requires *productivity* **or** *trade currency* **– one must produce what they need to consume or they must trade for it.** *Providing or acquiring the resources or the trade currency – the 'capital' – necessary to consume is 'capitalizing' consumption.*

The investment of resources to capitalize productivity or consumption can be in the form of *the resources themselves* **or it can be in the form of the** *currency required to obtain those resources* [aka 'financial capital'].

Providing the capital necessary for production or consumption is a *naturally occurring dynamically efficacious* **method of** *driving, manipulating,* **and** *managing* **their successful operation. It is, therefore, a 'derivative operating** *control'.*

However, the 'for profit investment of enabling or funding producers and

consumers' is valid *only* when contained within *ethical operational frameworks diligently enforced*. Unethical application of capitalizing inverts currency flows and can collapse an economy.

About Capitalization / Capitalizing:
an
Overview

TERMINOLOGY NOTICE II: Capital is a widely utilized term. In **productivity class** economics, we are only concerned with the **dynamic operating control** of **capitalizing productivity** and **consumption** – its basic *causation* and *application* principles.

Per the **second primary axiom**, all **productivity** requires **capitalization** – the provision of '*any and all of the* **resources** *necessary to* **produce** *and deliver a* **product** *or* **service**'.

One of the *fundamentals* of a **free market** system is *lenders* or **investors** *providing the* **capital** *for* **productivity** *or* **consumption**, *and requiring a fee or a portion of the* **profits** *to do so.* A **derivative dynamic operating** *control* is born. Born also is the '**capitalist**' – *a 'for profit' provider of* **capital**.

The practice of for-profit capitalizing of productivity and consumption is likely the single most powerful dynamic operating control in our micro-economic bag of tools. When **ethically** applied, it has **produced** more prosperity in human civilization than any other economic practice ever employed to advance the **productivity** and **basic purpose** success for entire economic populaces. [Possible exception: '**intellectual property rights**', an **organizational** strategy or tactic.]

However, applied *unethically*, outside of well worked out *ethical operating frameworks*, by the greedy, incompetent, ill intended, or self-serving, it can produce as much misery as any **inverted** economic practice. **Capitalizing** is a magnet for those who would **invert** the flows of **currency** toward themselves at the expense of others. Without ethical frameworks, **inverted capitalizing** can eventually **invert** an *entire* economic system, and eventually *collapse* it.

About Capitalization / Capitalizing:

Characteristics and General Factors

Capitalizing is *providing* or *acquiring* the **resources** necessary for *productivity* or *consumption*. *Period.*

'Free Enterprise' or *'Free Markets'* Is The System, Not *'Capitalism'*.

Ethically frameworked and enforced *'free enterprise' is the system* we operate in, *not* **'capitalism'**. **Capital***izing* is a **derivative operating** *dynamic*. We do not have a **capitalizing** *system* any more than we have a **risk** *system*, **supply** *system*, **price** *system*, etc. These are **operating** *dynamics*, not **operating** *systems*. And they function most effectively in the **ethically** enforced **operational** framework of a *'free enterprise system'*.

Capitalizing Usually Comes in Three Forms:

- **Retained Earnings** [i.e. *'saved'* from prior economic activities]

  Utilizing one's own financial capital to start a business; or income, from the operation of the current business, retained [saved] for further investment in that same business.

  Usually, **'retained earnings'** applies to the current **business's** or **organization's investment** 'savings' fund. However, when an entrepreneur begins a business using his or her own financial capital, this is still considered **'retained earnings'** because they **saved** it [retained it] from their prior **employment** or prior **business** earnings.

- **Credit**

  Credit is the term usually used when capital is provided as a 'loan' or in the form of a predetermined 'line of credit' [to be drawn upon as needed], *and the principle amount is paid back in one of two ways: a) a lump sum at an agreed upon later date – while a profit of an 'interest' percentage is paid in monthly or quarterly payments, or b) in incremental payments paying it back over an agreed upon time – with a profit of an interest percentage added to each of the payments.*

  For productivity: Loans are usually secured by an ownership percentage of the company or a company's **capital resources** *and other assets.*

  For consumption: Loans are usually secured by the item purchased, if warranted, or unsecured and reliant upon credit worthiness of the **consumer***.*

- **Investment**

  Investment is the term generally used when providing capital to produce a product or service *for an agreed upon share of the profits paid at agreed upon intervals, and the investment amount is to be paid back or renewed at an agreed upon later date or paid back in the form of ownership shares of the organization* [yeah, that's a lot, but if you reread it carefully, it's pretty simple]. *Investment is usually secured by a percentage ownership of the company* [aka *shares* or *stock*] *or a company's capital resources and other assets* [aka 'collateral'].

IMPORTANT INVESTMENT NOTE: 'Compound interest' or 'compound return' noun *For our purposes...* to add the interest income earned from a financial investment back into the amount invested [aka the 'principle' investment] so to collect the next round of interest on the now *larger principal* amount – done continuously on a long term investment [remember 'turnover'?]. [See **Currency**, page 92]

Capitalizing Productivity and Consumption

Providing the **capital** necessary for **production** or **consumption** is a **trade** of '*usage*-for-a-*fee*' and is a *dynamically efficacious* method of *driving, manipulating*, and *managing* the successful operation of the twelve **primary operating dynamics**.

Capitalizing *productivity*, and **capitalizing** *consumption* is each slightly different from the other, but interactive and supportive of the other. **Capitalizing productivity** provides *needed* and *wanted* **products** and **services** – *supply* – for **consumption**, and **capitalizing consumption** promotes the 'demand' for **production** of those **products** and **services**.

The concept of **capitalizing** is simple: *Investors – mostly private – provide financial capital resources to a producer or consumer for a fee or a share of the profit. That's it! There is nothing more to all this than that. A very simple concept.*

Until, of course, we **organize** it. Remember **organizing**? At first, **organizing** *simplifies*. Soon, however, everything '*develops more fully, expands exponentially, and becomes ever more complex and sophisticated*' – and if done right, '*more efficient, more productive, and, most especially, more consistent*'. And since **capitalizing productivity** and **consumption** is such a *powerful* **dynamic operating control**, '*fully developed, exponentially expanded, complex and sophisticated*' is what we get. [Done '*right*'? Well...]

Productivity Investing:

'A SECURITY' / SECURITIES noun *For our purposes...* **Stocks, bonds, collateral agreements are 'secured' investments and therefore called 'securities'. e.g. A 'stock'** *is proportional ownership 'securing'* **investment in a company; A 'bond' is** a loan *'secured'* by legal rights. Each instrument is legally binding and guaranteed by *laws* and the *issuer*, and therefore considered a 'secured' investment.

SHARES noun *For our purposes...* an ownership 'share' of a corporation or other valuable asset that entitles the holder a share of the profits proportional to the number of shares the corporation is divided into [*share* of **profits** are called 'dividends' as the **profits** are *divided* amongst all share-holders].

STOCK / STOCKS noun *For our purposes...* The *unit of ownership interest in a corporate entity* is referred to as *'share'* – you own 'x' amount of 'shares' of the economic entity [the corporation] and are therefore entitled to a proportional 'share' of the profits and to vote on company's directional policies. 'Stock' is a more general term referring to the *owning of shares* and means you have 'stock' in that company. The term 'stocks' usually refers to owning *shares* in *more than one* company [i.e. if you own *shares* in only one company, you own *a* stock in that company].

Most often, businesses will sell **shares** of **stock** so they can further **capitalize** the business without having to pay back the **investment** sum; or to sell a portion of the **company's value** to take personal **profit** from what they've built. Stock owners [**investors**], in order to liquidate their *stock*, have to sell their *shares* to some other **investor** – they cannot be 'cashed in' with the company. [Most **investors** buy **stock** expecting the **value** of the shares to go up. When **values (prices)** go up, they sell those shares to make a **profit** on the higher **price**. Until they do, they collect *quarterly dividends* – portions of the **profits** proportionally *divided* up between those who own 'shares' of the company].

BONDS (Etymonline.com*) noun Legalistic sense "an [legal] instrument binding one to pay a sum to another" [as in creating a 'bond' between two economic entities] ...1590s. (NOAD*) 2. An agreement with legal force [creating a 'bond' between issuer and purchaser, 'binding' the issuer to fulfill the agreement]; in particular, a certificate issued by a public company or a government promising to repay borrowed money plus interest at a specified time.

A **bond** is just a **loan** *from* the purchaser *to* the **company** *in the form of a certificate* – which is a document that '**bonds**' the company to the owner of the certificate. The **investor** purchasing the **bond** is **loaning** money to the company *for a fee* of a predetermined interest rate paid at predetermined intervals per the certificate agreement [quarterly, semi-annually, etc.]. At the end of the term of the **bond**, the company buys the **bond** back – i.e. pays off the **loan**.

Issuing **bonds** is another way a **company** can *borrow money* to raise **financial resources**. A **bond** allows a **company** to borrow more **money** – via *many* smaller **investors** [diluting the **risk**] – than it can from a bank or other financial institution. A **bond** can also be sold by one **investor** to other **investors** just like a **stock**. Also, a company can '*buy back*' [pay off] the **bond** at any time if it wishes, *unlike* a **stock**.

OPERATING CAPITAL [aka 'Rotating' or 'Roll-over' or 'turn-over' Capital] noun

For our purposes... **Financial capital used to operate the day to day productivity of the business – usually in the form of a line of credit drawn from and paid back monthly as revenue from that productivity comes in. Every month it is borrowed and paid back – plus interest – over and over again ['rolled over'] to** *operate* **the business.**

Banks, financial institutions, and private investors provide **credit** for **operating capital**. The degree of **risk** determines the *fee percentage* – the **cost** of the use of the **operating capital**; [*The riskier the investment, the more return required to entice an investor to invest or a lender to lend.*] **Costs** and contract stipulations must be added to **profit margins** and **administrative** procedures.

Now for the Marketplace

And so, we build a **marketplace** for buying and selling **stocks**, **bonds**, and every type of *financial instrument* we can think up – and, boy, can we think 'em up. And we simply call it the **'stock market'** – a **marketplace** where 'stocks', 'bonds', 'currencies', and other financial instruments are **traded** [bought and sold] from **corporations** to public, public to public, and oftentimes public to **corporations**.

Got all this? No? That's ok, this is just a primer.

About Capitalization / Capitalizing:

Principles and Concepts Important to Success

Funding a **business**, as stated earlier, usually takes two kinds of **capitalization**: The first is *'start-up'* or *'expansion'* **investment**; and the second is month-to-month *'operating'* **capital** to fund everyday **operations**. When making a decision to **invest**, **investors** must judge the *viability*, *profitability*, and *rate of return on investment*, etc. – a whole 'clockwork' of criteria.

This looks like a cumbersome set of chores, but *an experienced investor can 'eyeball' it all very quickly*. An inexperienced **entrepreneur**, however, would have to use a competently prepared outline as their first *preparation checklist* to prepare their approach to **investors**. The second checklist will be the one their **investors** or bank makes up for them to further do.

Consumer Credit: Pro's and Con's

There are many types of **consumer credit**: *mortgages, auto loans, furniture and appliance financing, credit cards, personal loans*, etc. Each has its own characteristics and most often different *interest rates*, different payment schedules, collateral requirements, etc. Although most **consumers** only want to know, 'How much do I pay a month, and how long do I have to pay it?', it is vitally important to know all of the *responsibilities* of **consumer** *credit* and **consumer** *debt*. A **consumer** should know how to take advantage of every type of **consumer capitalizing service** available – **consumer** *credit* – while at the same time avoiding the traps and pitfalls of **consumer** *debt*.

Consumers must be ever vigilant of *expenses*:

Every **household** is as much an **organized** *economic entity* as any **business**. The use of **credit** *adds* to the **costs** of every purchase. Good handling of **credit** has advantages that can add dynamic dimensions to one's **basic purpose** pursuits. Poor handling of **credit** can literally choke off one's **basic purpose** pursuits and destroy one's overall economic conditions.

Income to debt ratio [including vehicle payments]:

The 'income to debt ratio' is your '*monthly payment* vs. *monthly income* percentage'. At the time of this writing *monthly payments* at 36% of *monthly income* is considered an acceptable ratio. Over 36% reduces a **consumer's** ability to adjust to temporary adverse economic conditions, and so also reduces **credit** worthiness. Under 36% increases a **consumer's** ability to adjust to temporary adverse conditions, and therefore, also increases **credit** worthiness.

You need to understand this better than can be expressed in a primer. This is to initiate [i.e. 'prime'] your awareness. It is up to you to **educate** yourself fully about the handling of **credit resources**.

Economic Entrapment:

Legalized or unregulated '**consumer** entrapment' tactics by unscrupulous **credit** companies are abundant. **Unethical** lenders can easily 'entrap' *uneducated* or *undisciplined* **consumers** into borrowing at *interest rates and amounts* that can leave the **consumer** 'trapped' in a position of *perpetual borrowing* and *perpetual payments* – living in poverty or filing for **bankruptcy**.

There is, of course, inadvertent *self*-entrapment. This happens when through **credit** ignorance, lack of spending discipline, misjudging one's own future circumstances, etc. a person over-extends their **credit** balances or payment obligations and becomes entrapped in much the same way as described above. For the **consumer**, the end result is the same.

Bankruptcy:

Economically, **bankruptcy** is a state of '*insolvency*', *the inability to meet one's debt obligations*. *Legally*, **bankruptcy** is '*a legal process wherein one can appeal to the courts for relief from one's creditors due to an entrapment or* *insolvent condition'.*

There are several different types of **bankruptcy**, but what we mean mostly by 'filing **bankruptcy**' is appealing to the court for a legal *discharge of all debts owed* – secured and unsecured – leaving the **consumer** free to begin again.

No More Lender's 'Credit Judgement':

Today things are a little different than they used to be. Today a credit application is now usually sent electronically to a credit 'rating' company [formerly a 'credit bureau']. The credit rating company *'computer scores'* the application using an 'algorithm' of two to three hundred credit determining factors. The end result is a **credit** *'score'*. Loan 'officers' or 'committees' no longer make the judgement. Welcome to the twenty first century.

Consumer Credit Collections:

One of the most difficult, and distasteful, aspects of being a 'lender' is that one must also be a 'collector'. Regardless of how careful a lender is in determining **credit** worthiness, not everyone is going to pay their **debts** on time, or sometimes *at all*. Some of the *primary* reasons for **consumers** defaulting on debts are...

- divorce and the splitting of **income** to support two **households**;
- unexpected illness or inability to work;
- loss of primary or ancillary **employment**, or small **business** failure;
- over-extending **consumer debt** or uninsured medical debt.

These are the unpredictable changes in economic circumstances that commonly overwhelm **consumers** or that temporarily knock them out of their normal economic conditions enough to cause default on their debt obligations. Usually, but not always, when such circumstances occur, **consumer** and **creditor** can work together to resolve such conditions over time. When *either party* is uncooperative, the *lender* goes into *'collection mode'*. When they do, very specific **ethical** practices, required by law come into play.

THE PRINCIPLES OF INCENTIVIZING

Positive market incentives <u>operating in the public interest</u> are too few and far between, and are also up against a seemingly never-ending expansion of <u>perverse incentives and lobbying</u>. Author: Dr. Mohammed 'Mo' Ibrahim

About Incentivizing:

Productivity Class Economic Theory Statement

Basic purpose *needs* and *wants* compel into existence the five primary axioms and twelve elemental activities of economics. Basic purpose drive, therefore, is the *fundamental motivating force* driving *all* economic activity.

The first incentive is the basic purpose 'need to *consume*'. The need to *consume* incentivizes *productivity*. The next *productivity* incentive is the 'drive to *gain*'. The basic purpose need to *consume* and the drive to *gain* are the *primary* incentives driving all economic *productivity*.

Almost all *economic* incentives – consumptive and productive – are basic purpose based – i.e. economic incentives appeal most to producers and consumers when they are in the form of *gaining the material requirements* necessary to achieve *improved basic purpose conditions*, actual or perceived, toward themselves or others.

However, *anything* that motivates a human being to make economically applied *decisions* or taking economically applied *actions*, if ethical and *perceived* to be of value, can be a valid incentive if they produce *economically* applied activity – i.e. incentives usually considered *non-economic in nature*, utilized to produce *economic* activity, are also *economic* incentives.

Incentives induce producers and consumers to *action* on the *primary operating dynamics* and naturally *drive, manipulate,* and *manage* economic entities and conditions. Therein lies the basis of 'incentives' as a 'derivative operating dynamic *control*'.

About Incentivizing:
an
Overview

Anything that motivates a human being to decide upon ethical

*productive or consumptive action, is a valid incentive
if it is itself ethical and of value to the recipient.*

Material **incentives**, then, are not the *only* **incentives** that *drive, manipulate, or manage 'materially* **productive** *activity'.* Any **consumer's** *pursuit on the dynamics of living,* requiring a material aspect to pursue it, can be utilized as an economic **incentive.**

Further, economically speaking, *anything* that motivates a human being to taking any action that *causes* or *supports* economic activity can be a valid *economic* **incentive,** *even if the* **incentive** *is not economically* **gainful** *for the person motivated to take the actions* [e.g. basic human values, environmental conditions, the well-being of others, animal rights, status and recognition, etc.]. If they create *materially* **productive** *activity,* they are valid *economic* **incentives.**

About Incentivizing:

Characteristics and General Factors

The Two *Primary* Productivity Incentives

"The first incentive is the basic purpose 'need to *consume*' –
the need to *consume* incentivizes *productivity*.
The next *productivity* incentive is the 'drive to *gain*'."

All **productivity** begins with the **basic purpose** need to **consume.** As the scale of this expands into an advanced economic system, it is the **consumptive** *needs* and *wants* of the **consumer '*markets*'** that **incentivize** the '*productivity*' of **producers** [in their own drive for **profit** and **gain**].

All further primary axioms [axioms two through five] exist to improve and expand upon 'produce' – productivity – in order to better serve consumptive needs and wants.

Therefore, in advanced **'market'** economies, the economic community's need to **consume** for basic **purpose** *needs* and *wants* becomes a **producer's** 'consumer market incentives' to be utilized for **marketing** their **products** and **services** – while their own **gain** remains their *primary* **incentive** to **produce.**

About Incentivizing:

Principles and Concepts Important to Success

Targeting Incentives Toward Accomplishing Intended Goals and Purposes

There are two ways in which *every* **incentive** *must* be 'targeted':

- *Achieving, accomplishing, or delivering the promise of the stated* **incentive** *for the recipient*; and
- *Aiming the* **incentivized** *action to contribute to the offering party's purpose – directly or indirectly.*

For what should appear obvious, both are required to attain success:

Continued motivation depends upon...
realization of the incentive's promised outcome by the recipient;
and
accomplishment of the intended outcome by the offering party.

Marketing incentives:

Simply put, a **marketing incentive** is any *offer, appeal, feature, provision, encouraging tangible*, etc. that *motivates* or *encourages* a **consumer** to purchase or **trade** for a **product** or **service**. Such **incentives** are used to ***market products*** and **services**, and can be offered in *any* form: a philanthropy project tied to **sales**; a brand **consumers** desire to be associated with; **price** incentives; etc.

Pricing Incentives:

The effect that **price** has on economic activity cannot be overstated. From allocation of **resources** to **profit margins** to the general **marketing** of **products** and **services**, **pricing** is a full **derivative operating dynamic** of its own. And, as delineated earlier, the **dynamics** of **price** and **pricing** can be utilized as both **phenomenon** and **control**. The impact of **pric*ing*** as an economic incentive manifests its **operating** *control* characteristic.

Pricing designed to appeal to the **consumers** need or desire to *expend as little of their* **currency resources** *as possible* for their **products** or **services** has *a universal appeal for all* **consumers**. At the same time, **pricing** is key to **profit margins**, and the successful **producer** must skillfully balance the two aspects. As a result, **pricing incentives** are a ***primary operating tool*** of **producers**, and a ***priority incentive*** for all **consumers**.

Credit as Marketing Incentive:

Credit as **consumer capitalization** is also a full **derivative operating dynamic** of its own – a **dynamic** *control* just as powerful as **pricing**. *Credit provides financial capital for the* **producer** *and* **consumer** *both.*

As such, it provides a powerful **incentive** for **consumers** to *buy now* and *make* *payments over time, for a fee* [*interest*] rather than waiting to 'save up' for a **product** or **service**. Often enough, also, **credit** even allows a **consumer** to buy when they might not otherwise be able to buy at all.

For the **producer, credit** as a **marketing incentive** is a *powerhouse* **dynamic**. If a **producer** had to wait until a **consumer** saved up enough money to make a purchase, or lost **consumer** sales from those that can't afford to buy at all without **credit**, *at the time of this writing a good half of existing* **product producers** *would go out of business within weeks*.

Productivity Incentives:

Productivity incentives are, simply put, any *offer, provision, encouraging tangible*, etc. of enough **value** to **working producers, organized producers**, and **productive investors** to induce increased **productivity** along *any goal* or *purpose*. They are used to get **products** or **services** *made, delivered*, or **traded** [or to advance any other **organized productivity**].

Incentives to produce are generally successful in the form of
tangible reward
provided only when a *predetermined standard of productivity* is achieved.

Intangible reward, as those often used in **marketing incentives** [*fair trade practices, environmental responsibility*, or any other **consumer valued** purpose or ideal], are rarely effective as **productivity incentives**. *Status* and *recognition* rewards, such as '**producer** of the month' and other 'merit badge' types of reward are only good for morale. **Working** or **administrative producers** require *desirable* or other *valuable tangible reward* to increase **productivity** [*special privileges, pay raise percentages, extra vacation days, promotions*, etc.].

Working producers produce better with *ethically administered, well planned, graduated* **income incentives**, and **organizing producers** are better **incentivized** by wider **profit margins** – which also translates to **income incentives**. '**Produce** more and earn more' is usually the most effective **productivity incentive**.

Incentivizing Poor Producers:

More often than not **incentives** to **produce** more should be *withheld* from poor **producers**. Every **organization** should have a *well stated standard range* of **productivity** within which a **working producer** or **executive producer** should be **producing** as a *valued, accepted,* and *secure* **employee**. **Producers** who do not come up to these *basic company standards* should not be offered **incentives** to come up to standards –**employment** is the incentive [reward]. They should be required to participate in whatever remedial **training** or activities are required to get them up to *basic company standards* before any **incentive** program should apply, or face dismissal. The **incentive** to retain **employment** should be the only **incentive** for a poor, substandard **producer**.

Career Incentives

One of the best **incentives** for **productivity** is *gradiently increased* **responsibility** *and* **income** *positions – promote-from-within advancement.* Which means the best and most appropriate **working producer incentive** is a growing **organization** with *actual, achievable advancement to some level of better paying* **productivity** *or* **responsibility**, **administered** by standards of **merit**.

For those **working producers** that do not have the potential for **management** advancement or higher technology advancement, the best **incentives** are based on **employee training** that improves and expands other types of *same level* **expertise** or *number of tasks the working producer can do* – but only in **productivity** that benefits the **profitability** of the **organization**. [e.g. **apprenticeship** programs, industry standard **training** programs, etc.].

Finally, proper **industry standard training**, *especially with industry honored certification or qualifying degree*, improves the impact of any system of **productivity incentives** for both the **organized producer** and the **working producer**. The **organized producer** gains *confirmation of* **quality** *and usefulness of* **training**, and the **working producer** gains an *established level of increased personal* **productive value** – a certified training status – a sort of permanent training certification that establishes qualifications for better pay anywhere.

Business and Investment Incentives:

Profit is the **incentive** for all **business** and **investment productivity**. The number one **incentive** to **produce** is **profit**, as **profit** serves the entire spectrum from *the most essential levels of* **basic purpose** to the *upper limits of* **gain**.

Profit is associated primarily with the **organizing producers** [trades, professions, small businesses, companies, corporations, etc.], but the **working producer** 'profits', also. He or she **invests** their expertise in **trade** for an agreed upon weekly, bi-weekly, or monthly **profit** [income; paycheck; etc.]. They are, however, **incentivized** and remunerated differently.

THE PRINCIPLES of MARKETING

If the circus is coming to town and you paint a sign saying, "Circus Coming to the Fairground Saturday," that's *advertising*. If you put the sign on the back of an elephant and walk it into town, that's *promotion*. If the elephant walks through the mayor's flower bed, that's *publicity*. And if you get the mayor to laugh about it, that's *public relations*. If the town's citizens go to the circus, you show them the many entertainment booths, explain how much fun they'll have spending money at the booths, answer their questions and ultimately, they spend a lot at the circus, that's *sales*.
Author: P. T. Barnum

About Marketing:

Productivity Class Economic Theory Statement

Consumer 'basic purpose' needs and wants for the products and services produced by others *drives* the primary operating dynamic of *trade*.

However, *in order for trade to occur,*
a)   products and services must *have* the needed and wanted attributes consumers will trade for. Then,
b)   the 'orientation of consumers' using *specific communications* in *specific communicative forms* is required ['*what*' is communicated and '*how*' it is communicated], effectively utilized to
   1)   notify consumers that the product or service is *available* and *desirable*,
   2)   to draw the consumer to the product or service and its trading point, and, finally,
c)   to convince and help the consumer *to complete the trade transaction.*

This entire aggregate of activities is *required* for the successful trade in the *marketplace* – hence the term '*marketing*'. 'Marketing' is, therefore, an *operating dynamic* that *drives, manipulates,* and *manages* trade. It is, therefore, a 'derivative operating dynamic *control*'.

[In fact, if you add '*consumer basic purpose* research', '*communicative response research*', and '*transaction completion*' to the P. T. Barnum quote above, you get a good idea of **marketing** and why *effective coordination* of its activities is required.]

About Marketing:
an
Overview

The Driving Force of *Trade* is *Basic Purpose* Needs and Wants

Trade requires that a **product** or **service** be **produced** with the **basic purpose** attributes the **consumer** *needs* and *wants*, the **consumer** be made aware of the **product** or **service** and its attributes, and also that **trade** for it is available. Once the **product** or **service** is created by a **producer**, the **consumer** must then be *communicated to* in a manner [or sequence of manners] that *leads to a trade*.

**Therefore, marketing actually begins
with the development of the product or service
and doesn't end until the sale transaction.**

Even at the most basic level [familial, tribal, inter-tribal], all **trade** beyond a two person agreement to make a 'swap' involves **marketing**...

- **Producing** a **tradable product** or **service**;
- Bringing it to where it can be displayed, promoted, and offered for **trade** [**marketed**];
- Haggling [sales] over **price** [**money** or other **tradable** items];
- Closing the **sale** and completing the transaction.

As **trade** expands and becomes more sophisticated...

- 'bringing it to where it can be displayed and offered' becomes more sophisticated '*distribution*';
- 'notifying consumers of its availability and desirability' becomes *advertising, promotion, public repute*, and eventually *publicity* [even if only 'word of mouth'] – '**marketing**'; and
- 'haggling over **price**' and 'completing the transaction' becomes '**sales**'.

Later, '*marketing research*' is added to ensure more effective application of these fundamentals – all driven by **consumer basic purpose** *needs* and *wants* and the drive of **producers** to **gain**.

Here Enters The 'Organized' or 'Organizing' Producer...

As inter-tribal **trade** becomes centered around a single **trading** location, a '*market*', **producers** quickly begin to '**organize**' and '**specialize**' in specific **products** and **services** to **trade** as a method to fulfill their own *needs* and *wants*. **Employment** becomes common, and soon after, a **currency** becomes an accepted medium of exchange. It happens in *all* human communities.

When these conditions evolve, **organizing producers** begin to *flourish* and *prosper* – and along with them **working producers** and whole communities.

They do so by learning how to '*orient*' their **products** and **services**, their *presentations*, and their *communications* to '*serve*' and '*appeal to*' the **consumers** in their *marketplace* – i.e. '**marketing**' their **products** and **services**.

Marketing has Two Meanings to an Organizing Producer

The more *general* meaning of **marketing** is simply '*doing the business of symbiotic exchange in the marketplace*': *successful creation of a product or service that meets the consumer's needs and wants [consumer demand], placing it into the marketplace [supplying it to the consumer] where it can sell at maximum volume at maximum price, and generate the maximum profit.* That is the purpose of an **organized** commercial **business**, and the *general* meaning of '**marketing**' to an **organized producer**.

The more *specific* meaning of '**marketing**' to an **organizing producer** is its *primary* meaning [and its meaning here]: the *operating* **dynamic** of '**marketing**' – i.e. *orientation of* **product** *and* **consumer**, *promoting and presenting the* **product** *to the* **consumer**, and *completing the sale transaction* – taken together, that's the '*operation*' of **marketing**.

It is this ***organized operating dynamic*** aspect that makes for successful **trade**.

About Marketing:

Characteristics and General Factors

The need to **trade** for **basic purpose** *needs* and *wants* and the striving for **gain** compels the employment of an 'aggregate set of activities' that, *when in coordinated operation*, coalesce into the single **operating dynamic** of: '*the orientation of* **products** *and* **services** *to the* **consumer**, **consumer** *orientation to the* **products** *and* **services**, *and sale transactions*' – '**marketing**'.

Read the P. T. Barnum quote at the beginning of this section to see how each activity *coordinates and flows from one to the other*. Then from that description, consider each of the following *very basic* activities coordinated to **operate** [*function*] as a *single* activity:

- **Consumer 'Basic Purpose' Research [*before* and *after* purchase]**
  Research that determines actual **consumer** *needs* and *wants*, best design and presentation [appearance], **consumer** 'friendliness' [ease] of utility, acceptable pricing, etc. required in the **product** or **service** to generate the most **profitable sales**.
- **Produce the needed and wanted product or service**

This is not actually a **marketing** activity. It is the physical **producing** of the **product** or **service** *based upon* the above **marketing** *research*. It is the **consumer** desirable **product** or **service** *result* of the **marketing** research above.

- **Communicative Response Research [*before* and *after* purchase]**
  Determining 'what' to say and 'how' to say it for best **consumer** response: Proper *placing* of the **product** or **service** in the proper **market**; *attracting* the **consumer**; *drawing* the **consumer** in; *selling* the **product** or **service**; *completing the transaction* [**sale**] *and acquiring the **revenue**.*

NOTE: *The various methodologies and depth of knowledge and skills available to do the following are great and broad. **Marketing** is a complete **profession** unto itself and often may have an entirely different approach than you will find here in this primer. Think of this as a general orientation of the basic concepts.*

- **Advertising:**
  Basically this is simple awareness *'notices'* and *'announcements'* [signs, banners, emails, cards, and notices, etc.] designed to *attract* or *interest* **consumers** to the *existence* and *availability* of the **product** or **service**. The intent is two-fold: *a)* to *notify* already interested buyers of the availability of the **product** or **service** for purchase; and *b)* to *arouse* interest or curiosity of **consumers** within that **market** to *'look further'* [showing them, of course, where to look].

- **Promotion:**
  Campaigning for attention and creating a lasting, positive impression of *'***product** desirability' or desire to *'look further'* – i.e. *stepping up the game* [from advertising] and *making it stick.*

- **Publicity:**
  Spreading the word through media – making news worthy media announcements or creating any other type of 'news worthy' attention that will lead **consumers** to *'desire the **product**'* or decide to *'look further'*.

- **Public Relations / Branding:**
  Creating positive **company** and **product** *'image'* and *'repute'* with the **consuming market** – designed for best relationship required to maintain *maximum **sales** and **revenues**.*

- **Sales:**
  This is the place where the **consumer** *'looks further' to*, and *'actively convinces the **consumer** to make the purchase'* – i.e. *convinces* the **consumer** of *'the need'* or *'to want'* the **product** or **service**. 'Copy content' and **salespersons** go here.
  - **Transaction Completion** – aka 'closing the sale':

This is 'selling the closing'. Selling the '*closing*' is not the same as selling the **product** or **service** – selling the 'closing' is *convincing the consumer to complete the transaction* and *exchange the* **currency** *[your* **revenue***] for the* **product** *or* **service**.

It is this final closing transaction –
*the consumer deciding that the value of what is to be purchased
is more desirable to them than the value of their currency
or any other use of it* and then *completing the purchase,*
that is the whole point of marketing.

If you can do this, you will succeed in business.

About Marketing:

Principles and Concepts Important to Success

Segmenting Target Markets vs. Mass Marketing

Mass Markets, Segmentation, and Target Markets:

Mass marketing is simply *advertising* or *promoting* to the broad general public through **media** that *reaches* the broad general public. It is intended for **products** and **services** that apply to everyone [eating and coffee places, clothing stores, car repairs, general household goods, etc.].

Target marketing is *advertising* or *promoting* to a *specific group of* **consumers** *'likely to be interested enough to buy a product or service specifically for them'*. This simply means **consumers** whose *needs* or *wants* may not be shared with the rest of the general public. **Segmenting** is finding or creating **target markets** – *specific segments* of the *mass* **market**.

The Value of Segmentation and Target Marketing:

Target marketing requires consistently updated, and properly targeted, **market research**: Remember that a **target market** is a 'set' of *specific* **consumers** *'likely to buy'* a particular **product** or **service**. And **consumer** *needs* and *wants* fluctuate broadly [see **Demand**]. New **consumers** drift into **markets**, then drift out again, often because they've already made a purchase. So it is vital to be reaching the *new* **consumers** and not wasting **marketing resources** on **consumers** *no longer in that* **market**.

The *primary* use of target marketing is to make the most
efficient and *effective* use of *marketing resources.*

Promoting a **product** or **service** to the broad general public that only five percent were a *likely* **market**, would be a waste of ninety five percent of your 'marketing' contact budget'. If you were to *promote* in a particular **media** that reaches *only that five percent likely to buy*, your **marketing** would be *ninety five percent more 'on **target***, and likely ninety five percent more effective.*

Differentiation & Positioning

> *Differentiation* is presenting one's **product** or **service** as '*different*' in some *desirable way* from the **competition**.

Differentiating one's **products** and **services** as more appealing in **value** or *utility* to **consumers basic purpose** *needs* and *wants* than **competitors** or other **product** or **service** options is a vital part of convincing **consumers** to choose your **product** or **service** over others. **Marketing** must convince the **consumer** that the '*difference*' is in some way *better, more appealing*, etc. in addition to convincing **consumers** of the '*need*' or to '*want*'.

Positioning the **product** or **service** is *how* and *where* one '**markets**', '*situates*', '*places*', or '*presents*' the **product** or **service** in the **marketplace**. Only when the *difference* is determined can you know how to best *position* the **product** or **service** in the marketplace.

Differentation and *positioning*, done well, positively affects **consumer** *perception* of the **product** or **service** and, with excellent **target marketing**, *places* and *presents* it where it is most likely to *sell* successfully.

Trademarks, Copyrights, and *Competitive Marketing Uniqueness*

One of the *primary* methods of distinguishing [*differentiating*] a **product, service**, or **business** from **competitors** is creating distinguishing *titles, names, phrases* [slogans], *jingles, design, logos, ad copy*, etc. and establishing **trademarks** and **copyrights** to prevent any **competitor** from copying your unique presentation, appearance, style, etc. [More in **Competition and Competitive Advantage**.]

THE PRINCIPLES of COMPETITION

By killing transparency and <u>competition</u>, *crony capitalism* is harmful to free enterprise, opportunity, and economic growth. [Underline and italics mine.]
Author: Raghuram Rajan   Indian financial analyst; Distinguished Service Professor

About Competition:

Productivity Class Economic Theory Statement

The basic purpose drive to 'freely produce and trade gainfully' [requiring 'free market' economic systems] **generates into existence *producer competition* for the consumer's trade.**

Producing for *profit* drives *efficient use of resources* and *the highest obtainable prices* toward *increased profit margins.* Competition for the consumer's trade, however, *drives down prices – decreasing* profit margins. Lower prices, however, then drives *further improved productive efficiency* in order to still compete at acceptable profit margins at the lower prices.

Competition, therefore, improves 'productive and consumptive efficiencies' and lowers 'consumer prices', *improving both consumer and producer basic purpose conditions.*

'Intellectual property rights' is an 'organizing strategy' that grants 'legal monopolies' to producers – i.e. exclusive rights ensuring *'restrained competition'* in marketing, producing, and trading of inventions, innovations, and any other *registered* creative productivity:

- The advantages established by intellectual property rights encourages *creative productivity* by providing *exclusive command over productivity and prices* on the patented product. This further *generates* and *accelerates* 'competitive creativity', and therefore, consistent advancements in material accomplishments.

- *Time limits* on patent monopolies eventually bring invented and innovated products into 'competitive productivity' – i.e. competition on these better products by *any* producer. Competition for trade on 'patent expired' products *drives down prices* previously held high by 'patent monopoly'. Economic populaces benefit with now more available and affordable advancements in products [and services delivered with those products].

Competition, therefore, dynamically contributes to *driving, manipulating,* and *managing* trade and is, therefore, a derivative operating dynamic *control.*

About Competition:
an
Overview

GAME: (SOED*) noun A (form of) contest [with a goal or objective strived for] played according to rules [and structure of play] and decided by skill [education, training, practice, etc.], strength, or luck.

Economics, especially **business** economics, is a *game*, and don't let anyone tell you different. Many people, especially the more serious **business** executive, will tell you this is *'no game'* this is *'serious'* and you better not be *'playing games'*, you had better get *'serious'* – just fine if you *like* seriousness. But to think the whole thing is *'not a game'* would be a *'serious mistake'*.

Granted, this 'game' is *real life* and for *high stakes*. There are high rewards for winning and painful consequences for failing. But, of course, that's part of what makes it a game, isn't it – *rewards* and *penalties, moves* and *counter-moves*. But economics isn't really a game of *win* or *lose*. Economics is a game of **productivity**. And **productivity** is a game of *'degree of success'*. And the measure of success in economics is…

> *'one's level of achievement of basic purpose needs and wants through productivity and gainful symbiotic exchange'.*

And, as with all games of achievement, there are *competitors*.

Competition vs. Monopolies
[(mono = *one*) + (polein [poly] = *seller*) = *one seller*]

Monopoly means *'exclusive possession, control, exercise of action, etc.'* *'Exclusive'*, in economic terms, means 'no **competition**' [or 'no significant **competition'**] – monopoly means a **producer** has *exclusive possession, control, exercise of action of a needed or wanted commodity.*

A **monopoly** means the **producer** controls the **market** – the **producer** controls **prices** and **supply** and can sidestep the dynamics of **supply, demand,** and the **market equilibrium** that comes with the balance of **competitive** forces. A **monopoly** means the **producer** can be *inefficient, block the establishment of new **competitors*** in the **market,** *fix **prices*** high, *prevent or inhibit **invention** and **innovation*** in the **product** or **service** field, and *practice every kind of* *unethical* or *corrupt behavior* without suffering the *consequences* of the **consumer** turning to another **competitor** or an alternative **product** or **service**. And for those reasons, these kinds of **monopolies** are illegal. [See definition of 'trust' – **anti-monopoly** laws are called '*anti-trust*' laws.]

There Are, However, Legal and Beneficial Monopolistic Practices

'Natural Monopolies':

The best example of a natural **monopoly** is public utilities. There cannot be a hundred separate water lines, electricity lines, telephone poles, gas lines into a neighborhood of a hundred homes. The 'nature' of the **product** or **service** creates a '*natural*' barrier to **competition** – i.e. 'natural' **monopolies***. And for that reason, they are highly regulated to ensure **ethical profitability**.

[*At this time, however, new **organizational** configurations promoting **competitive consumer** benefits require electric, telephone, cable TV cables, cell towers, and satellites to share service usage with **competitors** for a regulated fee.]

'Intellectual Property Rights Monopolies':

Prior to any system of **intellectual property rights**, the only way to **profit** from an **invention** or **innovation** was to *keep it a secret* to prevent **competitors** from *copying* one's **productivity** and out **producing** the inventor in the **marketplace**. *This perpetuated very slow economic, scientific, and societal basic purpose material advancement – there was little incentive to **invent** and innovate.*

Intellectual property rights are a 'system of granting *legal* economic monopolies' – *legal economic rights to exclusive production, control, supply, or trade on one's intellectual creations – with specified limitations.*

The system of granting this type of **monopolistic** rights is designed to *forward* the economic and **basic purpose** advancement of a society by granting **monopolistic property rights** with a complete *absence* of **competition** in **producing** and **trading** an **invented, innovated**, or *creative* **productivity** – in the form of **patents, copyrights, trademarks**, and **trade secrets**. *Thus making it more **profitable** to **produce** and **trade** openly one's **productive** creations.*

The creation of a system of granting intellectual property rights
has been the direct cause of
*the most powerful surge forward in human quality of life
in all of human history.*
[With the possible exception of **ethical** systems of '**productive** *capitalization*']

Patents:

In the case of **invention** and **innovation**, we are talking about **patents** [not **copyrights** or **trademarks**]. Registering a **patent** is what grants exclusive rights to the **inventor** or **innovator** – the **patent** *holder*. Granted a **patent**, the holder can now withhold all **productivity** and **marketing** rights from any other **producer** and **produce** and sell the **product** or **service** themselves, or they can *license* **productivity** and **marketing** rights to other **producers** for a fee.

Patents are *temporary* legal **monopolies** that encourage **invention** and **innovation** by making it *more profitable* to **invent** and **innovate products** and **services** and *share them with the society* – instead of *withholding* them. A **product** or **service** that can't be **competed** against can't be stolen by a **competitor** and will command a higher **price** in the **marketplace**. When the time is up, **competition** can now **produce** and sell that **product** and drive **prices** down, making the **product** more **available** and **affordable** in the society. Now there is *competition* to get *inventions* and *innovations* to **market** quickly, creating *perpetual progress* in society's material **basic purpose** quality of life.

Patents are also a way to give **producers** time to recover *research and development* **costs** before **competitive** forces limit **profitability** and therefore limiting recovery of such **costs**.

Copyrights:

The **competition** in this type of **productivity**, is in the *creativity* itself. **Intellectual property copyrights** are designed to encourage *competitive creativity* by establishing and ensuring *permanent economic exclusivity* on every kind of *written, artistic*, or *musical* work [also including **marketing** *copy, art*, and *music (logos, phrases, titles*, or brand *names*, etc. are **trademarked**)]. Copyrights *do not* include subject matter, only the *exact* writing, artwork, or music itself.

Copyrights require some depth of intellectual effort.
Copyrights, however, last the creators lifetime plus seventy years.

Allowing this type of **monopoly** actually creates the *positive* economic effect of *encouraging creative work* without threat of *reproductive* *competition*. Copying and **reproducing** someone else's work *discourages* **productivity** and, therefore, economic growth of this type.

'Registering' a **copyright** can be done, but is not necessary. *One must only be able to show that they are the creator of the work.* Making the work public in some *datable, officially documented manner* is considered 'proof of origination'. For important work, however, it is best to register your copyrights and never have to argue over or prove what belongs to you.

Trademarks:

Trademarks are *identity* marks. A **trademark** is a *logo, word, phrase, symbol, image,* etc. that 'identifies' a **product, service,** or **company** – much the same as a 'brand' on livestock – while at the same time *differentiating* the **product** or **service** from all others with the **consumer**.

> **A trademark is a *symbol* that identifies [or is identified with] a specific product, producer, or service in the marketplace.**

Trademarks are by legal definition *'secured by legal registration* ® or *established by use* ™ '. *Legal registration* prevents a **competitor** from adapting that **trademark** and forcing a legal battle over who should have it. *Registration*, therefore, becomes vital from a **marketing** and especially an **investor**'s perspective. **Trademarks** can also be sold – which is *easier* and of far more *value* if *registered*.

Trade Secrets:

Sometimes something being used or done by a **business** *can't* or *shouldn't* be exposed with a **patent** or **copyright** and must instead be kept a *secret*. **Trade secrets** are just that – you keep it a *secret*. Any *practice* or *information* that is, for the most part, unknown outside the **company** or the **tradesman** utilizing it, but can't be registered as strictly their own, and must be kept *secret* from **competitors**, qualifies to be made a *trade secret*.

In order for an individual's or **company's** *'competitive or productivity secrets'* to officially qualify as a **trade secret** with all the entitled legal protections, it must meet the following qualifications:
- The **business** must apply reasonable *due diligence* – to *keep it a secret*;
- The secret must have *economic value* [knowing and using it must be *'shown to positively effect profit* or demonstrate **competitive** *advantage'*];
- It must be *documented information* – and best *witnessed* and *notarized* [similar to a **patent** or **copyright** having to be documented, but in this case kept secure but unregistered].

About Competition:

Principles and Concepts Important to Success

A Few Fundamentals of Competition

A Note About 'Absolute Advantage' and 'Comparative Advantage':
In **productivity class** economics, **absolute** and **comparative advantage** simply amounts to *'what can you produce to trade'*, and *'does that give you an absolute*

advantage – no real competition; or a comparative advantage – better able to compete 'compared' to other producers'. These are two completely different concepts than the academic and analytical concepts for the same terms. In **productivity class** economics, **absolute advantage** and **comparative advantage** are *not* fundamental economic principles, they *are simply* **competitive** conditions.

Competing in today's '*high tech* **consumer** *global* **marketplace**' requires much more **education** than an economic *primer* could possibly provide. Still, any primer worth its salt should acquaint the reader with the *fundamental principles* upon which all else of its subject is constructed:

Fundamentally, effective **competition** requires that a **producer**...

- If appropriate, establish firm/legal **intellectual property rights** to their **product**, **service**, and **marketing** essentials;

- Know *who* and *what* and *where* your **product's market** is;

- Know and understand your **competition** in every aspect of your business;

- Using the above, assess your **product's** '*strengths*', '*weaknesses*', '*opportunities*', and '*threats*' [aka SWOT in business terms (look that up)]

- *Go!* Establish **consumer demand** for your **product** or **service** – market hard [firmly '*distinguish*' and '*brand*' yourself or **product**] – *compete*;

- Out-**invent** and out-**innovate** other **producers** [**competitors**]. If that's not possible, *out-style* or *out-**produce*** them.

- Be *convenient* and *pleasant* to do business with, and *always* take care of your **customer's** concerns [aka know the **value** of *customer service*];

- *Close sales!* [*complete the transaction – get the* **product** *into the* **consumer's** *hands, or deliver the* **service***, and the* **money** *for it into yours]*

Each of these activities is a complete set of volumes unto themselves. **Education** in **axiom two** does *not* mean only '*how to make things*'. It also means **education** in how to **administrate** [that's what all the above is, **administrating**]. All this requires a good *depth of understanding* and degree of *skillfulness*. All **producers** must do their homework.

However, keep in mind, too, that all this can easily get *over* complicated. And it's important to remember that the *simpler* a **producer** keeps things, the more *successful* they are likely to be. Simple is better **administrated** and **managed** than complex.

MACRO-ECONOMIC
DERIVATIVE OPERATING DYNAMICS

Governments and Central Banks ['Federal Reserve Banks' in USA]

Governments and **central banks** fall square under the **primary** economic **dynamic** of **organization**. This how we, in our society, **organize**, **govern**, and **manage** *macro*-**economics**. They operate as *micro*-**economic** entities in charge of the **management** and **manipulation** of the *entire economic system*. i.e. **Macro-economic** *systems* are **governed**, **administrated**, and **managed** – **operated** – by **governments** and **central banks** *in coordination with each other.*

Keep in mind that **government** and **central banks** as *operators of the entire economy* utilize the **primary operating dynamic** conditions to *measure, calculate* and *reason,* and *their own set* of **macro-economic derivative operating dynamics** and **organizational strategies** to *drive, manipulate,* and *manage* the entire economy.

Governing is a '*derivative* **operating dynamic** *control*'.
[**Governing** is a *naturally occurring* form of
driving, manipulating, and *managing* any human group or society,
including a complete, self-sustaining economic *system.*]

A central bank is an '*organizational* operating *strategy*'.
[It is an effective and ingenious **organizational** *invention* for
driving, manipulating, and *managing*
economic **monetary** strength and stability,
but *not a naturally occurring derivative* of economic or **currency** activity.]

The *macro*-**economic** derivative/subordinate **operating dynamics** in the following sections are *organized* and *operated* by **governments** [*federal, state,* and *local*] and national **central banks**.

THE PRINCIPLES of
THE CYCLIC FLOWS of TRADE:
PRODUCTIVITY→ = ←CURRENCY

About the Cyclic Flows of Trade: Productivity→ for ←Currency

Productivity Class Economic Theory Statement

'*Economic flows*' are the *motion [or stream] of products and services in one direction → vs. ← currency in the opposite direction* created by the elemental activity of '*trade*'. Each product, service, or currency *exchanged* in a trade *flows* in the opposite direction of what it is exchanged *for – creating two parallel flows, each in the opposite direction.* Basic purpose 'drives' the flows.

Further, the basic purpose need for *continuous* consumption generates the need for *continuous* production of 'needed but expended' products and services – which further generates a <u>*self-perpetuating cyclic system*</u> of production and consumption. '*Self-perpetuating cycles' of parallel opposite flows* are formed.

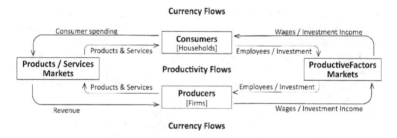

[Product and services markets are just that,
Productive factors markets are *resource* markets – material, capital, and human.
Honestly, it's not as complicated as it might look.]

These are a naturally occurring set of 'dynamic flows' that can be utilized to *measure, calculate,* and *reason,* or to *drive, manipulate,* and *manage* economic conditions and activity – as derivative operating dynamic *phenomena* and as derivative operating dynamic *controls.*

When this continuous 'cycle' of products and services form, they naturally accumulate into a *system* that must be effectively organized and governed if it is to service the basic purpose needs and wants of a *whole populace.*

IMPORTANT NOTE:

Products and **services** flow to an *end* user. **Currency** flows *continuous* from user, to user, to user, infinitum. [This is why a *'value equivalent medium'* (*money*) is called a *'currency'* – it *flows like a 'continuous current'* in the opposite direction of 'those things of **value**' it is **traded** for.]

An Additional *VITAL ASPECT* of Economic Flows:

Sufficient **productivity** and **currency** has to flow through *every populace in a society* for each populace within that society to **produce** and **consume** effectively and contributively, and for **basic purpose** drives to succeed and advance for everyone in that society. Although this additional aspect is a *vital requirement for economic and social stability*, it is *not naturally occurring*. It is simply an *'ethically required economic condition'* that *must* be **administratively** inserted, in order to prevent the impoverishment and suffering of entire segments of the society.

About the Cyclic Flows of Trade: Productivity→ for ←Currency
an
Overview

When you print money, the money does not flow evenly into the economic system. It stays essentially in the financial service industry and among people that have access to these funds, mostly well-to-do people. It does not go to the worker.* Author: Marc Faber: Investor and Investment Advisor

[*Be careful of misleading statements like this to the **working producers** of a society. Newly printed **money** is *not intended* to go directly to the **working producer**. It is printed by the Treasury according to *very careful assessment* of market **consumption/production** economic requirements. It is then sent to **central banks** so that it can be 'borrowed' from central banks by *commercial banks* and *financial investors* to invest in **productivity** that will **profit** over and above the borrowed interest rate. That **money** is supposed to then '*flow*' to the **working producer** *through that very productivity. All is paid for through productivity.* That's how everyone wins. To give printed **money** directly to the **consumer** ("the **worker**") only causes **inflation** as producers simply raise **prices** to meet the additional **money** available – and everyone loses.]

So The Cyclic System Works Like This...

'Organized producers' expend **currency** in *'resource markets'* for '*employees*' and for the use of '*investor's money*'. That's where **consumers** get *their* **money**: through **employment** and **investing**.

'Consumers' expend **currency** in *'products and services markets'* for, well, 'products' and 'services'. That's where **organized producers** get *their* **money, producing** and **supplying** the **products** and **services**.

The result is that *products* and *services* flow in one direction, and a flow of *currency* in *symbiotic exchange* flows in the opposite direction.

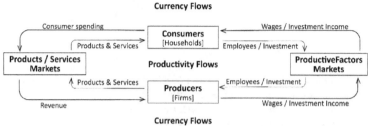

Currency Flows
[See? It really is much more simple than it looks]

It is this continuous 'cycle' of **products** and **services**→ flowing in one direction, and ←**currency** flowing in the opposite direction – taking place in many different *types* or *categories* of **products** and **services** – that creates an actual *system* that must then be **organized** and **governed** to effectively service the **basic purpose** needs and wants of a *whole populace* – an *economic system*.

A Naturally Occurring *System* – of Multiple 'Cyclic Trade Flows'
[in every different category of **productivity** and inter-related **productivity**]

All this then is a naturally occurring '*aggregate system of multiple smaller cyclic trade flow systems*' driven by **producing/consuming** economic '*entities*' **trading** through **product, service**, and **resource** '*markets*'. These '*markets*' and '*entities*' can be grouped into four distinct categories [as in the diagram above]:

Entities:

The '*entities*' actually driving the *flows* form two major categories: *producers* and *consumers*...

- **Producers:** the '*product and service producing*' organizations themselves – *businesses* [aka '*firms*' in economists terms; '*organized producers*' in **productivity class** terms]; and
- **Households:** the '*working*', '*administrative*', and '*owner*' producers – **employees** and **working owners** when *expending* [not when *investing*] their **currency** for **basic purpose products** and **services**.

Markets:

Markets can also be categorized into only two major **market** *types*:
- The '*Products and Services Market*': the **market** for **products** and **services**; and
- The '*Resources Market*': the **market** for *productive* resources* [aka the '*factors of productivity market*' in economists terms].

[*Productive *input* **products** and **services (resources)** purchased by *organizations* are distinguished as different from *end result* (*end user*) **products** and **services** purchased by *consumers.*]

As A Result...

- '*Productivity*' and '*investment*' flows from **'*households*'** through the '*human* and *financial resources market*' to the '*organized producers*' [in exchange for the equivalent **value** in **currency**]...
- The **products** and **services** they **produce** flow from '*organized producers*' through the '*products and services market*' to the **'*households*'** [also in exchange for the equivalent **value** in **currency**].

...all creating a 'cycle' of *productivity* in one direction and *currency* in the other direction – generating a parallel '*opposite flow*' – propelled forward *perpetually* by drives for **basic purpose** *needs* and *wants*.

So now you get the idea: **organized trade** naturally creates a *single* system of *two* parallel cyclic flows: one of **resources**, **productivity**, **products**, and **services**, and one of **currency** flowing in the opposite direction – *two* exchange flows creating *one* economic *system*.

Artificially Inserted 'Inclusiveness' in Economic Flows are the Responsibility of Governance

Every **governing** economic **authority** carries within its **ethical** purview the responsibility to ensure that *every part of a society or community has the wherewithal to successfully pursue* **basic purpose** *drives*. Sufficient **productivity** and **currency**, as well as effective economic **education** and **resources**, has to flow through *every* **market** *and populace in a society* for each populace within that society to **produce** and **consume** *effectively* and *contributively*, and for **basic purpose** *to advance* for everyone in that society. Period.

Every loss of *effectiveness*, every loss of *contribution*, and every loss of *basic purpose* advancement becomes a *burden* on that economy and that whole society. The greedy must be required to operate in **ethical** frameworks that bring them more prosperity **investing** in the overall society than for higher **profits** on *non-productive* or *non-contributive* endeavors.

'All-inclusiveness', however, is not a *naturally occurring* **derivative** operating **dynamic**. It is an **organizational/administrative operating strategy** *required* in **governing** in order to provide the economic and social *strength* and *stability* *required* in a society.

True individual freedom cannot exist without
economic security and independence.
People who are hungry and out of a job
are the stuff of which dictatorships are made.
Author: Franklin D. Roosevelt: 32nd President of the United States

About the Cyclic Flows of Trade: Productivity→ for ←Currency

Characteristics and General Factors

Basic Purpose is the *Drive* and Trade is the *Activity*

It is the action of making a **trade** – the '*exchange*' of one's own **productivity**, or its '*value equivalent*', for the **products** and **services** of others – that circulates the **products**, **services**, and **currency**. It is *not* the **currency** that circulates the **products** and **services** through **trade**.

The *development* and *use* of **currency** is a **primary operating dynamic**. It is, however, also an **organizational** *tool* for the *facility* and *efficiency* of **trade**. **Trade** is the actual *activity* that causes the *flow* of **products** and **services**, and therefore, also the **currency**.

The Fundamental Flow Is *Exchange* – 'Something Produced' for 'Something Produced'

'I'll **trade** something *I* **produced** for something *you* **produced**.' *It's an exchange*. In an exchange, 'what I **produced** flows to you, what you **produced** flows in the opposite direction to me.' That's it. You now understand economic '*flows*'. Brilliant you!

So why does it all seem so complicated? Because, as we become more and more sophisticated **organizationally** and add **markets** and **currency**, we expand the exchange 'activity' to many interconnected exchange '*activities*', and that means 'complexity': Instead of two 'entities' *exchanging* 'something **produced**' by each, you now have *two types of agents* **trading** plus *two markets* being **traded** in* plus *two separate activities***.

*Two separate **markets**: 1) the **resources market** as **employment** and **investment**. 2) the **products** and **services market** as **consumers**.
Two separate *activities*: 1) **Produce first, in **trade** for **currency** [in the **resources market**]. 2) **Consume** later, **trading** that **currency** for the **products** and **services** of others [in the **products** and **services market**].

Confused? Read it again more carefully, it actually makes perfect sense.

About the Cyclic Flows of Trade: Productivity→ for ←Currency

Principles and Concepts Important to Success

Productivity Must *Provide*, and Trade Must *Flow*...to *all!*

Every person in a society must be able to **produce** at the **volume** and **value** required to provide consistent **basic purpose** *progress*, and they must have the access and freedom to **trade** anywhere necessary to accomplish **basic purpose** drives. If such is not the case, that society is **misgoverned** [i.e. *mismanaged* by the **governing** body].

That also means that economic **education**, sufficient **resources** to **produce**, and **ethical**, unrigged frameworks to function successfully in, must remain accessible and obtainable for *every member of a society throughout their lifetime* if that society is to long hold together.

Lack of consistent doable economic potentialities *frustrates* **basic purpose** drives. **Basic purpose** *frustration* breaks down social judgement and the public's sense of responsibility to the greater good. They abandon *virtuous principles and values* for even just the *promise* of **basic purpose** progress. They feel their very *survival* is threatened when **basic purpose** success is out of reach. And under such conditions that society will *not* sustain itself.

Trade Flows

In addition to *cyclic* and *inclusionary* economic flows, **trade currency** *must circulate from* **investors** *to* **organizing producers** *to* **working producers, create productivity** *and* **trade** [and, therefore, **profit** and **gain**], *and back to* **investors**, *over and over again* [remember, **organized** and **working producers** *provide* the **investments**]. The purpose of economic structure is to advance **basic purpose** drives through *productivity* and *trade*. This all may seem the natural way of things as cyclic flows are a 'naturally occurring' **derivative operating dynamic**, but **unethical** manipulations often steer things otherwise.

Investments in **non-productive** money and commodity manipulations should be *taxed heavily* and those **taxes** *targeted* to specific economically **productive** purposes, such as infrastructure or the targeted establishment of economic *potentiality* and *opportunity* wherever it is needed. *This is not a punishment or penalty.* The reason for this **ethical** tactic is to discourage **non-productive** investment or to ensure *all* **investment**, even **money** and commodity manipulations, create actual **productivity**. This is simply the **ethics** of it:

The 'basic purpose' of *all* economic activity is to secure the *material* requirements necessary
- *to achieve a worthwhile quality of survival,*
- *successfully pursue the dynamics of living,* and

- *consistently improve living conditions.*

That goes for *individuals, groups,* and *whole societies.* Therefore,...

The basis of economic ethics is reasonable considerations for long term basic purpose well-being for all people, populaces, and environmental conditions included in, contributing to, or effected by the activities of any economic system.

In order to secure the *material* requirements necessary to
achieve a worthwhile quality of survival,
successfully pursue the dynamics of living, and
consistently improve living conditions,

humans actively PRODUCE what we *need* and *want,*
actively CONSUMING *when* we PRODUCE,
and through expenditure or utility, *what* we PRODUCE.

The whole point of economics is achievements of **basic purpose** *needs* and *wants.* And ***basic purpose*** *needs* and *wants are achieved through* **productivity** – 'all things economic begin with produce'.

Therefore, investment structuring must be '**incentivized**' [and sometimes *required*] to flow through *both* the **organizing** and **working producer** and all sluggish segments of a society, allowing the **working producer** to *gainfully* pursue **basic purpose** success *in every corner of an economy.*

THE PRINCIPLES of MACRO-ECONOMIC GOVERNANCE
Government's Role in Economics

Economics should be defined in terms of what it is about. It should be about how people ... pay taxes, how the government provides infrastructure with tax revenue, and how it conducts monetary policy.
Author: Ha-Joon Chang Dr. of Economics, University of Cambridge; *highly recommended* economics author

About Macro-Economic Governance:

Productivity Class Economic Theory Statement

Due to the broad spectrum of positive-to-negative and competent-to-incompetent variables in human economic, social, and civil behaviors, in order for civilized societies to establish themselves and flourish, all human societies must be *organized* and *governed*.

Government is the application of the *primary operating dynamic* of *organization* to a community or society for the purposes of establishing a *'shared culture'* and a *'system by which'* to govern it.

The purpose of government is to *unite the populace under a single set of agreed upon successful socio-political principles,* and to organize an operating system and framework that provides individuals and groups the necessary structure to create their own *efficient, productive*, and *consistent* way of life.

And further, the purpose of government is to manage and administrate the necessary institutions that empower the populace to pursue their own *survival* and *success* as individuals, communities, and as a society. That responsibility mandates that government *'serve'* the public, and that service be for the *greater good* – for the stable well-being of the whole of the populace and all constituent segments thereof.

It is, therefore, the responsibility of government to choose, administrate, and manage an economic system that is also the most *efficient, productive*, and most especially *consistent*, and that most ethically serves the basic purpose needs and wants of the community or society, its segments, and its individual constituents, as well as its relationships with other economies and trade partners.

In order to achieve its mandate and govern, a governing body must be endowed and empowered with the authority required to create necessary systems, laws, regulations, and enforcements.

About Macro-Economic Governance:
an
Overview

The purpose of a **government** is to create and maintain an *'operating system'* or *'operating framework'* within which every individual or group that makes up the entirety of the populace can *freely pursue their own life dynamics in a safe, orderly, and civil manner.* Such a purpose requires *uniting and **organizing** the populace under a single set of agreed upon successful socio-political, civil, and cooperative principles* that provide for an *efficient, productive,* and *consistent* way of life.

A **government** must further **manage** and **administrate** the necessary policies, actions, and affairs that *establish* and *institutionalize* the *highest quality of survival and success* of the populace that makes up the community or society.

Economically, therefore, it is the responsibility of **government** to choose, **administrate**, and **manage** an economic system that is also the most *efficient, productive,* and most especially *consistent,* and that most **ethically** serves **the basic purpose** needs and wants of the community or society, its segments, and its individual constituents, as well as its allies and **trade** partners.

A **government** comes with a myriad of tools and responsibilities required to **manage** and **administrate** a nation – tools for *legislative and economic structuring,* for *public service, infrastructure, defense, foreign affairs, economic **management**,* etc. Some economic 'public good' the **government** provides comes in the form of legislation, regulation, and the setting of **ethical** standards for how private **business** may **produce** and **serve** the public. Some 'public good' comes in the form of *government provided services, physical infrastructures, defense,* etc.

Therefore, there are *Taxes*

Services provided directly by the **government** itself requires *taxing the public* then *spending **taxes** collected* on the **costs** of such 'public good'. Therefore...

When a government *'taxes in order to provide'* for public good,
it is acting as a *'collective consumer'* for the public.

Therefore, a **government** must always consider, *just as any **consumer**,* "Am I spending within my means; spending as **'investment'** to advance **gainful** productivity; consuming for public *basic purpose* *requirements*; **taxing** enough to do the greatest good; **taxing** too much from private **productive** and **consumptive** economic activity so as to actually hinder it?".

Government, then, becomes the *necessary bane* of all economies.

Necessary because all economies need to be **governed**, and **taxes** collected and spent on public good; a *bane* because *political influence* is a wide open door for *corrupt* and *ignorant* **administrative management** of economic conditions and circumstances.

Economic Duties of Governments

The duty of **governments** and **central banks**, in macro-economics, is to *quantify* and *measure* conditions and circumstances of the whole and all segments within an economy and accordingly **administrate** and **manage** them*. *Quantifying* and *measuring* conditions and circumstances, requires *statistical tracking* of both macro-economic *derivative operating phenomena* and all *primary operating dynamics*. Administration and **management** of an entire economy requires effective data, reasoning, and **operating** *controls*.

*Note About Current Macro-economic Theories:
There are whole dynamic and **management** theories regarding **macro-economics** that range from Adam Smith's 'The Wealth of Nations' to Carl Marx 'Das Capital', John Maynard Keynes' 'General Theory of Employment, Interest, and Money', David Ricardo's 'Principles of Political Economy and Taxation' etc.

It is important to know that none of these treatise'
are theories of how economics works, but are actually
economic management strategies and tactics, and should be
utilized and combined according to circumstance and necessity.

'Organizational Operating Controls' [Primarily for 'Controlling Productivity and Growth Rates']

Together, the **government** and **central bank** *control the growth rate* of *a)* naturally occurring **inflation** of **prices**, and *b)* **productive** and **consumptive** *capacity* of the whole or any part of an **economy**:

Governmental macro-economic **organizational operating controls** *primarily* include [but are not limited to]:
1. *Setting Tax Rates*
   [Tax rates must be enough to pay for necessary public good, without hindering the forward motion of **basic purpose** pursuits of the populace or any segment thereof.];
2. *Spending* [as 'collective consumer' for the society]

[**Money** *competently* spent *within the general economy*, by the **government**, on **products** and **services** *necessary* for public good supports **employment** and **currency** circulation. (Including military spending; all types of research; **administrative resources**; Medicare; Social Security; etc.).];

3. *Infrastructure*

   [Roads, power (fuels, electricity, etc.), communications, transportation, etc. all contribute to **basic purpose** conditions. **Profitable** services are left to the private **producers** to deliver under **government** set standards; other services are provided by the **government** using private contractors also under **government** set standards.];

4. *Policy Making and Legislating*

   [**POLICY (NOAD*) noun A course or principle** *of action* **adopted or proposed by a government, party, business, or individual [or any organization or organized effort].**[**Governing** policies, laws, and regulations *create the very framework that is the economics system itself*, and therefore, also determine the flows of **currency** and the **profitability** and even *availability* of every form of **productivity** and **consumption** delivered to the populace.]
   ;

5. *Creating and maintaining ethically frameworked, competent economic organization, administration, and management – fair and ethical systems, regulations, and standards*

   [This includes determining and setting economic systems and structures (type of economic system; banking and financial industry; business and other types of incorporation; monetary systems; etc.) along with corresponding policies, regulations, property rights, promotion of broad scale populace **basic purpose** success, fair competition, etc. – which also requires *accurate* (not *politically fudged* or *economically rigged*) statistical tracking and usage – i.e. *measuring, calculating,* and *reasoning* of **derivative operating phenomena** and **primary operating dynamics**, and then **organizing, administrating,** and **managing,** according to accurate understanding of conditions, the appropriate *derivative* and *organizational controls*.]

About Macro-Economic Governance:

Characteristics and General Factors

Government is the application of the **primary operating dynamic** of **organization** to a community or society *– not necessarily only for economic purposes.* **Organization** *may be a* **primary operating dynamic** *of economics, but just like* **education***, it is also a* **primary operating dynamic** *for almost every human endeavor.*

The purpose of **organizing** a society and **governing** it is to '*unite the populace under a single set of agreed upon successful socio-political principles* [articulated in a 'constitution'], and to build that unity into an *efficient, productive,* and *consistently successful* way of life – as well as **manage** and **administrate** the activities necessary for *success* in every segment of society.

The complex activity of **organization** and **governing**, in addition to an economic system, is also required for *social* and *civil* purposes, requiring people get along in a non-destructive manner in which principles that give everyone the rights, freedoms, and responsibilities to thrive are provided, taught, and enforced. That very responsibility mandates that **government** '*serve the well-being*' of the whole of the populace, and all segments therein – *including economically.* There is no room for *ideology, incompetence, ill-intentions,* or tolerance of outside influence from *self-serving **inversion*** in **governing** others.

And Therein Lies Our Tie-In to *Economic* Governance

Whether in a family, a church, a **business**, a nation, or in an economic community, humans operate best when operating under [or within] *an agreed upon set of principles that **govern** behavior and relationships*. And such principles are best when they serve to causatively bring about success and well-being across all the *dynamics of living*. And considering our various proclivities and varying levels of **ethical** and moral concerns for each other, such principles only work when *agreed upon* and then *enforced.*

So, *when it is doing its job right,* the **government**...
- o   *creates* and *maintains* a complete economic system [with an **administration** (for economic **governance**) and a **banking** system (for monetary management)];
- o   **administrates** the system [**governing** the **banking** system, but lets it operate autonomously];
- o   then acts as '**collective consumer**' providing for the public good,

and does it all in a manner conducive to ***productive* prosperity** for the *entire* populace.

However, a **government** is such a large and powerful entity that controlling **taxation**, spending, infrastructure, policy making, and regulation, *to such an extent that it often is required to,* a **government** can sometimes...
- o   command as much as *fifty percent* of the **consumptive** activity of an *entire* economy;
- o   set policies that can expand, contract, strengthen, or cripple an entire economy; and
- o   extract so much **money** out of private economic circulation, from over-**taxation**, that *selective* **consumption** by the **government** can inflate some parts of an economy and depress others, while all the time hindering private economic endeavor and growth.

Competent, **ethical**, and economically **educated administrators** and legislators are a mandatory requirement if a nation's economic system is going to provide *participation* and *genuine opportunity* for **basic purpose** success for *everyone* throughout *all* of its varied communities and subcultures.

Macro-Economic Management and Governance

Government *measures, calculates,* and *reasons* what to do with an economy by *statistically tracking* the **twelve primary operating dynamics** and their corresponding *macro-economic* **subordinate operating phenomena** and then, using **organizational** and **derivative operating controls,** *manipulates, manages,* and *controls* the economy accordingly.

Government statistically tracks economic data far beyond the scope of an economic primer. Below is a 'smattering' of just a few statistics **government** tracks in order to *measure, calculate,* and *reason* appropriate actions to **administrate, manage,** and **control** the economy:

- o   Gross Domestic Product [GDP] [total and by state and region]; **Consumer** Spending Index; Personal **Consumption** by State; **Consumer** Confidence; Mortgage and **Credit** to **Income** Ratios; *Educational 'progress toward economic **productivity** and career';* Balance of **Trade** [imports vs. exports]; No statistics on *'economic* **ethics** data' is collected; **Corporate** and **Small Business Profits,** Personal **Incomes** and Outlays [**consumer** income and spending]; **Corporate** and **Small Business** Conditions; **Employment** Labor Statistics/**Employment** Rates; General **Monetary** Conditions; The Dollar's **Value** in 'purchasing' and 'in comparison to other **currencies';** etc.

Government compares the above statistics, *and much more,* to a broad scope of human demographics across national, state, and local economic regions to obtain a *complete picture of economic conditions* for each segment of the society.

With all of the above *measurements, calculations,* and appropriate *reasoning,* **government** then *manipulates, manages,* and *controls* the economy with a series of *derivative* operating controls and *organizational* **operating controls, strategies,** and **tactics:**

Taxing and Spending as Collective Consumer:

Acting as '**collective consumer'** on our behalf, **government taxes** us to provide public 'good[s]' that cannot be effectively provided by private industry but are needed for *a.* the operation of a nation [defense, transportation, infrastructure, etc.]; *b.* to ensure the economic success of the nation [**tax incentives** for **productivities, monetary grants** for research and **entrepreneurial** enterprises, etc.]; or *c.* are required for essential **basic purpose** needs and well-being of the populace [symbiotic support systems – like Social Security, Medicare and Medicaid, Food Stamps, Unemployment Insurance, etc.].

Building Economically Supportive Infra*structures* and Infra-*systems*:

Constructing and financing 'tangible supportive systems and structures' that the broad public utilizes to individually pursue their **basic purpose** *needs* and *wants* is the responsibility of **government**. Providing roads, power [fuels, electricity, etc.], communications, transportation, etc. all effect economic and **basic purpose** conditions. [See above.] This also includes the determining and constructing an economic 'operating system' – i.e. 'infra-system'. [See below.]

Legislating, Policy Making, and Administrating *'Ethically Frame-worked Economic Structure'* [an Infra-*System*] for Private Basic Purpose Activities to Operate In:

This is where 'the rubber meets the road'. Either we get it right or we end up in an economic ditch. Because an economic system is a 'clockwork' of activities, and every manipulation, shift, change, rework, etc. done in one part of the economy will effect a myriad of other parts of that economy and very often *every participating economic entity.* Every person we vote into office to represent us in **government** – *federal, state*, and *local* – isn't just 'representing' our philosophical and cultural viewpoints or desires. *We are assigning them an executive position in operating the economic system we and our entire community live in. Deciding who you vote for is not something you do hastily or half-cocked without thought for the total conditions and the whole populace that will be effected. This is important stuff.*

About Macro-Economic Governance:

Principles and Concepts Important to Success

Creating An 'Altruistically Supported, Symbiotic Exchange System'

Government determines the economic system in which all participants must participate. The alloying of **altruistic** support and remedial systems into the **symbiotic exchange free market** economic structure is a necessary element in creating a *fully functioning*, healthy, and strong economic system – a stronger, more resilient, and **productive** economy that serves the entire populace.

[Restated from Chapter Two – 'Symbiotic Exchange and Altruistic Support'...]
"Altruism *is necessary*, but it must be alloyed to **symbiotism** much the same as carbon is alloyed to iron to make steel. Iron remains the main ingredient. Carbon strengthens the iron, and the combination becomes much tougher, harder, and longer lasting – steel. **Altruism** is the secondary 'carbon-like' alloy in strengthening and improving **symbiotic exchange** – the 'iron' of economic structure. But, as in the making of steel, *only when __properly done__ , of the __right type__, and in the __right amounts__. Too much, badly structured, or poorly conceived* **altruism** makes for *weaker, poorer* economic structures and conditions.

Improperly Done Altruistic Programs *Subsidize* Inversion

Inversion [noun] [*short version*]: Perversion or corruption of the *innate* human intent to 'contribute to' others for reciprocal exchange into an *inverted* human intent to '*draw away*' , '*take from*' or '*deprive*' others to serve only oneself."

The adverse effects of inverted economic activities are only exacerbated by attempts to 'balance' them with improperly applied altruistic economic activities.

Inverted economic and business practices always create economic decline and suffering among the middle, working, and poorer classes – the **working producers** of a society. *Creating **tax** paid programs to handle the adverse effects of **inverted** economic behaviors, **without eliminating those behaviors**, only subsidizes the **inverted** activity, while further exacerbating the economic stress on the populace with the increased **taxes** upon it.*

The only true solution to such conditions is the construction of **ethical** frameworks that *solve the **inverted** behaviors or practices* and prevent them from happening in the first place.

Whenever business or cultural *irresponsible, corrupt,* or *poor behavior* creates conditions *adverse to public good, that area of society must be governed* – government must step in and 'govern'. *...competently* and *ethically*.

THE PRINCIPLES of CENTRAL BANKS
and
Macro-Economic Monetary [Money] Management

About Macro-Economic Monetary Management:

Productivity Class Economic Theory Statement

In order to function, a *monetary system* and the *currency* it supports must have the confidence of the populace required to use it. Therefore,...

 a) the currency must be backed by the government as '*legal* tender' [all businesses must be *required by law* to accept it for trade], and

 b) the '*volume of circulating currency*' must be properly balanced with the '*actual rates of productivity and consumption*' in the marketplace [leaving enough extra to encourage growth in productivity (employment) and consumption – without causing inflation].

 c) The currency's value – in comparison to products and services – must be determined by this balance and supply-and-demand principles.

When those three *organizational operating dynamics* are applied, fairly and equally to everyone, *confidence in the currency is generated* and *the currency becomes functional.*

[A secondary commodity of agreed upon, stable value (gold, silver, etc.) can also be used to support *confidence* in currency. This is done by the *governing body's agreement to take back its currency 'notes', upon demand, in trade for the agreed upon* commodity (in actuality, a *backup* currency).

However, in order for an economy to fully mature, 'the volume of currency circulating' and 'its value' must be determined by 'productivity and consumption' and 'supply and demand' principles and cannot be limited by or determined by the amount of a single specific resource of agreed upon value.]

In order to *organize, balance,* and administrate *monetary* conditions for an entire economy, an operating authority must be instituted by government – e.g. that government's *treasury department* or a *central bank* with government oversight.

The monetary operating authority's purpose is to bring a *stable, orderly,* and *organized* application of successful currency operating principles to an economic system.

About Macro-Economic Monetary Management:
an
Overview

Why Central Banks?

In order to *organize*, *balance*, and **administrate monetary** conditions for an entire economy, an **operating authority** must be instituted by **government** – usually, that **government's** *treasury department* or a *central bank*. The **monetary operating authority's** purpose is to bring a *stable, orderly*, and *organized* application of successful **currency operating** principles to an economic system.

Although banks themselves may seem inevitable, they are not. A **government's** treasury department could be **organized** and *authorized* to do the same job.

Banking, therefore, is not a **derivative operating dynamic**. It is, however, a vital *organizational* **operating strategy** of **currency** economics. When currency **volumes** and **values** in an economy are determined by **politics**, and not by *ethical, competent* **banking** and **currency** principles, **political** *corruption* and *incompetence* collapses that **currency** and, inevitably, that economy. A non-political, competent, **ethical central bank** is the best choice to administer **monetary** 'organizational operating dynamics'.

An economy, in order to **operate** effectively, *requires a very specific* **monetary** *'liquidity' balance* – a balance of **money** *'flow'* [liquidity] in the economy that, while holding **prices** stable, allows for **producers** to **produce products** and **services** effectively and for **consumers** to afford to, and be willing to, purchase those **products** and **services** – with enough extra [discretionary] money to promote economic *growth* [ever *increasing* **productivity** and **consumption**].

Put too *much* **money** in an economy and **producers** raise **prices** simply because the **money** is there to be had [this balances the additional **volume** of money available with the **volume** of products and services available] – **prices** *rise* ['inflate'], while **products** and **services** stay the same, leaving those without commensurate increases in **income** unable to meet their own **basic purpose** *needs* and *wants* – **inflation**.

Put too *little* money in an economy and **consumers** and **producers** are *afraid to spend* – they want to hold onto what little they have – and **production** and **consumption** recedes – **recession** [economic slowdown] occurs and **producers** can't **price** their **products** at what they are worth – prices *de*flate – **deflation** [the opposite of **inflation**].

So this 'balance' requires enough **money** in an economy to **produce** and **consume**, and also enough *extra* [discretionary] **money** [together creating a free

flow of currency – '*liquidity*'] to make **producers** and **consumers** feel that it is ok to *invest* and *spend* and so participate in **gainful** economic activity.
Providing the **currency** and maintaining this *monetary 'liquidity balance'* – the proper '*flows*' of **currency** in the economy – is the primary purpose of a **central bank**.

'Central':

A **central bank** is just that, the **bank** at the *center* of the entire **banking** and financial industry. Its overall purpose: to provide the **currency** for the nation [or geographical economic community, as in the European Union] and control [**manage**] the **monetary** aspects of the *entire* economy – the **volume** of **money** available; the **interest rates** at which it is available; the strength and stability of its **value**; **prices**; **employment** stability throughout the economy; etc. As such, it has certain regulatory authorities [granted by the **government**] over other **banks** and other financial industry **banking** services.

All responsibilities and authorities of a **central bank** are granted and enforced by the federal **government**. Once granted, **operational authority** to act *independently from* [*but in coordination with*] the federal **government** is then also granted in order to prevent **political** ideologies and biases, or corrupt political pressures, from perverting **monetary** policies and **banking** activities and damaging economic conditions.

In order to ensure a **central bank** only functions as an '*agent of strength and stability*' to the **monetary system**, and to prevent *operational conflicts* with the very **banks** it is mandated to support, a '*central*' **bank** *is not allowed to compete* with the '*commercial*' banks to which *it provides the very **money** with which they operate*. That means that although a **central bank** is an *independently operated for **profit** bank*, *it may not serve the private commercial economy directly*. It may only operate as a '*federal **monetary** reserve **bank**'* supporting [and contributing to the regulation of] the entire **monetary** system and '**banking** services' industry – making it, therefore, '*central*' to the *entire system* of **banking** and **monetary** services of an economy.

The '*Dynamic Operating Controls*' of a Central Bank

The *organizational operating dynamics* and *responsibilities* of a **central bank** are *primarily*...
   o   Issue the **money** [**currency notes**] printed by the **government's** treasury department;
   o   Be the **bank** for the **government** [*federal reserve* **bank**];
   o   Be a **bank** for other **banks** [mostly commercial **banks**];
   o   Be the 'lender of the last resort' for the economy [explained up ahead];
   o   Control macro-economic **credit** rates [rates charged *for the **money***

issued to commercial banks and financial markets]; and

○ Control the monetary exchange rate [exchange rate of its county's **currency** for other country's **currencies**].

Providing and Controlling Currency and its Circulation

To 'provide' currency means to <u>lend</u> the currency
printed by the Treasury
to commercial banks and the financial industry...
...who further lend it to
consumer banks, businesses, investors, and consumers.

A nation's **central bank** is the *only bank* legally authorized to provide the **currency** [notes *and* coins] printed or minted by or for the **government's** treasury. When providing **currency** to the economy through such a system, a **central bank** must charge an **interest rate** that...

a. still allows *commercial* **banks** to charge a higher rate – in order to **profit** – but that **businesses** and **consumers** can afford to borrow and still **profit** themselves – allowing for effective economic **productivity** and **consumption** [which creates the conditions conducive to 'productive prosperity', employment, etc.]; and

b. control the '**volume** and rate of flow of **money**' within the economy [aka '*liquidity*'] – allowing for **productive prosperity** while at the same time controlling **inflation** and guarding against economic **recession**.

Lender of Last Resort:

A **central bank** is also responsible for providing **funds** to the entire economic community, or any segment of it, in the event *commercial* **banks** are, for whatever the reason, in *short* **money** supply and economic stability *requires* that supply. In that manner, a **central bank** is responsible for preventing **bank** failures or financial industry collapse from lack of access to funds. This is the *only* time a **central bank** can supply **currency** *directly* to the private sector. Hence the term '*lender of last resort*'.

'Open Market Operations':

In addition to *lending* Treasury printed **money** to commercial banks at a controlled **interest rate**, **central** banks are also *authorized to buy and sell* **government** *bonds* [*only* **government** bonds (federal savings bonds, treasury bonds, treasury notes, etc.)] through the *same markets as everyone else* ['open market'] – called **central bank** '*open market* operations'.

Purchasing **government** bonds *on the open market* injects **money** into the open economy [see **Investing** for how **bonds** work pg. 145] and causes a *decrease* of **interest rates** [the increase in **money supply** into the 'open market' lowers its costs – see '**supply-and-demand**']. Selling them back on the **open market** reduces the **money** available to the open economy and causes an *increase* in **interest rates** [decrease in **money supply** in the '**open market**' increases the cost of **money**]. Thus, the use of '**open market operations**' becomes an **organizational operating tactic** that **central banks** use to the control **monetary** *volume* and *circulation rates* in the economy.

Controlling Inflation and Stabilizing Prices:

*Setting **interest rates*** controls how much **money** commercial banks or the financial industry is *willing to borrow* and provide for **business** and **consumers** – higher or lower **interest rates** decrease or increase **profit margins**. **Volume** of **money** in circulation controls inflation and deflation. As stated above, an economy, in order to **operate** effectively, requires a *'liquidity balance'* of money in circulation that allows for and encourages **producers** to **produce** and **consumers** to **consume**. The raising and lowering of **interest rates, open market operations**, and determining **interest rates** for new **currency** [called the *'discount rate'*] are the most effective **operating dynamics*** [or tactics] for controlling the **monetary** *'liquidity balance'* within an economy.

*Since charging **interest rates** for **money** borrowed is the same as charging **prices** for **products** and **services**, *controlling* **interest rates** is a *derivative operating dynamic* – it is naturally *derived* from the **operation** of the **twelve primary operating dynamics** [a '**trade**' of 'charging for the *use* of money']. **Open market operations** above, however, is not a **derivative operating dynamic**. It is a clever and effective *organizational operating tactic*.

Interest rates also determine access to **credit** – a **derivative operating dynamic** – for everyone, **businesses** and **consumers** alike.

Monetary Policy:

A **central bank** is also responsible for setting **monetary** *policy* regarding what *interest rates, financial reserve requirements [**money** held in reserve to cover financial obligations]* for **banks** and financial industry **banking** services, and its own buying and selling of **government bonds** will be. Ninety nine percent of **central bank** policy, however, is nothing more than **managerial** decisions on **operating** already *known and instituted* **operating** *mechanisms*. The intent is always the same – as stated above:

> *Maintain the correct volume of **money** in circulation,*
> at ***interest*** *rates* that allow for *effective **productivity** and **consumption**,*
> at an *acceptable rate of naturally occurring **inflation**.*

Its purpose: coordinating with the **federal government** to *create **monetary** conditions conducive to consistent **basic purpose** advancement and **prosperity*** for the economy as a whole.

A Final Note on Economics:

Economics Is A Game of Real Life Consequences, but It Is Still A Game!

Sounds like a lot, doesn't it? – from **basic purpose**, to the **five primary axioms**, to the **twelve elemental activities/primary operating dynamics**, to a couple of fists full of *macro-* and *micro- economic* **derivative operating dynamics**.

Now you now know all the **base principles** – *cause-and-effect* and *application* – that make up the **operating dynamics** of economics. *Real life, active, productive economics*. Not just the academic '*top down theories*' they teach in school, but the real life *make-a-living, build-a-business, build-a-society* stuff they should have taught in the first place.

And, no, it's not *easy* to succeed at it. But it is *simple*, and it is *doable* by anyone of average intelligence willing to work at it – *real work*. This is not a game for the lazy or faint of heart. This is tough stuff. There may not be any 'easy' in all of this – but anyone or any group or society can do it. We were born to it. The activities and functions of economics are already in our DNA.

So, after all this reading, do you get it yet? Can you finally see it? Look up in any dictionary the definition of a '**game**'. *Economics is a game* – a '*work hard* and *smart*' *game* with *real life consequences* for success and failure.

The game of economics consists of a) personal *basic purpose* goals to achieve, with b) *operating dynamics* to skillfully apply to a self-determined level of desired success, within c) an *organized* framework of *natural* and *organizational* rules, regulations, and laws.

And it is *never* a 'win' or 'lose' **game**. It's a '*measure of success*' **game** – a **game** of achievement.

So the question is never, '*Will* you succeed?'
The question is always, '*How far* will you succeed?' …and
what *contribution* in **productivity** will you offer in **trade** for that success?

Oh, and by the way, *life* created this game, not man. So you are in it whether you like it or not. And because you have evolved to be here, you were born with all the necessary capacities for playing it. You were born to *succeed* at it.

And now you know how to play!

[Yeah, I know. This where the **glossary** and **index** should start.
A **glossary** and **index** will be included in the 'alpha' version.]

CPSIA information can be obtained
at www.ICGtesting.com
Printed in the USA
JSHW031143290121
11194JS00001BA/1

9 781734 708837